Notes of appreciation

"Personal, global, reflective, and written with clarity, it has all of the elements of the protagonist's journey in great literature that captures and keeps the reader's attention to the last page."
Barbara Ballard, Writer, historian and ex-colleague at Davidson College, Davidson, NC, USA

"This is a book of life, loss, and longing. Desai's narrative straddles beginnings and ends, love and despair, the past and the present, affect and anecdote, the strange and the sublime -- their compelling calls and uneven textures."
Saurabh Dube, Professor of History, Centre for Asian and African Studies, El Colegio de México, Mexico

"Imagined Memories brings together stories - evocative, poignant, and with gentle humour that reveal the inextricable link between the personal and the cultural and political and reminds us of the power of memory as a bridge between generations and between our own different selves."
Shirin Rai, Professor of Politics and International Studies, University of Warwick, UK

"The book is a sumptuous read and brings back many of my own memories of Delhi ... It blends the geography and personal history of childhood and young adulthood, recalled from diasporic distance. I enjoyed the panorama of memories very much."
Nalini Natarajan, Professor of English Literature and Theory, University of Puerto Rico, USA

"Jackie captures our emotions by vividly describing the sights, smells, and tastes of slices of time in places near and far, as though it all happened yesterday."

Jaideep Kapur, Director of the UVA Brain Institute, Professor of Neurology, University of Virginia, USA

"Jaikishan Desai is a talented chronicler of evocative personal stories. All of them are conveyed to the reader in an easy and engaging style. It is a pleasure to read."

Robert Gregory, Emeritus Professor of Politics, School of Government, Victoria University of Wellington, New Zealand.

"Jaiki's book evoked a flood of memories, impressions, and emotions of a time and place long ago when I had returned with my young family to India - Pantnagar, near lovely Nainital. His writing made me relive a cherished chapter in my life."

Dipak Mukherjee, Former Professor, Department of Civil Engineering, GB Pant University of Agriculture and Technology (1972-74).

"Jaiki's style is one that carries you with him in his memories, imagined or otherwise."

Michael Hogan, Former housemate in Chapel Hill.

"I thoroughly enjoyed reading your book as you passionately bared your soul. A masterpiece!"

Mohini, Classmate from Modern School (India)

"Desai's writing paints such a beautiful and vivid picture of our youth. "

Sandeep Kishan, Childhood friend of 50 plus years.

"Shiny pieces of an age clutched so tight."

Shabi Hasan, Childhood friend of 50 plus years.

IMAGINED
MEMORIES

Imagined Memories

Jaikishan Desai

"But how will you ever die when your time comes, Narcissus, since you have no mother? Without a mother, one cannot love. Without a mother one cannot die."

Hermann Hesse, Narcissus and Goldmund

Contents

Prologue

This is a book of memories, not a typical memoir with a continuous narrative that tells a big story. I didn't go looking for the memories that make up this collection; they just came along and landed on the welcome mat I laid out somewhat inadvertently a decade ago. It may sound quirky, but that's how the book came about. There is a little story behind that, and I might as well tell it, because … well because, if there is a story, it should be told.

It all began in 2011 when I was about to turn 50. I was sitting in a small Suzuki Swift car on the side of a hill on Bedford Street in Wellington, New Zealand waiting for my daughter, Tishya, to finish her piano lesson. It was a classic "Windy Welly" day, and the howling wind was shaking the car from side to side. Intending to do some work, I had brought along the Asus EeePC netbook I used to carry around in those days. But instead of working, I opened a new page in OneNote, Microsoft's note-taking program, labelled it "50-for-50," and went about listing moments in time that I would want to write about. The memories came quickly and by the time Tishya emerged from the lesson, the list had built up to number 49. In the weeks that followed, at those very piano lessons, I added details to the entries but only made it to number 19 on the list. The 50th entry was never added to complete the list, and I gave up. Like many of my other castles-in-the-air, "*hawai kile*" in Hindi, it stayed unfinished.

Fifty came and went and not much happened for a couple of years, but without knowing it, I had tickled memory's toes, and it started spilling bits and bobs. It wasn't the first time I had moonwalked through memory, but this time it was different. Memories would float in from nowhere and land on the welcome mat I seemed to have laid out with the incomplete list. If I wasn't doing anything serious, I'd ride them to wherever they took me and write them up. If not, I'd make a note of them—on scraps of paper, notebooks, my phone's notepad app and in OneNote.

A collection of activated memories is a suitcase of eager beavers screaming to jump out. We all have those suitcases, but most of us have secure latches on them. Mine has a particularly loose one, and the beavers are particularly eager ones. They regularly peep out and let me know that they would like some space to stretch their legs. If the mood is right, I oblige and give them lengthy words to tell their story; if not, I add notes and put them back.

At some point in 2014, I started posting tidbits from that OneNote notebook on Facebook. You could say that was attention-seeking, and I wouldn't dismiss that out of hand. It was, but it was also about sharing fun stuff and tickling others' memories. Friends would comment on the ticklers and periodically urge me to collect the musings and write a book. I was flattered, thought about it now and then, but shelved the idea as something to come back to some day.

That's how it was going till last year—a regular academic job and then some frivolous wanderings into memory's bylanes. Then came the pandemic and a lockdown and restrictions. When things finally eased up, for no reason other than to take a break from work, I copied the meaningful stories into a new OneNote section and printed them all out. It was only then that I realized that little by little, the collection had grown to a couple of hundred pages. I thought—Holy mackerel, maybe there actually is a book here!

Walking back home from work on that sunny day in May 2020 with a stack of pages in my backpack, I had a skip in my step and a song on my lips: "*Chala jaata hoon, kisi ki dhun mein, dhadakte dil ke taraanen liye.*" It is a classic Kishore Kumar song from the Bollywood movie "*Mere Jeevan Saathi*" and filmed on the hero, Rajesh Khanna, driving to meet his love, Tanuja. I have never seen the movie, have no idea what its storyline is, but the song had floated in just as I had started walking back home. It fit the skip in the step and seemed to perfectly capture the entirely bearable lightness of being that I was feeling at that point. I even had a book title in mind!

The euphoria lasted only a day. Going through the document I realized that while there were upwards of 100 Facebook posts which could be stories, they were all over the place and had no coherent theme. Some were from the 21 years of growing up in India, some from nine years in tertiary educational institutions in America, some from living and working in America after that, some from travels to different countries, some from two years of life in Mozambique, some from five years in Bangalore, and some from what is for now the final destination—Wellington, New Zealand.

When the river of life has meandered about from one shore to another over such a long period of time there are bound to be umpteen stories to tell. The Facebook posts had covered some of that ground, but the "ditties" were all over the place. They needed winnowing down and then reworking. There was no time for that so I decided I would wait till the end of the year, take two months leave and figure out what to do with the collection.

When December came along, I got back to the document and decided to pick 60 pieces and flesh them out. Why 60? Well, the journey had begun with "50-for-50" and I was going to turn 60 in a few months, so it made sense to go 60-for-60 and select the ones that fit the time frame for when the title of the collection first popped into my head.

A long time ago, around the time I was finishing my doctoral thesis in economics, I wrote "IMAGINED MEMORIES" in orange ink on the white label of a three-and-a-half-inch diskette. I am not sure whether that was November of 1991 or April of 1992, but I am sure it was one of those two dates. I don't have the diskette anymore, but I do have in my head a clear image of writing that phrase in the early morning hours after a night of working on the thesis and smiling at the choice of words—for a label. I like quirky things, so it is no surprise (to me) that the moment I realized the possibility of a book of memories, I wanted it to have this title. The timing of its writing is just a convenient selection criterion for the collection.

The coining of that phrase might have just been something that emerged at the end of one journey and the start of another, but it is an apt title for this collection. These are memories—of events, people, places—and while the experiences they recount are real not fabricated, I am aware that our memories of the past are selective, defective and malleable. In simple words, we don't remember everything that happened in the past, remember only bits and pieces, and are liable to revise and reinterpret our recollections. In that sense, memories are ... imagined!

This is a collection of 60 imaginations of the past. Some have been triggered by sounds, smells, sights, tastes and thoughts in the present, others have just come along because ... they felt like it. The selection is not entirely deliberate, and the collection is by no means complete. Sometimes I think of myself that way—not entirely deliberate, not yet complete!

I have many people to thank for making this book happen. For starters, there are all the friends who've prodded me to collect the Facebook posts into a book. There are too many to list here so I will just thank them on that social media app. There is no doubt in my mind that without your indulgence, this wouldn't have got started, so as they say in North Carolina, "Thanks y'all." A bigger thanks to Bob, Shirin, Madhav, Nalini, Dev, Shabi, and Saurabh for reading the first draft; sorry it was so here and there, and thanks for the feedback. And then there is my dear friend of 40 plus years, Punita Singh, who painstakingly edited drafts and made numerous suggestions for improvement—all while doing the gazillion things only she can manage at the same time. Thanks Pu, I dread to think what this would have looked like without you.

Finally, there is my family—my dear wife Sumi and my delightful daughters Tishya, and Anushka. This book covers a life phase that precedes your arrival into my story, but you are very much part of the walk back into that phase. You let me have the space to lay out that welcome mat for memories and tolerated—the glazed looks, the drifting off in conversations, and the missed turns on roads. For all of that, I would dedicate this work to you but ... this one answers a different calling.

Twenty-five years ago, in late 1996, I had a dream—that I was in the auditorium in Miranda House, the college my mother (*Amma*) taught at in Delhi University, and she was on the stage to release a book I had written on gender issues in Vietnam. I had been involved in the country's first national household survey, had written a lengthy report based on the data, had thought of transforming it into a book, and even had a publisher lined up for that but ... never wrote it. I am glad this one has come to be. This is for *Amma*, who appears in several places in this collection. I'll be hoping that dream, or something like it comes along. It would be nice. If not, I might just have to—deliberately—imagine it!

1

Namesake

What's in a name? For some, it is their whole identity, which must be why people get all upset if you don't remember their name or mispronounce it. I even had a childhood friend who would vouch for his tall tales by putting his name on the line with—"*Main sahi kah raha hoon. Maan ja nahin tho naam badal doonga*" (I am telling the truth. Believe me otherwise I'll change my name). I never understood that threat of his, and sometimes wondered if he would actually change his name if I didn't believe him. Those exchanges occurred in a school bus numbered T3, and when I was just about 7 or 8, so one could say I didn't know anything then. Of course, I sort of feel that way even now, 50-plus years later. I wonder if that has anything to do with not feeling bound in the identity of a name ... and having more than one —name and identity.

While I was in her womb, *Amma* (my mother) used to listen to a Marathi devotional song with something about "*arunodaya zhala*" which, she said, was about the rays of the rising sun. She was Tamilian, had grown up in Hindi-speaking Benaras, and didn't speak Marathi so she couldn't have known the song's meaning; my father, who was Maharashtrian, must have told her. Whatever it was, and wherever it came from, she decided that I would be her daughter Aruna. She didn't know that the X chromosomes had already crossed the Ys and Aruna I was not to be. When the Rubicon was crossed, and out popped me with a bit of extra, she had no choice but to call me Arun, the closest she could stay to the original. She loved telling me the story of how in Vrindavan hospital in Mathura, a Malayalee nurse had brought me to her all swaddled and said, "Here is your Aaaaroon."

The name story didn't end at that. If it was not confusing enough to have wished-for-sex be different from realized-sex, and a name change right at the beginning of life, along came the customary reading of the Hindu horoscope, which said the name should begin with J. At that point, my grandfather, a devotee of the god Krishna, suggested Jaikishan (glory to Krishna), which was what went on my birth certificate. Of course, he promptly forgot that name while taking out a life insurance policy for me, so when I got to be 18, I had to go to court to get my name changed—from Arun to Jaikishan.

The formal name didn't make an appearance in the first few years of life in idyllic Pantnagar, a small university town we moved to after I was born. Even something quasi-formal, like a nursery report from age four lists me as Arun, not Jaikishan. Formality started creeping in when we moved to the capital city, Delhi, and I enrolled in Modern School—as Jaikishan—but my mother never really accepted that name and continued to call me Arun. I don't remember her ever calling me Jaikishan, not even when she was mad at me. Many parents go all formal when they want to rein in wayward young'uns, and I sure gave her a lot of occasions to go formal on me, but never once did she deviate from the rays of the rising sun.

My entire family—immediate and extended—were the same, and other than the nuclear four, I doubt anyone had any idea that I really was not who they thought but someone else, or.... oh well, never mind. There was even a time when a relative was taking a nap in the bedroom where sat the telephone, and when it rang and someone asked for Jaikishan, she said, "there is no one by that name here." I was outside the door and wanted to correct her, but she had hung up by the time I could. So it was Arun and Jaikishan, one name for home, family and 'hood, and another for school. The two spheres did not overlap, so it was easy to maintain a dual identity.

Then at some point in junior school, a third name emerged when some people started calling me Jackie. I am guessing my friend Madhav had something to do with it because of all my friends he was most tuned in to the American world, and Jackie Kennedy-Onassis held sway over the world's popular imagination in the 60s. Besides these three names, many also called me by my last name, so in effect, there were four names to respond to.

A fifth one appeared in the last year of high school when I had my head shaved off for no reason at all. How that came to be is a story told later in this collection so no point detouring from this one and start reflecting on what the head-shaving says of me. That one began with *Takla*, the Hindi colloquialism for the bald one, and transformed to Tuck and Tuckles. But hair being hair, it grew and the new names withdrew; only two of my dearest friends still call me that.

People may have called me different things in school and college, but I doubt I referred to myself as Jackie—till I left India. The change came the first time I had to introduce myself to a non-Indian ear. In the summer of '82, on my way to the US, I stayed with my aunt and her family in Geneva, Switzerland for six weeks. She had arranged a job for me at the neighbourhood convenience store and when I went to meet the proprietor, Jackie Steiner, I sensed that he didn't quite catch the more complicated sounds in Jaikishan. Jackie came in handy, especially since he too was one. Of course, that was all through my cousin Rajeev because Steiner spoke no English and I spoke no French.

Taking a cue from that first experience, I soon became Jackie to the other workers in the store and all the non-Indian ears I encountered after that in America. I never wrote my name that way, but for others' ears, it was Jackie, not just in America but also in the 14 odd countries I visited for work. In first meetings with non-Indians, I would introduce myself as Jaikishan but then make it easy for the other person by telling them to call me Jackie. I didn't care one way or another. They were fully functional names so why not use one instead of the other? Occasionally, I had to explain to indignant Indians who thought I had "sold out" and "Americanized." I doubt they ever bought my explanation that I was Jackie well before landing in America. Then again, if figuring out who you really are and what you really believe in is selling out, maybe I had sold out well before leaving, and am still not done selling.

At some point, someone might have said something to make me aware that Jackie was a female name, but by then I had also learnt of the great baseball player Jackie Robinson who was instrumental in integrating segregated baseball in America. The sports and civil rights associations greatly appealed to me, so when asked for an explanation, I would joke that maybe that is how I got to be Jackie; I am quite sure that was not the case.

I've used that Jackie Robinson association more since moving to New Zealand and realizing that it is an entirely female name here, and an entire cohort of 50-somethings is named Jackie. I am told it has something to do with a lot of girls born in the early 60s being named after the elegant Jackie Kennedy. At one point, my wife and I both had bosses named Jackie, accomplished and poised in their own ways, but not quite the queen of Camelot that Jackie Kennedy was.

That should be the end of the namesake story, except ... a slight twist has appeared in recent years. I have noticed that people in the university and elsewhere have started to completely strip me of my official name and use the first five letters—Jaiki—in official documents. It is one thing to have an abbreviation of your proper name appear in an email address, and quite another to ... officially be a shortened form of yourself. A couple of people even pronounce my five-lettered name in its spelt form—with an emphasis on the 'i.' In my more insecure moments, it is a bit disconcerting, but for the most part, just amusing. Fuzzy names suit the fuzziness of my sense of identity just fine!

2

Stand by me

Late in the 80s, when I saw the Rob Reiner film, "Stand by me,"
I was reminded of the first few years of life and pre-adolescent summers and winters in sleepy Pantnagar, a bucolic university town at
the foothills of the mighty Himalayan mountains in India. My years
in Pantnagar were nothing like those in Castle Rock, Oregon, the
setting for the movie, but there was something about the tall grass
and sleepiness of Castle Rock that took me back to a time I hadn't
exactly forgotten, just not thought about much.

G. B. Pant University of Agriculture & Technology was founded
in Pantnagar in 1960 with technical assistance from the universities
of Illinois, Pennsylvania, and Tennessee and modelled on the great
Land Grant Universities of the US. The university, and several
other institutions of higher learning, were part of the vision of Pandit Jawaharlal Nehru, the first prime minister of India.

Not long after the university was set up, we moved from
Mathura to Pantnagar. My father (*Appa*), who had been employed
at Mathura Veterinary College, took over as the Head of the Department of Animal Sciences in the College of Agriculture, and my

mother (*Amma*), who had also taught in Mathura, took a teaching job in the College of Humanities. The move from a reasonably large and well-connected city to a small, artificially created town in the middle of nowhere must have been a big change—more for my mother than my father. After growing up in Benaras, a culturally vibrant city, *Amma* would have found little of the arts and music culture she cared for in agriculture. My brother and I were too young to note the difference or care and, quite simply, thrived in the open spaces of the small town.

I would have been around two and my brother about four when we moved into a four-bedroom professorial bungalow with a large amount of land all around with boundaries marked by tall hedges. A highway runs through Pantnagar, and our house sat on the right side of a minor road that ran off to the right of that highway. It is nearly 50 years since I last was in Pantnagar, but the image I have in my mind—of the layout of that part of town—is as clear as what I see on maps on the internet.

In the information highway in my head, I can visualize driving into town on the highway from Rudrapur, the nearest town, taking a right at the bus stop next to the aerodrome, going 100 feet or so, and turning right into the long driveway of the house. That part is very clear, but rewinding the movie of life to remember "littul" adventures of "littul" boys with altogether too much spirit, too much curiosity, and too much energy makes for a grainier replay. I'll take that; it is better than a blank slate.

The cognoscenti of cognition say that our earliest memories are typically from sometime around four years of age. That is just about right for my assortment of memories that revolve around a friend from a nursery run by an American and an Indian, a beloved dog, and adventures with various small animals.

Brijpal Singh and I, and a girl named Tata, lived in adjacent houses and attended a home-based nursery run by Ms Phyliss Regnier and Mrs Nene in a house close by. I don't remember much of Tata, and I don't remember much of what we did in that nursery, other than one distinct memory—of us toddlers taking turns to feed a tiny fawn with an infant bottle. I am not sure how that came to be but have to guess the fawn was found lost and wandering in the forest nearby. Brijpal, I remember more of, because I spent more time with him and because ... he was a bit different from me.

I have a certain image of myself in those early years—of being spirited, curious, full of energy, and somewhat wild. Of course, how we see ourselves is always biased and self-serving and questionable, but it is the only window we have in the unobservable workings of people's minds. What others observe and make of us also has biases, but it provides a second look which can be very useful in making sense of things. It is, therefore, interesting that in a nursery report I have from 1965, Mses Regnier and Nene describe me as—having "self-confidence and self-assertiveness" and "unselfish traits," but also needing to "develop a sense of sympathy toward those younger ones he topples over."

They would have written a report for Brijpal, and while I quite obviously have no idea what they wrote, I have a particular image of him in those years. I remember him as being ... tentative and cautious and preferring to have someone else test out the unknown. Most of the time it didn't matter, but occasionally it tested my patience.

He lived in the house to our right and would come over now and then, always with a chaperon because of Lucky, our beloved and beautiful Alsatian dog. There are several stories of her, of how she came to be in our family through Raja Bajrang Bahadur Singh, an actual (provincial) king and the vice-chancellor of the university at that time, of how she was devoted to my father and much more, but I'll leave all of that for another time. Fact is, as gentle as Lucky was, she did look ferocious in the way Alsatians do, and Brijpal was scared of her. When he'd come over to play, he'd insist that Lucky be on a leash, and only when that had been done would he let go of the hand that had brought him in.

I only went to his place once or twice. I don't think his mother cared much for my free-spirited ways. It was either that or the fact that the one time she had let me have a taste of the strawberries his father was growing, I had more than the one I was allowed. It might also have been because I had gone over to their house by crawling through a gap in the hedges that separated the compounds, and not come down the driveway like Brijpal always did. Whatever it was, it was always him over at our house, which was better anyway because in our house there were fewer restrictions on where to go and what to do.

The house had a large lawn with a circular patch of beautiful rose bushes at the front, a vegetable patch on the left side with some fruit trees behind it, another vegetable patch at the back, and another big stretch of land on the right that had a papaya tree and grew something I don't remember. In short, there was lots of room to wander about, be curious and discover things, and encounter others who moved about in that space—the proverbial birds and bees, and *chhipkalis* (lizards) and *mendhaks* and *daddus* (frogs and toads) and *girgits* (chameleons).

Brijpal was scared of *girgits*. I wasn't. I just didn't like them, mainly because I couldn't catch them; they were too fast. I also didn't quite like the way they'd stare straight with shifty eyes, tauntingly wait, and if I took one step towards them take off. The worst was that they never changed colour. I was told chameleons change colour, but these didn't. I didn't like that at all.

Brijpal had no feelings other than fear. It was that simple. When he'd come over to play, we'd wander about and at some point, invariably end up climbing the guava trees on the left side of the house. True to the characterization of my traits in the nursery report, I would rush to climb the trees, always testing out the higher and thinner branches to see if they could hold my weight. Brijpal went about the climb more tentatively.

If it was winter, we'd look for ripening guavas. We had learnt quite quickly that the dark green ones were raw and tasteless and hard to bite into, but as they matured, the green turned lighter and sweetness slowly made its way in. We liked the light green ones that were still firm, not the greenish-yellow ones that were sweet and gooey, not even the ones that were pink on the inside. When we'd find one of the slightly light green ones, we'd stay up in the tree sitting straddled on a branch nibbling away and chatting—for as long as little-boy restlessness allowed.

Nothing grew under those trees, and in winter months, there were plenty of dry leaves on the ground, a direct result of the cooler air of the *terai* region. We'd tread somewhat carefully because it was not always clear what was under those leaves—possibly *girgits*, maybe even snakes.

One time, being the mean little boy I could be sometimes, I climbed down from the high branches and told Brijpal that I had just seen a *girgit* under the leaves. That was it. He refused to come down. It went on like that for a few minutes … till he started crying, and I felt bad and assured him that there weren't any around. At first, he didn't believe me, but when I persisted, he gave in and climbed down, and we continued playing and then foraging through the vegetable patch in front of the guava trees nibbling on tomatoes, green beans, and whatever else the *mali* (gardener) had planted.

Girgits were elusive, but the other small animals were more gettable, and their pursuit was a central feature of our lives in those early years. I don't remember Brijpal being part of any of those adventures. He couldn't have been there when my brother and I would try to bring down the *chhipkalis* (lizards) from the ceiling with long bamboo sticks but only succeed in chopping off their tails which would fall to the floor and wiggle about for a bit before going still. That was at night when we'd lie in bed and look up at them and feel jealous of their ability to move on all surfaces at all angles. We didn't have sleepovers back then, so he couldn't have been there for that adventure.

He could have been there when the monsoon rains came and the *mendhaks* and *daddus* (frogs and toads) appeared, and we'd cup our hands to catch them and squeal when they squiggled inside the cupped hands. It is possible, but unlikely because my memory of those adventures has the face of another boy who lived behind our house, not Brijpal. If he wasn't part of that story, then he surely couldn't have been there for the more gruesome bit when, pretending to be biologists, my brother and I cut open a frog with my father's set of dissecting instruments. It was not a pretty sight, and I cannot imagine Brijpal being there for that event.

Those were my first few years in the foothills of the Himalayas. They were carefree, secure, and full of magic, even after girgits and Brijpal had moved off the radar and replaced other things. My little-boy adventures were different from those of the somewhat older boys in the movie, Stand by Me, but their essence—of life in a small town in a simpler time—is the same.

When I first saw the movie in the Student Union theatre of the University of North Carolina at Chapel Hill in America 20 odd years later, memories of Pantnagar came flooding back, and I had a big smile on my face throughout the movie and after it. The memories didn't come in the defined story form of a film, but in images and video clips of little things that occurred at different points in time. That was all a long time ago, but I still think of them every now and then and quite like the wistfulness they evoke. They surely have stood by me all these years and even urged other memories of those years to come out of the dark. More will surely emerge and want their own accounting. I will be glad to oblige.

3

Guns and neighbours

When G. B. Pant University was founded in 1960, some forest land must have been cleared for its vast campus. As often happens in these cases, the forest inhabitants were not quite ready to give in to "townies" and tended to wander back in. In the minds of little boys, *that* translated to—"wildlife roamed at night." I never saw any wild animals at night, but vaguely remember hearing strange sounds at night and seeing a paw mark of something large one morning. That's not much by way of evidence, but small boys with large imaginations don't require much to cook up a story and that was the storyline I pitched in school in faraway Delhi—that we were told not to go out at night because there were wild animals outside.

Our house was in a part of town that had large professorial bungalows. The bungalows to the left and right housed, quite appropriately for that point in time, lions, or as the infamous Bollywood villain Ajit would have said "loins." To the left was a Rajput Dr Singh and on the right was a Sikh Dr Singh (Singh, a common last name, is Hindi for lion). Their kids, Tata and Brijpal, were friends of mine from nursery school.

The regional and religious affiliations of the Singhs were not part of our household chatter, and I don't think those things were part of the national discourse either. Then again, I was not even 10 back then, so what do I know? Those were still the early years of independence, "unity in diversity" was the nation-building story-line, and we were all just Indians. Sadly, times have changed. People seem to prefer wearing their faith on their sleeves or cloak theirs in fear. Some like proclaiming they are Punjabi or TamBram or Marathas or Biharis or all the regional trappings that define diversity, not unity. And then some think unity lies in conformity to some majoritarian idea of a national colour, a creed, and a set of narrow beliefs. Sunil Khilnani's "Idea of India" and the greatest so-far-successful experiment in representative governance in human history is lost on all of them, but that's how it is. I prefer those quiet infancy-of-independence times but recognize that maybe those are just misty-eyed memories of an idyllic childhood.

Anyway, Dr Singh on the left had guns. I know because there was this one time when we heard that they had shot a tiger, a maneater at that, and brought it back home. Whether the tiger had gone rogue or not didn't matter; we'd heard of Corbett National Park and Jim Corbett's book, "Man-eaters of Kumaon," and that was enough to get us all excited and curious.

Wanting to see the great Bengal tiger up close, my brother and I snuck through the hedges that separated the two compounds and showed up in Dr Singh's driveway to see for ourselves. There was a small crowd of onlookers gathered around the back of a military truck and we snuck through tall adult legs to get a glimpse. It was quite a sight. The big cat lay sprawled on the ground, majestic in orange, black and white, and even though we knew it was dead, we were just that little bit worried. I remember thinking ... "What if it isn't dead? If it wakes, it will surely come for the smallest ones here." We kept looking for signs of movement, but there were none. At some point, we lost interest and went back to our side of the hedge and continued with whatever we were playing at that time.

Dr Singh on the left, and maybe also the one on the right, and possibly others at the university and in that area might have regularly gone on wildlife hunts, "*shikar*" in Hindi, but we had nothing to do with guns and hunting. Our involvement was very indirect and came about when Dr Singh's guns, implicated in the shooting of the maneater, came in handy later when we borrowed them and his marksman to solve a little problem of our own.

At some point after the encounter with the tiger, it was decided that my mother would move with us boys to Delhi. The decision had nothing to do with the tiger encounter but everything to do with ensuring we got a better education than what Pantnagar or the boarding schools nearby had to offer. My brother had attended a boarding school in nearby Rampur for one year and been miserable, and my parents had decided that the experience was not to be repeated.

The move might also have had something to do with my parents meeting Mr. MN Kapur, the principal of Modern School in Delhi. MNK had a farm in Rudrapur and likely came into Pantnagar seeking advice and met my parents and convinced them of the wonderful school he ran in Delhi. *Amma* told me that he also offered her a job with accommodation in the senior school premises. She was tempted, but after having taught in three universities for nearly 20 years, that was too much of a step-down. She declined his job offer but took up the school admission offer for my brother and me, and we moved. It was the only way we could get a good education without going to boarding school, and to my academic parents, nothing was more important than that. *Appa* stayed on in Pantnagar and would visit every couple of weeks, and we would go back there for the winter and summer holidays.

One summer, when we came back to Pantnagar, we found that my father had converted part of the enclosed brick backyard of the bungalow into a small-scale poultry farm and had several hens ... that laid eggs, that he thought he could sell for a profit. He was a professor of animal husbandry and advised Puranchand, a businessman from Mathura who made poultry equipment, so he knew a thing or two about chicken and other animals. He also had two young nephews from Maharashtra staying with him, so he must have figured he could put two and two together and make ... at least five, if not twenty-two.

That henhouse was a source of great excitement for us boys, and my brother and I had a great time going in there and feeding the hens who would get all excited at the sight of somewhat similar sized creatures that they quickly learned to associate with food; going around the place and collecting the eggs that had been laid added to the magic. That it allowed us to make a connection between omelette and egg, farm and plate, was a secondary educational benefit. I didn't think much of that till much later in life when I encountered a kid from New York City at a boys' summer camp in the mountains of North Carolina in the US who insisted that ... "milk comes from cartons."

The henhouse enterprise wasn't making my father any money, but well before he came to that realization, he discovered that every now and then one of his hens went missing. There appeared to be a hole in the roof, and the considered opinion was that a fox was coming through and making away with them. The thieving fox had to be taught a lesson.

Dr Singh's marksman was hired, and a great trap was laid. A floodlight was set up in the backyard and the marksman was stationed on the roof. In an otherwise pacifist household, this was a special event, so we were allowed to stay up that night to watch the "*shikar*." We waited, and waited, and waited. The hours slipped by with no sight of the fox. Our little-boy eyes started finding it difficult to stay open, so *Amma* bundled us off to bed, and *Appa* promised to tell us all the details the next morning.

Morning turned out to be anticlimactic—there was nothing to tell. The fox hadn't come. Maybe he didn't want to be in the spotlight, or maybe he had other commitments. No one knows for sure. The set-up was laid for another night, and he still didn't show up, and so the trap was shut, and not much came of that. The hole in the roof was repaired and that was that.

A couple of months later, my father decided that the hens weren't laying enough eggs to make it worthwhile. I don't know what his thinking was, but I think the hens might have been spooked by the fox and decided to hold back. Too bad for them because when the entrepreneur packed up that enterprise, a couple of them ended up on our dinner plate, which, if you think about it, is way worse than being ... backed up.

Those two, possibly three, chicken dinners were events in themselves because the birds were cooked and consumed outside the house. My mother, being a fastidious vegetarian, would not allow her utensils, kitchen, and house to be used for any meat cooking and eating. She didn't object to us eating *that* stuff, just not inside the house, so the chicken was cooked in the "servant's quarter" adjacent to the henhouse and eaten in the backyard. You can call it a barbecue, but it wasn't. It was a proper chicken curry, either based on one of the Singhs' family recipes or improvisation of my mother's various vegetarian recipes. I have to guess it was eaten on the porcelain plates that were used for guests, for it is highly unlikely my mother would have allowed her beloved stainless-steel plates to be used for "non-veg" food.

That poultry farm was one of my father's several entrepreneurial forays. None succeeded, but he never learnt that while he was sufficiently risk-taking, he was too much of an academic softie to cut it in the rough and tumble of the business world. Years later, during college years in Delhi, when I read VS Naipaul's brilliant, 'A House for Mr. Biswas,' I thought of all of my father's attempts at being someone he wasn't and had a good laugh.

Years on from that laugh, when I now think of my 17 odd years in international development working for various organizations in various countries and trying to be someone I just couldn't be, I have an even bigger laugh. You can call that genetics, and people love to, but that's just bad analytics. The ways in which the now-cracked genome tangles with the far more complicated mix of upbringing and environment—over a long period of time—is a very complicated puzzle that really can't be solved with just one piece.

Guns didn't make any killing appearance in my life after Pantnagar. In high school, I did get to fire a .22 rifle in the National Cadet Corps (a junior wing of the Indian Armed Forces), but that was only twice a year. The activity was exciting in adolescence, but firearms held no appeal, not in college when I encountered members of the "rifle shooting club" who occasionally went on hunts, and not in adulthood when I landed up in America, the land of guns and gun-related violence. Our move to New Zealand wasn't based on a desire to get away from the random but regular shootings in America, but I am glad there are no guns in our neighbourhood.

4

Aid to deviance

The university bungalow of many childhood adventures in Pantnagar had a long driveway that, in the initial stretch, ran over a storm water drain that was parallel to the road and carried excess rainwater during the monsoon season. At the point where the driveway crossed over the drain there were two whitewashed concrete blocks. We called the blocks *pulia* though, technically speaking, *pulia* is the Hindi translation for culvert, meaning drain. They were meant to mark the culvert and stand watch over it ... so overly curious and excited little boys who didn't often pay attention to the undulations of terrain didn't fall into it while pursuing critters and cricket balls. That the *pulia* served other purposes, including aiding deviance, was not by original design but user intent.

In north India, winter is sugarcane harvesting season, and trucks laden with "*ganna*" (sugarcane) stalks regularly went by our house. My brother and I would sit on the *pulia* and wait for a truck to pass. Since the *pulia* was a bit off the road and partially hidden by a couple of bushes, the driver wouldn't notice us sitting there, not that a couple of little boys would have attracted much attention anyway. If the truck was overladen, as it often was, it moved slowly.

We'd watch a truck approaching, look away just when it had passed, and then run after it, making sure to get squarely behind it so the driver would not be able to see us through the side mirror. The trick then was to quickly spot a sugarcane stalk sticking out more than others, grab it with both hands, and then lock down feet on the road as much as possible. If the stalk was a loose one, the truck's forward motion and a little bit of holding pressure would pull it out of the stack. If it didn't budge, you had to let go and quickly latch on to another, all while running. If that didn't work, then you just had to let go and wait for the next truck. It was harvest season, and several went by, and they were always overloaded, so we were never disappointed.

The reward was a long stalk of sugarcane to take back to the *pulia* and get busy. The incisors would grab hold of the tough outside cover and unsheathe it by pulling the stalk away from the mouth. The first cut was crucial and took a bit of effort, but once that was done, the others were easy. Fully unsheathed, one end of the stalk would be stuck into the mouth and small pieces bitten off and chewed to suck out the deliriously sugary juice and spit away the remains.

That sequence—of ripping, biting, chewing, sucking and spitting—was repeated till there was no more of the stalk left. What remained was a very satisfying mess of sheath strips and chewed husk all over the ground with bits and pieces sticking to the clothes and dried juice dripples around the mouth. The glass of *ganna* juice bought in town at roadside vendors had more juice in it, but never that taste—of deviance and it's (un)just reward.

Winter was sugarcane season, and the holidays were short. Summer was cantaloupe and watermelon and mango season, and the longer holidays offered greater possibilities for play, especially in the second half when the rain-bearing monsoon winds had been turned back by the Himalayas.

If the monsoon rains came in time, which was always earlier in the foothills than further south in the plains, the culvert would fill up with rainwater, and little fish would appear. The *pulia* would become the best place to dangle makeshift fishlines—strings tied to bamboo sticks with unwilling earthworms threaded through an upturned safety pin. The fish were usually too smart to take the bait, but once in a while, they did. The initial excitement of a catch would quickly dissipate when the haul had been brought up and found too small to make a meal, not that *Amma* would have ever allowed them to be cooked inside the house. Fish was "non-veg", and my mother's domain was strictly vegetarian. We'd untangle the catch from the safety pin hooks, throw back the small ones into the culvert and keep the marginally larger ones in a small stainless steel flower vase that had an open mesh top. That only lasted a couple of days because eventually *Amma* would find out, and not wanting them in the house would force us to put them back in the culvert.

Fishing was in the early years of life, and the culvert was the only place to do that. The more productive use of the *pulia* came a bit later—from its role in learning to ride a bicycle, with a touch of deviance. *That* had long term implications, longer than whatever might have come from pilfering *ganna* and catching inedible fish.

There was a *mali* (gardener) who came every day to tend the vegetable patch and fruit trees. One day, my brother and I discovered his bicycle unlocked in the garage and decided to teach ourselves how to ride it. We were too little to ride a bike like adults, so we figured out how to ride it sideways—in what is called "*kentchi*" (scissors) style. That involves being on one side of the bicycle, holding the handlebar with both hands, slipping a leg through the triangular frame to reach the pedal on the other side, and riding the bike crouched and suspended on the side of the frame, not atop the seat. It wasn't easy and required twisting the body in an awkward way and having someone hold the bike straight till it got moving. Learning involved a good bit of falling, but the advantage of *kentchi* riding was that when the bike fell, as it often did in the early stages of learning, it was usually away from the rider. That meant fewer noticeable bruises, an essential part of deception in the practice of deviance.

A few days of *kentchi* riding had boosted our confidence, and we were ready to take the next step and ride like adults, except we weren't tall enough to get up on the seat while standing on the ground, but just enough to reach the pedals when they came up to the top of the chain wheel. Of course, we weren't supposed to ride that bike at all, and most certainly weren't supposed to go on the road ... but young boys don't have particularly good hearing, and not that much between the ears either, so we did what we weren't supposed to.

The obvious solution to not being able to get up on the seat was to line up the bike next to the *pulia* with one pedal up at the top of the chain wheel so we could get a foot on it while being seated. Then we'd climb up on the *pulia,* stride one leg over the central bar and settle into the seat. With that done, we got going by pushing off the pedal that had been aligned on top of the chain wheel, and doing the same when the other one came up. It was a bit tricky because contact with the pedals was made only when they came to the top, and so you had to anticipate the rotation of the chain wheel while holding the handle steady and looking in front. Miss one pedal, and the tendency was to look down to find it and thus lose the balance that came with looking straight ahead. It took several tries to figure out the mechanics with many a bruise sustained in the process, but once we got the hang of it and got a few wheel rotations going, we were off.

There remained two challenges. The first was making a right turn on to the road because the left went to the highway, and we weren't allowed to go that way. It wasn't that hard to solve that problem because even though a wobbly handle could make you go whichever direction facilitated balance, there was enough distance from the *pulia* to the road to steady the wobble and turn with intent instead of randomness. It took a little bit of work and some falls, but once the steadying of the handlebar and turning had been worked out, it was blissful to be on the road.

The second challenge was stopping the bike. This wasn't easy, especially when the right turn had been successfully executed and we were on the road. In the early days, an approaching tractor would cause enough panic that we'd want to get off the road and off the bike. Our legs weren't long enough to reach the ground to stop the bike, so we'd just veer off the road and crash into the tall grass on the sides. No one noticed because ... there was no one on those sleepy roads. The only nuisance was that to get back on you had to walk the bike back to the *pulia* and go through the complicated process all over again.

As confidence with stabilizing and turning grew, we were able to find space further down the road to turn and get back to the house. That was a major achievement except ... the stopping challenge hadn't been solved, just postponed to when a final turn was made into the driveway. Initially, the stopping was done by applying the brakes to slow down the bike, with the person on the ground grabbing the bike from the back to stabilize it enough for the rider to somehow get off the seat and on to the ground. That wasn't easy to do, but over time we figured it out and then went a step further by learning to use the brakes just right—so as to align a stop alongside the *pulia*, put down a stabilizing foot on it and be able to get off the bike without getting off the seat. At that point, all basic learning had been completed, and it was only a question of negotiating with each other about who would ride for how long for the few hours the *mali* was busy with work. *That* was much harder than learning to ride a bike!

Getting comfortable on the bike in Pantnagar was transformational. It gave me the confidence to rent bicycles from Refugee Market in Delhi on the weekends. I was already used to roaming around in the Bengali Market neighbourhood where we lived at that time, but with a bicycle I was able to go further—to Shanker Market and Connaught Place. It was liberating and would get even more so when we'd move to Poona, and I'd get a bicycle of my own and start riding to school and back, and going all over the city with my friends.

It is safe to say that without that *pulia* it would have taken me much longer to learn to ride a bicycle and just might have compromised the independence that would come later in adolescence. On the other hand, not having that aid to deviance might have made me conform a bit more, which ... I don't know, might not have been such a bad thing.

5

Entomologist

Restless little boys need things to do and are a handful to raise. I was one but didn't raise any, so I can't be entirely sure but … I think it is reasonable to say that young boys present a greater parenting challenge than girls. It might be one reason parents are happier during the school year because someone else has to give boys things to do in those months. Holidays pose a challenge for parents and little boys, which was greater back in the 60s in India when there was no TV, no computer games, and nothing but friends. My brother and I didn't have even that when we'd go back to Pantnagar because we didn't live there during the year and knew few kids our age. We had to come up with things to do, and we sure did.

Each summer produced its own adventures, but none was quite like the summer of '71 when, pretending to be a budding entomologist, I ran around the tall grass and bushes of Pantnagar chasing six-legged creatures. That it came about because bull semen from America came chilling in liquid nitrogen cylinders and then rode around town in Styrofoam makes for a story worth telling.

The university had some sort of crossbreeding program attempting to develop higher-yielding varieties of cows by artificially inseminating Indian Gir cows with semen from American Jersey and Holstein cattle. The sub-continental four-legged creatures were hardy and adapted to the local conditions but produced a tenth of the milk made by the chubby American ones who were adapted to the cooler climes and more abundant feeds of North America. Inserting a bit of one into the other was the technology transfer effort the initiative was all about.

It is a bit of a shame that the contribution of the crossbreeding program and other technology adaptation efforts has been obscured by the success of the nationwide milk cooperative movement launched by Verghese Kurien. There is no question that the "White Revolution" ushered in transformed milk distribution in the country and increased availability of milk in urban areas. Supply-side efforts, like the crossbreeding program, did not have a similar impact on milk production— in the immediate term—but those efforts built a scientific outlook and research capacity that has paid dividends over the longer term.

That summer, when we got to Pantnagar for the holidays, there were sheets and sheets of light white Styrofoam everywhere, as in everywhere that mattered—our house and my father's office in the Department of Animal Sciences. The big sheets were cut to size with thin hacksaws and used to line the insides of boxes, which served as insulated chambers in the same way camping "chilly bins" work these days. That is what, I am guessing, bull semen rode once it emerged from the liquid nitrogen cylinders that had flown in on aeroplanes or sailed the oceans and seas to get to India.

I hung around my father's office quite a bit and came across a wooden box with a Styrofoam base with an array of butterflies and moths quite still and neatly spread out and labelled. One of the lab assistants told me how they had gotten there and how they could be caught and made to pose in a box. The age for catching little frogs, fishing with safety pins and earthworms, and chasing chameleons had passed and I was looking for a new adventure, so I asked him if he'd show me how to catch them.

He helped me make a butterfly catcher with an old badminton racquet and mosquito netting and showed me how to sneak up on unsuspecting insects and catch them in a swoop. Then came the best part—getting them ready for posing. For that, he gave me a large empty glass bottle and a small bottle of chloroform. I was to soak a small piece of cotton in the sleepy liquid and drop it in the large bottle. Every captured creature was to be put in there, which wasn't easy because they didn't want to go in there, and the mouth of the racquet was much bigger than that of the bottle. Aligning those two required twisting the mosquito net to narrow the space and aligning it with the mouth of the receiving bottle.

The lab assistant showed me the basics, and then I had to figure out the adaptations because some insects were more reluctant than others. I was encouraged to be curious about insects in the wild and when caught in my net, but not so once they were in the bottle. And I certainly was not to be curious about that wad of cotton. I wasn't much for instructions, but those I didn't disobey.

For the next month or so, I ran around that sleepy town catching little insects and putting them to sleep in the big glass bottle. Except for the ordinary housefly, which wasn't novel, everything was fair game, including that fly's colourful cousin—the green bottlenose fly—which hung around in cow dung and carcasses of dead birds and other small animals.

That summer, I learnt all about butterflies and moths and dragonflies and beetles and grasshoppers and praying mantis, and more generally, about all the six-legged creatures that were called insects. There was a healthy degree of wariness when it came to honeybees and wasps because they fought back, and I had some experience of the stingers they had left behind in a previous summer. I never caught a spider ... because it had eight legs, two too many to be an insect. That was just fine by me; I didn't like them anyway.

At the end of each day, I would take the bottle home, and *Appa* would help me take them out and get them to pose on pieces of Styrofoam with their beautiful delicate wings neatly spread out and held apart with tiny pins. The butterflies and moths were pretty in an undeniable way, but extending their wings required care because their pretty colours got easily dusted off if the wings were held too firmly. I liked them, but it was the others, especially the dragonflies that "helicoptered" over tall grass, that really grabbed my attention; their wings were sturdy and had intricate weaves and patterns that were more beautiful than those of butterflies and moths.

As the days passed, my collection of insects grew, but it was also messy because it was on salvaged bits and pieces of Styrofoam and sat around here and there and everywhere. *Amma* wasn't too happy with that, but on my father's, urging let it be. At the end of the summer, I wanted to take the whole collection back to Delhi, but that was not possible because there was only one wooden box available for the final ride. So, a "best of Pantnagar" selection was picked out, and only the select ones made the car ride back to Delhi and then to school.

Mrs Pandey, our science teacher, gave me a "good chit" for that effort. I was mighty proud of that because I only got two in junior school, and it was earned with good effort. From then on, I declared to anyone who cared to listen that I was going to be an entomologist; nothing like a big word and familiarity with the unfamiliar to impress my friends. I even bought a small yellow book on insects at a book fair in Delhi and read it cover to cover multiple times.

That six-legged career ambition lasted only a couple of years. Adolescence came along and laid waste to it. It might also have been because of *Appa*'s retirement from the university three years later and the severing of ties with that sleepy town where I had put several insects to sleep. Either way, I lost interest in them, but memories of that summer chasing insects are still alive and always bring a smile, especially when I get to correct people on the six-legs classification, which keeps out spiders and centipedes and millipedes and other critters—with legs too many.

6

Mangoes

Amma loved mangoes. She loved all varieties, but *langda* was, without an iota of doubt, her favourite. The regular yellow and orange ones could not stand up to the tangy sweetness of the one-legged green one. I suppose if you grew up in Benaras, how could you not like *langdas?* They even carried the name of your hometown—*Benarasi langda.* The sweeter varieties that came in the drier but hotter summer months were ok, but nothing compared with the *langda,* which came later with the monsoon humidity. You could even say that the others were just part of the welcoming party.

Appa said Alphonso, grown in his native Maharashtra and called *aapus,* was superior and had a more refined taste. You can argue about that, and I am sure many in India would be willing to, but he didn't. He liked some things in life but was not fussy or adamant about them, and I think he would have readily agreed that in our family, *langda* was king and the others were ... let's just say, lesser kings.

Like millions of Indian families, our summers were defined by the arrival of mango, the king of fruits. Southeast Asians might dispute the noble title and bestow it on the exotic durian, but in South Asia there is little doubt who rules the roost. The boozy cantaloupe and watermelon— *"kharbooza"* and *"tarbooz"* in Hindustani—come early in the blast furnace-like dry heat of May and June, but once the mango varieties get going, there is no competition.

My annual love affair with the mango began earlier, well before the king had turned sweet and was still hanging from the trees in varying stages of sourness. There was a patch of mango trees on the left side of my father's university bungalow in Pantnagar, and I spent a lot of time there watching the raw mangoes ripen and fatten and bite-checking them to monitor their progress.

The real young'uns were bitter and tough, but as they grew, the skin thinned and the taste turned sour and slowly sweet. *Amma* said they were thinking about things and that ... thinking and waiting was what made them sweet. I am not entirely sure she actually said that. Maybe I am just imagining it all, but she did say many things to foster patience, so perhaps my imagination is not too far from the truth.

In Pantnagar, we didn't give the raw mangoes much time to think and wait because their transformation from sour to sweet drew parrots who would descend in droves and have a nibble or two. Instead of letting them hang around for that, we would get them all down early and bury some in hay ... so they could think in peace. That never really worked well, so *Amma* would chop up the others while they were still green and pickle them by putting them in large vats with oil and spices, once again to let them think about things, but differently and for longer.

We had clear instructions not to disturb the pickling ones for a few months, not till the flesh had softened ... but in a kid's life, a month is an eternity. I could never hold out that long, so I would sneak in and check on their progress—with a lick here and a bite there— sometimes washing off the spices under a tap, sometimes just wiping them off on my shorts. It could have gotten me into trouble, but it never did. *Amma* was a softie, and it being all about mangoes, she didn't think one could do much wrong with them.

There were always two lots of pickles she liked to make. One was what she called UP-style *aachar*. It was made with mustard oil, mild spices and some fennel thrown in. That, to me, had to be had with UP-style food—*rotis, aaloo sabzi* and *moong dal* with a hint of *ajwain* (oregano). The other was the fiery Tamilian *avaka* with a healthy dose of red pepper that turned the oil red. The internet says it is *avakaaya*, but I don't remember *Amma* calling it that, so it is *avaka* for me. I liked the UP-style *aachar*, but it was the *avaka* that held my heart and still does.

Back then, the closest store-bought variety to match the *avaka* was Bedekar's mango pickle. That was Maharashtrian *aachar*, which held its own appeal with my father being from that part of the country. It was not quite as fiery as *avaka,* and we'd get it when *Amma*'s was gone and had left a hole in our hearts. Bedekar's mango pickle was good, but not quite the same as *avaka*. Now there is "priya's" *avaka* that is available in Indian grocery stores abroad. It is very, very good, but not quite the same *as Amma's*. It never is. If you dance to the tune of little taste buds, and are finicky about small ticklings, and just have a multi-layered memory that strings back in time, then nothing is quite the same as the original.

The nice thing about *Amma's achaar*, regardless of its styling, was that the tangy twangy love lasted all through the year. The same could be said about *aam papad*, the dried and spiced strips of mango that can tingle the tongue, and *amchoor*, the dried mango powder, which can light up curries of all sorts.

The real and true love, though, was in the ripe and sweet ones, and those only came along in the summer months and were always brought in by the vegetable and fruit vendors who came around every day. In my younger years, it was *Amma* who picked out what to buy and what not to buy, but once I had gotten to college and started going to the university grounds in Old Delhi or the stadium in Model Town for evening athletics training, it became my job to buy them. I knew which ones came when in the season, where to get them, what price was right, and how to pick out the good ones.

At home, it was also my job to cut and serve them for dessert. My brother would set the table, and I would clear it, and in summers, after clearing, I would wash and slice the ripe mangoes in the kitchen and bring them out to the dinner table. The flat sides were always sliced close to the pit, "*gutli*" in Hindi, and sometimes further sliced into two pieces along their length. Everyone in the family preferred the pit less slides which could be eaten in "natural" ways by scooping out the flesh with one's incisors, or in sophisticated ways by scooping it out with a spoon. The *gutli* was treated as a leftover, but I preferred it because you could only eat it the natural way and savour it for longer by sucking out every morsel of flesh on its sides.

Mangoes were the only bright spots in the miserable dry and humid summers of Delhi, but you had to be careful. It was widely believed that the fruit carried heat, and eating too many caused the skin to break out into an itchy rash called "prickly heat." That happens in the monsoon season when the temperature is still in the 30s, the air is humid, you sweat more, and wet shirts and tops stick to the skin longer. I happen to believe it is *that* and not the mangoes that cause prickly heat. I certainly preferred the second explanation and didn't let the first one dictate consumption of *langdas* which came during those humid months.

My summer dalliances with mangoes ended in the summer of 1982. When I left home for the US via Denmark and Switzerland in July, I carried a fake red Adidas sports bag with a couple of kilos of *langdas* for my aunt in Geneva. Arriving in Copenhagen at five in the morning with a connecting flight to Geneva in the late evening, I decided that I would venture into town instead of spending the next 11 hours at the airport. I didn't have a visa, but the world was simpler back then. All you had to do was ask, and I did. Satisfied that I had valid onward travel intentions, the immigration officer gave me a day pass or something equivalent.

On my way out of the airport at the security checkpoint, when another official had me unzip the sports bag, the hitherto confined *langdas* collectively let loose their angst. He was a bit taken aback. He'd never encountered a mango before and asked me what they were. Imagine that, I thought … and I couldn't. I told him they were a type of fruit for my aunt. He didn't quite understand but smiled and let me go.

I carried the *langdas* into town, napped with them in Tivoli Park before dawn broke, and spent the whole day with them. They even got to see the famous Little Mermaid statue by the waterside. At the end of the day, they went back with me to the airport to make the last journey to Geneva where my aunt got to taste what she had grown up with in Benaras.

I didn't get to eat *langdas* for the next 20 odd years; the timing was always off. By the time I aligned my presence in India with their seasonal arrival, the *langda* lover was gone. Time had ticked on … but not without providing one last story, not of the king of kings, but of the generic *aam*, Hindustani for mango.

In the summer of '96, I was working as a poverty advisor for the Government of Mozambique, and living in the capital city, Maputo, with my wife, Sumi. It was a two-year contract, and the plan at that point was to head back to India after the three months remaining in the contract and take care of my ageing parents, who were finding it hard to manage on their own.

Life's twists being what they are, that didn't come to be. One weekend, I got a call from the young tenant who lived in my parents' house in Indore to say that *Amma* had been admitted to the hospital and was in the ICU. Sumi and I scrambled to put together the cash needed to purchase a plane ticket, and I rushed to Indore, going straight from the airport to the hospital. She was stable and still had that incredible spirit of living that had carried her through tough times. *Appa*, in his 80s at that point, was there beside her.

Amma wanted me to be with her in the ICU that night but let me go home to catch some sleep because I hadn't had any on the way over from Maputo to Johannesburg to Bombay to Indore. When I came back to the hospital the next morning, her first words to me were— *"Aam khaya?"* (Did you have a mango?).

It was late June, and mango season was in full flow, and even though she was diabetic, my father let her have a small piece of the king of fruits after a meal. I reckon she was looking forward to the arrival of the king of kings, the *langda*, in July. She had, all through life, and I cannot imagine it not being on her mind that year. It didn't come to be. A couple of days later, she passed very gently in much the same way she had lived her life.

I've had mangoes since, including the one-legged one, and it delights me no end that my daughters, especially Anushka, love mangoes. I do still like them, but I don't crave them anymore. The taste is gone. Time has truly ticked on.

7

A serenade

No one likes being caught in a traffic jam, but if you are going to be stuck in one, there are few places better than State Highway 1 in New Zealand—between Pukerua Bay and Paekakariki. On that stretch, the road is mildly winding with a steep cliff on one side and Tasman Sea on the other. The sea view is quite simply stunning and can get you imagining all sorts of things, but ... it isn't enough to get you thinking of a serenading song with a waltziness about it. For that, you need a bit more.

Earlier this year, Sumi and I were heading back to Wellington from a long road trip up north. We were on the cliffside of that stretch of the highway, traffic was backed up to a crawl in our lane but not the one coming in our direction, and I was driving. That put me on the seaside with a breathtaking view of the glimmering water. It was mid-afternoon, the sun was out, and Wellington, which can be downright witchy even in summer, looked welcoming.

For reasons unknown, I had the Bollywood playback singer Kishore Kumar on my mind, not KK in general, but his romantic songs. It might have had something to do with the damsel in the passenger seat and having gotten her to laugh in that delightful way she does at my silly stories. Whatever it was, I asked her if she would play "*Phoolon ke rang se dil ki kalam se*" on Spotify. She was Whatsapping with a friend but obliged, and on came the melody of melodies that, in my mind, is easily in the top 10 of KK's romantic songs. In my memories, it is forever linked to a Maharashtrian summer get-together one evening in 1970 in Pantnagar.

By the time the 70s rolled in, G B Pant University of Agriculture & Technology had been in operation for a decade and was well established, with students and faculty from different parts of the country. Even though we—my mother and the two of us boys—had moved to Delhi sometime in 1966, we spent summer and winter holidays in Pantnagar. As a result, we still had a reasonably active social network. I say "reasonably" because I am pretty sure it was mostly centred around my mother who nurtured the network and kept it going. That's just how she was—in Pantnagar, in the different parts of Delhi we lived in, and in Indore after she retired.

The interesting feature of the Pantnagar network was that it was made up of a large number of Maharashtrians, a bit of an anomaly because my mother was Tamilian and had grown up in Benaras, and it was my father who was Maharashtrian but not much of an initiator of social contacts. The contacts in that social network were primarily junior faculty, often with young families and post-graduate students my father was supervising for masters and doctoral degrees.

How the network got revived each time we were back in Pantnagar is a bit of a mystery. The revival was usually incremental, with people just "dropping by" informally. The configuration of Pantnagar, with separate houses, made that informal contact a bit more difficult than in more densely packed Delhi, but it happened nevertheless. *Amma* needed people and people seemed to need her, and when you've got that type of motivation, contact is not constrained by topography.

Large get-togethers of the social network were not the norm but occurred once in a while. In fact, I can think of only one such occasion sometime in the summer of 1970. It was a potluck dinner, and everyone had brought along a dish. *Amma* had made some things, and *Appa* had arranged for strawberry ice cream that had come in a stainless steel container submerged in packed and salted ice in a wooden barrel.

People were milling around, and my brother and I were hanging around doing what *Amma* had asked us to do—very simply to behave ourselves and not go wild, which was our wont at that stage in life. We were doing our best but ... it was proving difficult. A simple bit of cross-language pronunciation had us sniggering.

It being summer, the mangoes were fattening up, and parrots were starting to descend to nibble at them. My mind, quite naturally, was on "*thothe*" which is plural for parrot in Hindi. Nothing to snigger about there, but we had just been introduced to one of the dinner guests, a young Maharashtrian academic, Dr Thote. The second t in Thote is meant to be pronounced as the sharp t in tea, but ... in our mischievous brains was playing out as th in that, and had our tongues going—Dr Parrots, Dr Parrots, Dr Parrots. It is juvenile, but that's the age we were then, and that is how we could be at times. Dr Thote had added to that by admonishing me for patting his baby's bottom by saying not to do that because "*usko thatti aa jayegi,*" (he will shit). We were used to the sharp t in the Hindi word for shit, but much like my father's pronunciation of the same word, Dr Thote had flattened the sharpness by adding an h to the first t. This was more than juvenile; it was gross, and we knew that we could get into trouble. That, and the uncontrollable laughter that had resulted from the pronunciation switch, had led us to running away to another room.

What brought me back to the living room was the sound of a young man's sweet voice singing "*Phoolon ke rang se, dil ki kalam se.*" At that point, it is improbable that I had any idea of the movie origins of the song, though it is quite likely that I had heard it on the radio because the movie, "*Prem Pujari,*" had been released earlier in the year. SD. Burman's score in Dev Anand's directorial debut movie is quite simply magical, and it would have had to be riding the airwaves of All India Radio in those days. The young Maharashtrian academic who sang it that night had a voice very different from Kishore Kumar's, but his rendition had the same serenading effect as the original. I heard it in that drawing room when I wasn't even ten and never forgot it.

Years later, when we lived in Bangalore, I bought a CD collection of "Best of Kishore Kumar" and made sure it had "*Phoolon ke rang se*" on it. The nice thing about recording the song is that I don't have to go to YouTube and watch Dev Anand's over-the-top acting in entirely unrealistic settings in Switzerland; I can focus on S. D. Burman and Kishore Kumar's divine music.

The song has a waltziness about it and is a serenade to Waheeda Rehman, my favourite Bollywood actress and a beautiful woman—much like the one sitting next to me in that traffic jam. Midway through the song, I realized that the trigger for it was not the stunning scenery of the Kapiti coast but the Whatsapping damsel by my side. It brought a smile. When that song ended, I requested another romantic song by Kishore Kumar, and then another, and then some more. The smile that had come on during the serenading song, it stayed ... all the way back home.

8

A doctoral journey

Five years ago, Ali stopped by my office to say hello and update me on his three-month-long trip back to the Maldives to collect data for his doctoral thesis. He said things had gone well, and he had ended up interviewing more people than he had planned on, was getting the recordings transcribed and translated and would then start analysing them. When he was done talking, I talked, and he listened. I told him that the phase ahead would be tougher than the one before because now there would be no visible hurdles to jump over, no benchmarks to mark progress, but only benches to go lazy on. I warned him that it would be a wander through darkness that would lead to discovery, not just about what he was researching, but more importantly, about himself.

I had told him that the year before when he presented his proposal to the department's research committee, and I repeated it all, and then reassured him that I would hold his hand through it, but only if he was willing to walk the walk.

"Are you up to it?"

"Yes," he said quietly.

Then he dug into his bag and handed me a souvenir he had brought back. It was a beautiful orangish-red-black vase made of wood, wide at the bottom, tapering in and stretching out to a wide middle, then narrowing again to widen out right at the top. The more I looked at it, the more it seemed like an off the shoulder woman's full-length evening dress, not that I know anything about those.

One look at the vase and I had a memory trigger take me back almost 50 years to Sawantwadi in Maharashtra. We had driven down from Pantnagar to my father's hometown for his nephew's wedding. That would be Prakash, my first cousin, but really, he was my father's nephew. Relationships are like that. Formally you can connect dots to make someone's nephew be your cousin, brother be your uncle, and daughter be your niece, and everyone be related to everyone, but there are always some connections of those dots that hold more meaning than others. It was like that with Prakash and with his other nephews.

My father's siblings had married early, and he had married very late, and childbearing patterns being what they were, most of his nephews and nieces were closer in age to him than to their parents. That, and the fact that he had made it out from challenging circumstances in a small town and gone on to do a PhD in America on a scholarship meant they also admired him and sought his guidance. He, in turn, watched over them and did what he could. It is a universal pattern, possibly more so in some places than others.

We had driven down from Pantnagar in the north to Sawantwadi in the southwest of the country, a distance of nearly 2000 kilometres in the white Standard Herald car my father had at that time. It being an auspicious occasion, other moments got tagged on to the wedding and my brother, and I had our heads shaved for the Hindu "*janev*" thread ceremony. I can't imagine my father being the instigator of that; it must have been *Amma* who liked the little rituals of Hinduism. It was sold to us as a rite of passage, but to what? My little brain did not ask then and struggles to understand now.

I only thought about what was promised as a reward—mussels curry. If you've ever had Maharashtrian meat curry from those parts, you would know what I am talking about, if not, oh well. Next time you are in Goa, skip the chicken cafreal and xacuti and fancy foods at the resorts and go up north a bit, and you'll find it across the border in Maharashtra. I haven't done that myself since then but hope to at some point.

In those few days, my father took us here and there, and to the house, he had grown up in. Someone else was living there and was running a "*karkhana*," a mini production unit, making wooden knick-knacks on a lathe machine. I had never seen one before and stood there transfixed while the owner demonstrated how a piece of wood was clamped between two spinning metal parts and how a woodworker with steady hands could work a long sharp chisel on the surface of that piece of wood and carve out whatever they wanted. The result was the same as what a potter would get on a potter's wheel—symmetry from shaping a spinning object. Once done, they would use the same lathe machine to apply colours in neat circles to put out brightly coloured things for sale in the local market.

What Ali had brought back was something very much like what I had seen 50 plus years earlier. Naturally, I told him a shorter version of that memory-triggered story; I couldn't resist. What I did, though, was tell myself a forgotten story of a very modest wedding, a head shaving, threads across the chest later forgotten in the Aligarh Muslim University guest house on the drive back, mussels curry and a lathe machine from half a century ago. When I was done, I looked up at him, and he smiled. He said that was in-

deed what it was—a lathe-turned wooden ornamental vase with local motifs.

Back to business, I suggested he draft chapters which I promised
to read carefully and redline as I had done before. I also told him that
he should reasonably expect to write at least two if not three drafts
of the thesis. All that seemed to unnerve him a bit. To assure him
that I was no harder on him than I was on myself, I sifted through a
stack of A3-sized papers on which I had been writing detailed chapter outlines of what I hoped would be a book one day and pulled
out one page. On it, I had written, entirely to myself, and in red ink:
"GARBAGE - This is not an outline for writing." He smiled again.
This time it was a bit wider.

He went away to work on the thesis and two years later handed
me a draft. I did what I had said I would—redlining the hard copy
from end to end with edits and comments, and suggestions. He
went away to rework the draft and did the best he could in the time
that remained before the deadline to submit the thesis for examina-
tion. I was concerned that his revisions might not be enough to secure passage.

The thesis went out to three examiners, and a few months later,
he had his final oral defence. The examiners complimented him on
a well-written dissertation and then asked questions to which he
calmly and humbly provided answers. I sat there listening, taking
notes, smiling inwardly, and thinking … maybe I had contributed a
teeny-weeny bit, and maybe my being so demanding had done him
some good after all. When it was all done, the examiners congrat-
ulated him on a job well done and told him that subject to some
manageable revisions, he would receive the degree he so very much
wanted and had worked so hard for. A few months later, when he
returned for the graduation ceremony, he brought me another souvenir—a beautiful wooden ship in a glass display box. It didn't trig-

ger any memories, and he didn't have to suffer through another story of mine.

Two more PhD students have followed in his footsteps, one very self-assured and confident in his abilities, another a challenge far greater than I could have imagined at the start. With the latter, I had to be thesis supervisor at times and a stern and caring father at others. His finishing brought an even bigger smile and some silent tears.

When I think of the five students I have shepherded through the doctoral journey, I am reminded of my father and his doctoral and masters students in Pantnagar. He had many more. They would often come home, and he would lecture, instruct, and give them all sorts of suggestions. He was committed to them, and they were forever grateful to— *"Daksahab"* (Dr *Sahib*)—for holding their hand through their journeys.

9

Who do you love?

It was a conversation only overly confident pre-adolescents are capable of. I was just about that. The year would have been 1971 or 1972, but it doesn't really matter, and nor does the conversation—in any substantive way. It's just that I remember the conversation, the conversationalists and where it took place so ... might as well tell the story.

Those were the years we lived on Todarmal Road in Bengali Market, in the very heart of New Delhi. I am not entirely sure why we moved there from Lucknow Road in the Mall Road area of North Delhi. That had been a reasonably short walk from Miranda House, where my mother taught, while this was a longer commute for her by bus and autorickshaw. Maybe *Amma* had gotten tired of being in the relatively low culture northern part of Delhi and wanted more of the music, dance and drama of the Mandi House area. Or maybe she was willing to take on a longer commute so we could have a shorter one to our school. Or maybe it was just chance. She said she had been in Bengali Market for some reason and had just walked up to the proprietor of Nathu Sweets, one of two sweetmeat shops that defined that marketplace, and asked him if he knew of any rentals in the area. He had pointed her to a potential vacancy in number 14 Todarmal Road, and she had gone and met the owner, and that is how we had ended up moving. Whatever it was, all of us loved living in Bengali market.

Todarmal Road was and still is a long run of row houses. The house numbers began at 10 and then progressed in twos, which, now that I think about it is a bit strange because there were no odd numbers on the opposite side. It's quite possible that the odd numbers were in the master plan, but then the government took over the land and built government flats. It wouldn't be the least bit strange in the Indian landscape where plans are often just plans—to be appropriated, improvised and ignored as power sees fit. All capital cities swoon with power, but there probably are few places in the world so intoxicated with it as Delhi.

Anyway, the even-numbered row houses were all one storey high till you got to number 28. That one, and the one after that, had a couple of extra levels, and that might be because they were completely redone from the original. Most owners on that stretch were professionals of modest means, but I think those two houses belonged to business families with larger means. I had a play-friend in one of them, and we used to call him "*atthais*" which is Hindi for 28. That's how I know. The nice thing about the shared roofs between 10 and 28 was that the roof dividers were only ankle high, so you could hop across them, sometimes to catch kites, and sometimes for no reason at all.

We lived in number 14. Dr Chopra, the owner, had been a university professor in Delhi and had recently retired and moved to Chandigarh to live with his son. He hadn't completely given up on his memories of life in Delhi and kept them in three of the four rooms, renting us one. After the first year, he must have started building new ones in the "planned city" because he let us have a second room so we could build our own memories in his house. In the three-four years we lived there, we surely did.

My life revolved around number 14 where we lived and number 12 where my friends Richa and Bittu lived. We never really knew the folks in number 16. I am not sure why, but it is quite possible that it was because they were elderly and preferred not having to deal with young kids. Numbers 18 and 20 housed young girls, but they were older and had no eye for us.

Number 10 was relevant only because there was shared schooling with the occupants. The girl who lived there must have been 17 or 18 and was several years senior to school. Her mother also taught in our school. I don't think there was a father around, but I am not sure. Maybe he was, or maybe he had moved on, which way I don't know. I wasn't nosy then, and I am not now. That has its upside and downside. The downside is that I am rather clueless about things around me. The upside is, well, I don't really know what the upside is, other than that I don't interfere in others' lives.

When we moved to Bengali Market, both my brother and I were in Junior Modern School, which was a few kilometres away on Humayun Road. It was not on one of the school bus routes, so we had to figure out how to get to school on our own. There was no direct bus from Bengali Market to Humayun Road, so we'd end up walking to Mandi House and catching a public bus from there. Not being particularly timely in getting ready, we'd often be late and get into trouble for that.

The shorter commute meant we got back home earlier. I'd get back, drop off the school bag, and head out to play or loiter about—still in the very identifiable blue school uniform of Modern School. *Amma* would plead with me to change out of school uniform, but I couldn't be bothered.

It was on one of those evenings of street loitering that I happened to be somewhere on Todarmal Road, between numbers 10 and 14, and got into in an animated conversation with my school senior from number 10 about—who was a better playback singer, Kishore Kumar or Mohammed Rafi. In today's stupid world, that question might easily follow religious lines about Hindu and Muslim, but back then—in the early 70s—religion mattered not. It was all about whether Kishore Kumar's sharper voice scored higher than Mohammed Rafi's mellifluous crooning. Rajesh Khanna's blockbuster movie *Aradhana* had been released a couple of years earlier, and Kishore Kumar had sung its songs in a voice ... pre-adolescent boys waiting for voices to crack hoped for, wished for, prayed for. Naturally, I liked his manly voice more than Rafi's sweet tones, which she preferred.

I was just about 10 or 11, and she was closer to 18, but that age difference and the fact that she was a senior in school meant nothing to me. I knew what I loved and was willing to stand up for it, and she knew what moved her and was naïve enough to engage a pre-adolescent in an argument that couldn't go anywhere. It didn't. I don't know how it ended, but I am quite sure I didn't give in.

Over the years, I came to appreciate Rafi, and the other great male playback singers of that time, while never giving up on Kishore Kumar. Before I left home for the US in 1982, I recorded as many Rafi and Kishore Kumar melodies as I could from the radio, and then years later, I bought cassette tapes and, still later, a collection of "best of" CDs of both singers. Whatever was not in that collection I have now picked up from YouTube, and all of the radio memories of those days, including those of the other great playback singers, are complete.

I don't compare Mohammed Rafi and Kishore Kumar anymore. Each fits a mood, memory and space the other can't, and that's just how it is. What Rafi did with OP Nayyar, Kishore Kumar couldn't have, and what KK did with RD Burman, Rafi couldn't have. I wouldn't want to argue about that with anyone, but I did a very long time ago. When I think about it, it is mildly embarrassing, but retrospect is like that—a mixed bag. I have made my peace with it.

10

Idli-Dosa

If you drive from Madras to Bangalore on National Highway 4, the Murugan Idli Shop appears on the left, well before you get to Vellore. They've changed the names—Madras to Chennai and Bangalore to Bengaluru—but Vellore is still Vellore. Its name has not been changed. I don't know why. Maybe it is because the British never changed it from something else to Vellore, or it is too small a place to score a political point. I don't quite understand the current penchant for name changing, so best to move on to memories of unchanging *idli-dosa*.

A couple of years ago, we were on National Highway 4, driving from Madras to Bangalore, and just around lunchtime saw a sign for the Murugan Idli Shop. Sumi had heard that it was famous for good quality "tiffin" food, and so we stopped for *idli-dosa*, the quintessentially South Indian snacks with pan-Indian, and even global appeal.

The interesting thing is that, linguistically, *idli* is *idli*, but *dosa* isn't really *dosa*; it is actually *dosai*, which is what Tamilians call the savoury crepe. The rest of India and the rest of the world may call *dosai dosa*, but it isn't. In restaurants in south India too they may call it *dosa* but in the home setting, it most definitely is *dosai*, the 'i' adding the homeliness that comes from the crepe being smaller and frumpier and not as golden and pretty and crispy as the restaurant variety *dosa*.

Idli and dosai were a regular feature in our home, not as staple as many Tamilian homes, but still a core part of the food pyramid. My mother was a Tamilian from the south who grew up in Benaras in the north and married a Marathi-speaking Maharashtrian from the western part of the country. While she did throw in plenty of Tamil words into family conversations, no attempt was made to teach us Tamil, and so ... I don't remember if *Amma* called the crepe *dosa* or *dosai*. It doesn't really matter.

Amma had a slight preference for *idli*, quite possibly and very reasonably, because she was the one who made both, and the making of *idli* is not as laborious as that of *dosai*. The batter is the same, but *idlis* get steam cooked so you can put them all in a cooker at one go and have them all come out steaming happy at the same time. *Dosai*, on the other hand, are made one at a time, so you have no choice but to stand in front of a frying pan for an extended stretch, and *that* is not fun in the hot temperatures of India.

Amma used to say there is nothing like a hot *idli*, one that flops but doesn't fold, and in its eagerness to be more than itself, sponges up the flavours of others. You could say that in that sense it is very Indian; it would be very consistent with Pavan Varma's idea of what "Being Indian" means.

An *idli* can't really be had by itself—it is too bland and needs company. The simplest of those is a sprinkling of oil on *modhapadi*, the crunchy red powder of mysterious ingredients. I know it is *molgha podi* not *modhapadi* but that's how I remember my mother's reference to it, and I prefer imperfections in the memory of a perfect mother to the perfections of a language, so I'll hold on to that quirk. If nutty gun powder is not on offer, as it often isn't beyond the southern firing range, you can sponge up a bit of fresh coconut chutney or dunk the *idli* in *sambar*.

If you are from anywhere other than the Tamilian south, you might not know that the generic *sambar* has several avatars; India isn't polytheistic for nothing! There is the one that is heavy on tamarind, the one that has devilish little onions (shallots) in it, the one that has drumsticks, and my favourite—the sweetish one with tomatoes. *Amma* could make all of those pitch-perfect. That is not my obviously biased opinion but the assessment of Chandru mama, my uncle who is a famous dancer. He once told me that she could make a *vengayam* (onion) *sambar* like no other! I happen to think that artists sense things more finely than others, so I am happy to go along with that confirmation.

At home, I tolerated *idli,* but it was the *dosai* that really had a hold on me. When dosai and I became acquainted is frumpy in one part and crisp in another. I don't quite remember the eating origins of *dosai* in our household other than that it was there as early as my pre-school days in Pantnagar. *Amma* had a big two-stone grinder like a mortar and pestle that was used to purée the soaked rice and *urad dal.* Every now and then, she would work that grinder or get someone to do that for her. For some reason, I remember that but not the *dosai* being dished out in the kitchen. They must have been turned out in Pantnagar because she taught the Garhwali cook, Satram, how to make them and then, when we moved to Delhi, encouraged him to start a *dosa* shack.

He did set one up on the side of the highway that ran through town and made *dosa* not *dosai.* They were crispy and restaurant-like, and his thatched-roof shack did great business. I once told

Amma that I liked his *dosa*s better than the home-cooked *dosai*. If she minded that she didn't say it. She knew, and I knew, even though I was not much more than seven or eight, that no shack or restaurant could make *dosai* what it really was—homely and warm.

The origins of my own making of *dosai* are crispy clear. I was about 12 or 13, and we lived in the Bengali Market area of New Delhi. One weekend before school exams, my friend Madhav had come to study, but instead of hitting the books, we'd spent the whole day playing "*gulli danda*," a simple little game with a big stick (*danda*) that is used to whack a small one (*gulli)* that has tapered ends. We played *gulli danda* all afternoon and studying never really happened.

By day's end, we were hungry, and *Amma* wasn't around. I confidently offered to make *dosas* even though I had never really made any before. The first two or three were all messed up, but once the *tawa* (pan) was evenly heated, and I'd gotten the hang of pouring out the batter in the middle and spreading it out in ever increasing circles and flipping the *dosa* when one side was ready, it went smoothly. I made, he ate, and we didn't keep count.

All of this was running through my head at the prospect of encountering the Murugan Idli shop. The butter *dosai* I ordered came with four chutneys, and a *sambar* and each one was divine. I am used to just one chutney, the coconut one, so to have four on offer was a bit overwhelming. To really enjoy the taste of each, I had to go slow and pay great attention to the chutneys and no attention to other things. It was well worth it.

The food came on the traditional banana leaf but was set in a stainless steel cafeteria tray. That serving combination makes for faster and easier serving and clean up. It is also more environmentally friendly, though I suspect there is a subtle marketing angle in that combination because it allows the deeply ambivalent Indian consumer to make a comfortable transition from traditional to modern.

There was so much chutney, and sambar left over that I just had to indulge and order another *dosai*, and then filter *"capi"* (coffee). You couldn't possibly have grown up in a Tamilian home and not want that heavenly finisher. The filter coffee arrived the way it always does in the southern part of India— in a stainless steel *"tumbler and dabra"* set, which is quite simply a small glass inside a small bowl. The coffee comes "piping hot" in the tumbler (glass), and people like to pour out small amounts into the *dabra* and drink from that. I don't like it that way, preferring to drink the coffee straight from the *tumbler* when it is at its hottest.

Immensely satisfied with lunch, I paid a visit to the restroom, which was spic and span, an oddity of sorts in the sub-continent and a welcome sign of progress. There was an attendant present, and he was busy cleaning and singing to himself. I quite like people who sing for no reason and for no one but themselves. When on my way out, I handed him a tip, he was a bit surprised and told me it was not necessary and that it was not a pay-to-use *Sulabh* toilet. My limited Tamil vocabulary did not allow me to counter that argument, so I just smiled, rolled my head in the typical Indian way, and insisted. He relented and continued with his singing. That itself was worth the tip.

As if all of that was not enough, there was a sweet shop that was part of the complex, so we walked in there. In southern sweet shops I have always looked to see if I can find the smooth variety of *Mysorepak*, the kind that my mother used to make. Most often, you get the bubbly crunchy variety which tastes similar but does not have the same texture as the *barfi*-like smoothness of *Amma's* preparation.

The *Mysorepak* on offer was smooth, not bubbly crunchy, so I was tempted, but one look at the colour and texture said it wouldn't be the same. We still bought a few pieces, and when I tried it later, it wasn't the way I wanted it to be. I should have been disappointed, but I wasn't. Some memories are best left in their original ... *barfi* smoothness!

11

Salem

Salem isn't exactly between Bangalore and Madras. Actually, it is nowhere close to either of the two southern megalopolises, both of which are sprawling and teeming with people but quite different from each other. Bangalore, officially Bengaluru, is chaotic and reluctant to embrace its mega-size, while Madras, officially Chennai, is more orderly and assumes its size and stature with confidence. I am not saying that because I am part Tamilian, but that is how I see it. As frustrating as Bangalore is, there is no other place in India I would rather live in. Its lovely climate and cosmopolitan culture are hard to beat. That said, times are changing, and it remains to be seen whether the garden city will be able to hold on to its cosmopolitanism in the face of exclusivist winds coming from the right side of Indian politics.

I wasn't thinking of the contrasting cities and the oncoming sauna of the south-eastern coastline of India when we drove out from Bangalore to Madras. I was just salivating at the prospect of a breakfast of masala *dosai* and filter coffee at Adyar Anand Bhavan and wondering if, like the stop at Murugan Idli Shop the previous year, it would trigger memories. Given that state of being, it was somewhat surprising to find my mind pick up a road sign for Salem just before we got to AAB. For someone who regularly misses exits, that was noteworthy.

Before I could start wondering why that road sign had registered, we arrived at Adyar Anand Bhavan and attention got focussed on the super efficiency of the roadside restaurant and its superfast assembly line production and delivery of *dosai, idli,* and *vadai.* Business schools might associate the assembly line production method with Henry Ford and talk about how it revolutionized automobile production, but what the assembly line methods of south Indian tiffin shops do in high-volume low-income settings is, in many ways, far more impressive. The organizational and management principles one can extract from them, not to mention the principles of complex combinations of Indian spices, are worthy pedagogical material.

When we got back on the road and turned left on the highway to head to Madras, my head, just a little bit dizzy from excellent *dosai* and filter coffee, got back to thinking about Salem. Why had it registered? I've never been to Salem and, as far as I know, have no family from there. My brother did work for a couple of years in a coffee plantation in Yercaud, and while that is in Salem district, I don't remember him telling me any stories of Salem. And, I surely hadn't been thinking about the infamous Salem witch trials in 17th century Massachusetts in the US. So why Salem?

It might have been the whiff of coffee lingering on my moustache that kept the southern India connection alive, for I soon realized that it all had to do with a washerwoman back in the early 70s when we lived in Bengali Market in the very heart of New Delhi.

Like most middle-class families in India, we had household help who would come every day to sweep the floors and wash clothes and do dishes. In Pantnagar, we had a big house and live-in help, but in Delhi, the rental accommodation was smaller, and so helpers did not stay; they came every day, did the work and left.

I want to be very honest about the use of these terms— "household help" and "helpers" — and the superficial dignity they lend to those who were called "servants" at that time and were essentially dispensable. The gulf between their lives and ours was so enormous that it would be an insult to airbrush the reality of those times with pleasant-sounding words that make things less queasy— now.

Kandai came every day to clean and wash clothes. *Amma* said she was part of a group of "Salem women" who did housework in Delhi households and once every few years would head back to Salem for a month. They lived on the outskirts of the city, which, back then, was Shakarpur or Trilokpuri or one of the other illegal settlements which miraculously got legalized come election time. Their south-to-north movement is part of the great internal migration story of India, something that was brought into sharp focus during the short-notice stupidity of the Covid-19 lockdown last year that threw the lives of Salem-like people in complete disarray.

There is, of course, also an external migration story, one that I am very much a part of and in a somewhat unique multi-continent multi-country way. In both movements, money and materials are, and always have been, prime motivators. How well ideas and values and, more generally— culture—piggyback on those and go back and forth is, in many ways, the more interesting story.

Kandai was very regular and usually on time, but then one day, she didn't show up. When she didn't come the next day as well, and then the next, we wondered what had happened. We weren't averse to doing household chores, and so we weren't too concerned about the daily cleaning—"*jhadoo* and *poncha*"—that is a necessity in Delhi because of the desert dust that hangs in the air and settles on everything. In that respect, I suppose, we were a little different from typical better-off families—all over India—who throw a fit when "my maid" doesn't show up and can be downright miserly in paying household help.

A classic illustration of that came many years later when we lived in South Bangalore in the 21st century in Adarsh Palace, an upscale apartment complex. One day, one of our seriously well-off neighbours, a highly educated professional at that, called up to ask if we could send over our household help because her maid hadn't come. When Muniamma, the woman who worked for us, went over to help them out, we were shocked when she was handed 20 rupees as compensation—by someone who was in a fix, and whose monthly income was probably a hundred thousand times that amount, and whose assets most surely were in the millions.

Back to the 1970s in Bengali Market, Kandai returned after a couple of days, and all went back to normal. I asked *Amma* what had happened, and she told me that Kandai said to her that she had gotten pregnant and to deal with that had been eating a lot of *pappalimaram*, Tamil for papaya. She believed that papaya was an effective morning-after-pill and "washed it out." When I asked *Amma* what was washed out and how papaya could wash out things, she said I was too young to understand, and that poor people lived life in different ways from us and ... that was how it was.

I didn't know anything about anything then, and I didn't ask any more. I am pretty sure Kandai did not know anything about estrogen and progestin and levonorgestrel, and I don't know whether that papaya ingestion was just a Salem belief or had genuine biochemical effects like modern contraceptives. All I know is that it was salient enough to stick around in my head this long.

It was only later in graduate school, when I studied biostatistics and the mathematical modelling of demographic phenomena and hung around multi-disciplinary demographers at the Carolina Population Center for several years, that I came to understand a bit more about all of that. There are still many things I don't understand and many questions I have—about why humans don't do obviously beneficial things like use contraception, get vaccinations, adhere to prescribed medications, et cetera—but I better leave those aside and get back to completing this story.

Sitting in the front seat, next to Raju, the multi-lingual taxi driver who could function in English, Hindi, Tamil, Kannada, Telugu and Malayalam, I thought about all these things and smiled and chuckled to myself. I had let my mind wander, and it had followed a thread from a Salem road sign to Bengali Market and Kandai, to papaya and contraception, and to the Carolina Population Center and triggered much more along the way. What more could one want from a long drive fuelled by *dosai* and filter coffee?

12

Cooking with inspiration

Anna Lou Ashby left Delhi to return to America in 1972. I don't know what month it was or whether it was even that year, the year before, or the one after. I also have no explanation for why I remember the name and departure of a person I never met. It might have something to do with the sound and novelty of her three-piece name, but the real reason is that on leaving, she sold her gas range and handheld mixie (blender) to my mother. ALA could not have known that her departure and the transfer of those appliances would mark a critical stage in my gastronomical development.

Until then, the tastings at home had come from a two-burner gas stove and a circular electric oven that depended on erratic electricity supply. Now they flowed in sync from the reliability of a gas cylinder which fired the combination appliance—a large oven and a multi-burner stove on top. Gas was a more dependable energy source, but it came in a red cylinder, and most families had only one. When the cylinder ran out, you had to wait for a replacement cylinder's delivery, which always took a day or two. The acquisition of the gas range automatically led to us having a second gas cylinder that served as a reserve. It was a luxury of sorts in the controlled economy of the 70s when things were invariably in short supply and access required either money or "connections," which ordinary folk like us didn't have.

The stovetop still put out authentic Tamilian, Maharashtrian and UP fare that *Amma* would dish out day after day, but the space below now had an expanded workload. There were scones and hot cross buns, and breads and cakes, and apple pies and soufflés, and pizzas and whatever caught my mother's fancy or looked interesting in the little spiral-bound baking cookbook she had. Everything that she had enjoyed in her days as a student in Leicester and London was reproduced, and then some. We were always willing to help with mixing things and trying whatever she made; the magician had a new wand, and she had eager knaves ready to do her bidding.

It was never quite the same after that year. You could say that thence began the life of a pig. I'd just say that that's when I became bound to the 'papillae' of life—'dem tiny taste buds that sit atop the tongue and have a stranglehold on me. It was *Amma's* doing. She was, quite simply, the most versatile and amazing cook I have ever encountered, quite possibly because she cooked with the most important ingredient—inspiration.

Of all the baking that emerged from that gas-powered oven, a few things had special standing, though ... they didn't have much of a chance to stand or sit around for long. One was a chocolate cake that was legendary, so much so that people unknown would request it now and then, and people known would want "Aunty" to teach them how to make one. Her cake was moist but also had a backbone, and it was finger-lickin' good—all the way from batter to pan scrapings. She could make it with eggs and without eggs, in her oven and in others' ovens, and once even in a relative's microwave oven. I am guessing that if she had had to, she could have even baked it without an oven!

The chocolate cake had no frosting because the one time she had put that on, the frosting had been so embarrassed at spoiling the show it had pleaded to stay away in the future. It did. It was the same with the other cakes; they too refused to be layered. The only exception was a lemon cake, which was a rich pound cake with a drizzling of sweetened lemon juice. That one liked the lemon juice because it would soak in a bit and enrichen its already rich flavours.

There was another version of the pound cake that didn't get to have much of an opinion. It was because it became the bottom layering for a trifle that had fruit and cream sitting on top. By the time you got to it, there was no cakey identity left. That trifle was a dessert fixture for special dinners for a couple of years, and no one liked it as much as my friend Madhav who could put away a good bit of it and put out effusive praise in return. *Amma* loved that.

There was also a banana bread that appeared more regularly because when bananas got a bit aged and squishy, none of us would eat them. So, instead of tossing them into the garbage, she would toss them in with some flour, baking powder, eggs and sugar. The inedible would transform into something that would leave an indelible mark on those same papillae. People who ate that banana bread never forgot it.

And finally, there was the cake that appeared towards the end of the year but announced its arrival weeks ahead of time. It was dubbed a Christmas cake because it came around in December and was anchored in *Amma's* memories of student years in England when she had enjoyed being part of the travelling choirs that went around singing Christmas carols.

The Christmas cake was special because it was the only time my simple and straight mother went deviant. Every year she would procure rum and soak the dry fruit in it for a few days. How she figured out where to get exotic baking ingredients at a time when those were available in only one or two shops in all of Delhi is a mystery. How she got hold of the rum was an even bigger mystery because there was no alcohol consumption in our home, and I doubt either of my parents knew where to get any. I always had the sense she was a bit embarrassed about that. It's not like she hadn't tried alcohol, but, as she told us at one point, the buttons she used to see with just a sip or two were buttons she didn't like to see.

The rum in the cake might also have been the reason why she insisted we didn't have more than one slice per day. She couched that instruction in terms of the cake being too rich and heavy and how we'd get sick if we had more than one slice, but I have the feeling it was also about the alcohol and the buttons. She had somewhat similar instructions about the other baked stuff, but we didn't follow those too closely; it was always so good, you couldn't. The Christmas cake one, we did.

You'd think that with such a rich heritage of refined baking and the sustained gluttony resulting from it I would have learnt something and tried my hand at baking. I haven't. Baking entails following recipes and directions to a T and for some reason I am averse to doing that. That hasn't stopped me from cooking what I did learn from watching and helping her while I was in high school and college.

Cooking learnt from her served me well in graduate school in America when I'd eat mostly at home and make myself proper meals, not the macaroni and cheese and microwave dinners a lot of my friends had. It made living on little very manageable and entertaining friends very affordable. It continued to serve me well when I had a real income and my own family, though they must surely wonder how the same dish tastes a bit different each time, sometimes finger-lickin' good and sometimes just ordinary. When they ask me how the good ones have been made, I have no answer, quite simply because I follow inspiration, not the perspiration of formulaic recipes. That bit, I got from her.

13

Refugee Market

I shouldn't have, but I did. I don't know whether it was relief at having finished all the assignment marking for the year, the crisp baguette with tuna salad from a hole-in-the-wall Cambodian lunch place, the languorous walk back from a rarely taken lunch outing, or just the warm November sun. Whatever it was, I shouldn't have ... just burst out laughing when I saw the back of a Wellington city bus advertising free bra fittings at Farmers, a local department store.

My reaction wasn't voyeuristic. I wasn't led off into imagining anything, and it sure as hell wasn't a cynical old fart look-what-the-world-has-come-to laugh. The involuntary reaction resulted from the memory trigger the ad had provided to a world gone by—of pre-adolescent indulgences in tamarind and pomegranate delights, of playing with marbles and spinning tops, of bicycle rentals and adolescent savouring of simple flavourings—in a market that has a distinct history but does not feature in the recordings of history.

The adolescent bit was in years 11 and 12 of high school when my school "batch" held sway as the senior-most class and came and went as we pleased. It came to be so because in the great wisdom of reality-removed Indian policymaking, the education ministry had introduced a new 10+2 system and extended schooling from 11 to 12 years, and we were the first lot to experience it. The grand plan was to have a vocational stream emerge after year 10 except, it had little anchoring in the workings of the labour market on the supply and demand sides.

In those golden years, one day, I tagged along with friends to savour the much-talked-about one-rupee *'bun-samosa'* at the nondescript Refugee Market at the back of our high school. There was nothing to the *bun-samosa* but a bun sandwiching two *samosas* doused in *saunth*, that devilish tamarind concoction that lights up many an Indian snack. Then again, there was everything to it because the taste and price hooks had me go back to it again and again and never forget the experience. When the organizers of our 25th high school reunion arranged *bun-samosas* for the get-together, it was a special treat except ... biting into that no-star delicacy in the five-star antiseptic atmosphere of Le Meridien hotel just didn't have the street flavouring of chaos and commotion in it.

Until recently, I had no idea how and why Refugee Market had that name, and I'll bet—two *bun-samosas*—that none of my friends did either. It is only now, when details are of interest, and the internet offers easy access to them, that I have learnt that the origins of that name lie in the partition of India at the time of independence. The migration of 14 million people across arbitrarily defined borders produced a lot of refugees who settled in various parts of Delhi. Some of them ended up operating that small market, which came to be called Refugee Market.

That logic does not apply to the nearby Bengali Market, which had nothing to do with Bengal, the state in the east of India. According to the not-entirely-reliable Wikipedia, Bengali Market was founded in 1930 by Bengali Mal Lohia. It doesn't say whether BML was from Bengal and how he got that first name; someone with the brilliant writer-historian William Dalrymple's digging-for-detail ability would need to figure that out.

Sadly, no one has bothered to put in an entry for Refugee Market. You have to go to both markets to see why—Refugee Marlet is on the low end of the retail-space scale, and Bengali Market is on the high end, and while all realities have histories, only the upscale have recordings; the downscale just pass by. Such are the ways of the world.

Those *bun-samosa* trips reminded me of an earlier time when I roamed the streets of that neighbourhood without much of a care. Those were the days we lived on Todarmal Road, which was, and still is, a stone's throw from Bengali Market, our go-to place for groceries, stationery, and snacks and sweetmeats from the famous Nathu Sweets and Bengali Sweet House. Refugee Market was further away and not for our household needs. It was my go-to place, not for learning history, but making my own ... with *kanchas* (marbles), *lattoos* (spinning tops), tennis and cricket balls, the mango-tamarind-pomegranate delights of *aam papad* and *churan* and bicycle rentals. All those childhood essentials were only available at Refugee Market, not at the more upscale Bengali Market.

The only exception was a *gulli*, sometimes also referred to as *gilli*—a short piece of wood with tapered ends that is born to be whacked by a longer piece in the quintessential street sport of *gulli danda* that is played all over South Asia and, according to Wikipedia, as far out as Turkey and Italy. I never looked for a *gulli* in Refugee Market because somehow, and I don't know how I found out that for 50 paise, you could get the attendant of the coal shop at one of the backstreets of Bengali Market to make you one from firewood. I can explain the mechanics of *gulli danda*, but what's the point? You can catch it all on YouTube, another internet invention that has rendered DIY books redundant.

Most of my transactions at Refugee Market were at two little shops with a bylane in between. They were small-scale convenience stores and sold basic stuff—things like pins and needles and thread and undergarments and whatnot—that people needed to keep their lives running. All that was really for the adults; kids' lives don't run on that. They need *kanchas* and *lattoos*, and little delights that cost little money that parents are willing to spare or happen to leave around... for wayward kids to pick up without their noticing its absence.

And so it came to be that one day, back in those pre-adolescent times, I was at Refugee Market looking to buy a spinning top. It was my third or fourth one, and by then I had become quite proficient in its operation—capable of winding the rope around the top reflexively, tucking the knotted end of the rope between the pinkie and the fourth finger, holding the top between the thumb forefinger and the other three fingers, and letting rip. Hitting the aimed-for spot was the first mark of skill, but the real one was to let it rip and get it back directly onto one's hand without touching the ground. That bit marked you out as notable to other kids who would then want the top to spin on their hands and would beg you for that privilege.

I had gotten past all of that and was now ready to graduate to the mean side in a game where the ultimate objective was dropping my spinning top onto the opponent's top to split it—so the other kid would be topless. It is admittedly mean-spirited, and I don't know what today's guardians of political correctness would say about it, but that's how some games are, and that's how that one was played.

So there I was at Refugee Market, ready to buy a bigger, fatter top with a thicker and sharper nail for the spinning end. Setting up any top required time because the lathe-turned wooden tops came without nails, and the shopkeeper had to hammer in a nail at the spinning end, then cut off the head with a pair of pliers and file the edges, so it was ready to spin. Smaller tops could make do with a thin nail, but a big top needed a thick nail and lopping off its head was not a straightforward scrunching of the pliers but needed a bit of working around. All of that took more time.

When I asked the shopkeeper for a bigger top, he said to wait because he had other customers to attend to. In today's times, I would probably whip out a smartphone and get smart, but back in those days, there wasn't much to do but hover around the counter, and so I was hovering. Indians, of course, are world leaders in that activity. Go to any railway counter, airline counter, bank counter, any counter of any sort in India, and there is a good chance you'll find the transactee surrounded by one or two others on the side with elbows resting on the counter. The counter-dwellers are either trying to cut in the queue or just watching over the transaction—in your interest, in their interest. At times, they even offer unsolicited advice. If you are the privacy-loving kind, it will drive you nuts, but it is normal practice, quite likely picked up as little boys and girls at places like Refugee Market.

Hovering in that shop, in the hope of getting a meaner top, I didn't hear what she said, but I caught what he said: "*Katora size thik rahega*" (cup size will work). My ears perked up, and my attention hoovered in to see what it was all about because it was a knickknack shop, not a kitchen utensil store, and there were no "*katoras*" i.e., cups in sight. It was when he brought out a box of brassieres for her to see that I realized what the *katora* was about —it was his assessment of her chest size. I don't remember how I reacted, but there was no reaction from here or him. She was comfortable getting a bra fitting from him, and he was obviously comfortable providing advice. It was a market transaction, and that was that.

I am guessing the free bra fittings offer at Farmers in Wellington, New Zealand, was similar in essence, though probably not in the mechanics of the process. I can't be sure because, well ... let's just leave it at that. The bus advertisement had made for a laugh and provided a ride back to a place that had made me many smiles a long time ago, and that's all one needs to know.

14

The Invisibles

He appeared from nowhere. One year he was there; the year before, he wasn't. Of course, he may have always been there, and I might have only "discovered" him one day. It happens all the time to all of us. We are so busy going about our lives and so focused on some things that we don't notice our surroundings—things that are always there—and then are surprised when we notice them. My "discovery" of the neighbourhood *tandoori roti walla* was like that. It had little to do with his arrival in the surroundings, but once I had noticed him, his functioning was of great interest.

His little *jhopadi* (hut) with a below-ground *tandoor* oven was behind my friend Ashim's flat on the little back street that ran off Todarmal Road towards Triveni Kala Sangam in the Bengali Market neighbourhood. Much like my early life wanderings in Pantnagar, I was here and there in that neighbourhood, and likely "chanced" upon him while loitering about, and then got transfixed by what he did and how he did it. He made *tandoori rotis* and *paranthas* for a small fee, charging by the piece one price for *roti* and a marginally higher one for *parantha*.

I loved going over to his *jhopadi* and sitting there on my haunches and watching him do his thing with absolute admiration and fascination. The whole process began by kneading the *atta* (flour) at home and taking that and dry *atta* over to his *jhopadi*. He would start by putting a small amount of the dry flour on a wooden board which was somewhat bigger than the typical rolling boards at home. Then he would pluck out small amounts of the kneaded flour, roll them up into little balls and set them in one place. After that, he would wet his fingertips, pick up each ball, slap it up and down on the wooden board to flatten it out, and then flip the flattened dough from one hand to the other to spread it out to about the size of a quarter plate. That would then be put on a smallish cloth pillow, the type workers in India use to settle the things they carry on their heads. With one hand, he'd open the underground oven's lid and, with the other, dive into the hot oven with the little pillow and stick the wet *roti* to the earthen sides of the *tandoor*.

The procedure would then be repeated with the next ball of dough. In between, he knew exactly when to take two long iron prongs and pick off the baked *rotis* from the side, just before they were ready to fall onto the burning hot coals at the bottom. The sequence of actions was a little bit different for *paranthas* which needed the application of *ghee* at the start and at the end. Everything was done seamlessly and with the fluidity of an artist, and there was a certain rhythm to the whole routine.

If you took a napkin along to wrap the stack of hot tandoori *rotis*, they would stay dry and fresh through the short walk home, and you could have a restaurant-style meal without ever leaving home. My mother was an incredible cook, and every meal was better than what you could get at a restaurant, but the one thing she could not make was *tandoori rotis*. Those needed a below-ground earthen oven, and in urban settings, that was not possible. The coal-fired *angithi* was about the closest you could get and, while that had a charm and a flavourful odour of its own, it wasn't a *tandoor*.

The *tandoori roti walla* was honest to the core. He never kept any of the flour or the *ghee*, never charged an extra paisa, and refused the extra my aunt offered for the spectacle when she was visiting from overseas. He had almost nothing in that hut, most likely was sending money home to a family back in some village far away and would have certainly benefitted from siphoning off a bit here and there, but he didn't. I suppose he wasn't willing to cut out the honest corners of those *rotis*.

He also made a *dal* which he served to labourers with *rotis*, but we didn't go for that. One time I begged my mother to let me get some, and we tried it, but it was very thin. That's when I learnt how poorer people make do—same taste, less substance. We weren't poor, so ours had less water, and since he didn't have anything special taste-wise, we didn't continue with that trial.

Who he was, where he was from, what stratum of society he occupied was of little interest to us, and I also suspect others who went to his *jhopadi* to get *tandoori rotis* and *paranthas*. In that respect, he was not that different from all the other "informal sector" workers who greased the giant Indian urban machine—their identities were invisible. In today's world, leftists and, more generally critics of economics love dumping on the market economy for the inequality it breeds, the waste and environmental destruction it brings, its connections to politics and shaping of policy, and more. While there certainly is some truth to all of that, the invisibility the market economy affords is a valued feature, especially for those who have few alternatives to make a living and are caught in the suffocating strangulations of rural society in India.

I don't remember his name and likely didn't know it then either. To me, and likely to others, he was the *tandoori roti walla*, or quite possibly just the *roti walla*. "*Walla*" is a commonly used suffix and denotes a person who performs a particular occupation, sells a particular good or provides a particular service. With female workers, called "*wallis*," the entire workforce can be labelled in terms of work identity, though the term is used more for informal sector workers.

There was a whole range of *wallas* and *wallis* in Delhi, some fixed in one location, but many more itinerant. They sold their goods and services from door to door, or at the places where people congregated for different reasons. The *roti walla* could be found in the same location, much like the "*pani walla*" (water seller), "*churan walla*" (condiments seller), "*mungfali walla*" (peanut vendor), "*istri walla*" (clothes ironing person), "*mochi*" (cobbler) and "puncture *walla*" (bicycle tire fixer).

Our *roti walla* lived and slept in his hut, but the others lived in the invisible outskirts of town and magically appeared in the same spot every day, walking the many miles or riding rickety bicycles and taking public buses. It was much the same for "*jhadu-poncha wallis*" (cleaning women) who came home every day and the "*sabzi-phal wallas*" (vegetable and fruit vendor) who wandered the streets and would stop by our homes when called. These were the regulars, and then there were the ones who came periodically, some on weekends, and some seasonally. There was the "*dhobi*" (washerman), the *mali* (gardner) and the "*kabadi walla*" (waste purchaser) who came every weekend; the "*chhurri walla*" (knife sharpener) and "*talai walla*" (copper and brass pot refurbisher) who came by occasionally; and the "*dhunai walla*" (quilt refurbisher) who came at the start of winters.

I am deliberately mentioning each and every one that I can remember because I loved watching all of them do their thing in their unique ways. In much the same way as I remember the details of the *roti walla*'s craft, I also remember little details of who did what and how and can recount those, but it would take too long. And the thing is this—while all that would be fascinating, it would say nothing about who the *wallas* and *wallis* actually were.

A lot about the identity and lives of those people was invisible, but not all of it. In younger years, I was oblivious to a lot of things, but as I grew older, I became increasingly aware of the wide gulf between our lives and theirs. It didn't alter my way of living and functioning, and I would never claim that I was "holier than thou" because of that awareness, but they were not invisible to me then, and they are not invisible to me now—whenever I visit India.

I see now as I used to back then, but there is a difference—now it is with a perspective derived from working on development issues for many years, thinking about these things all the time and teaching an undergraduate course in development policy. Every year I think about the *wallas* and *wallis* when I get students to appreciate the complex web of economic connectivity that links up people's lives in a country and ... how the poor are always the most fragile and most invisible parts of that web.

India has grown and changed enormously in the 50-plus years since I took flour to the *roti walla*'s *jhopadi* back in the early 70s, but it still has millions and millions of people who scratch an informal living in towns and cities. They are often invisible to those whose lives they grease. Sometimes that comes into sharp relief when Indians are shocked when confronted with the—fact—that while there is the ballyhooed "Indian middle class" of 300 odd million, the country also has an equivalent number of poor people, the most of any country in the world.

What is even more shocking is how the *wallas* and *wallis* are invisible to people who have the power to make policies that affect their meagre livelihoods. If only the current government had seen them when it went about demonetizing their lives at short notice in 2016, demeaning them again with a short-notice lockdown in 2020, and entirely ignoring them during the second surge of the pandemic! Pity, they were and still are, invisible and dispensable to a government that has built its case for ruling in terms of unleashing market forces and transforming India into a trillion-dollar economy.

15

Men in white

He came every week, always in a white *veshti*, plain shirt and leather ch*appals*. It was always in the evenings after his day job at All India Radio, and always during my cherished playtime. For that, I hated it—so much so that I would wait for him till the appointed hour, give it five more minutes, and if he wasn't there, run away to play. If he did show up, *Amma* would have to send someone to fetch me. Sheepishly I would come back and then complain to her later. In the three-four years he came, I don't remember him being late more than once or twice. While he was there, though, I loved it.

Mr. Panchapakesan taught me to play Carnatic music on the violin and was both infinitely patient and greatly frustrated because he said I had talent, music sense, and the right fingers for the violin, but I didn't practice. He said if I practised, I could be a good violinist, but I had no desire to wear a *veshti* and play music on All India Radio. The cusp of adolescence in Bengali Market in the carefree early 70s held many innocent distractions, and I had succumbed to them entirely.

I desperately want to remember how it all began but can't. You can say music was inevitable, inevitable given that my mother played the *sitar* and I attended a school where academics wasn't everything and where art, music, dance, drama and sports were equal partners. Still, stars can align one way, and lives can manage to walk away in a different direction.

Why I didn't go to Triveni Kala Sangam to learn to paint like my brother and instead chose to play music, and that too the violin, a difficult instrument, I will never know. Was it because *Amma* took me to the Carnatic music maestro Lalgudi Jayaraman's concert at Bharati Vidya Bhawan, and I liked it even though I fell asleep? Or was it because she knew Dr N Rajam, a Tamilian but one of the finest Hindustani music violinists from her Benaras Hindu University days? Or was it the start of weekly painting, music, clay room rotations in Junior Modern School? I have moonwalked through memory many times but have not found the definitive answer. It doesn't matter; a fuzzy memory of the start doesn't take anything away from the beauty of the journey that unfolded thereafter.

Whatever it was, a violin was bought, and Mr. Panchapakesan was employed to teach me the fine bowing and fingering needed to play Carnatic music, the south Indian style of classical music. Why *Amma* didn't tune me into Hindustani music, which she played on the *sitar*, and instead lined me up on the south side of town is another mystery that is too late to investigate.

Initially, the violin was a run-of-the-mill one acquired from the Rikhi Ram music store in nearby Connaught Place. Then, when *Amma* went to see her sisters in Europe in 1972, she brought me back a German violin. I have to guess Mr. Panchapakesan suggested it was time for me to move on to a more finely tuned instrument.

The beauty of those musical years lay in the diversity I was exposed to—Carnatic at home and Hindustani at school, Mr. Panchapakesan at home and Mr. Choudhary in junior school, one a Tamilian the other a Bengali, one in shirt and *veshti* the other in pant and trousers, one a professional violinist the other … I am not entirely sure, other than being a strummer of *sarod*.

I have long wondered how many countries have two seriously classical and codified musical traditions that run in parallel, several other folk music streams, and the popular stream connected with movies. India might get a lot of things wrong, but of the few things it surely gets right is music. To that, add the other arts and the art of the gut—food—and it would be hard to find another place that does the "*gana, bajana, khana*" (singing, playing, food) combination better.

That is how the first few years of music went for me. The rhythm of that charming phase of life turned a different beat when life began in senior school on Barakhamba Road, and I landed at the doorstep of another man in white.

In junior school, we had rotated between the different art forms, getting exposure to music, painting and clay modelling. In senior school, there was more, much more to choose from. In our school timetable, we used initials of our teachers' names to mark out different classes, but for extracurricular activities, it was a simple acronym—MAC. It stood for Music-Arts-Crafts, but the Arts-Crafts part of that included a variety of activities that included woodwork, sculpture, metalwork, tie-dye, photography, radio engineering and more. If you think about it, it is pretty remarkable that so many activities were on offer in a regular high school.

The bigger difference between the two levels of schooling was not variety but the fact that you had to choose one activity in senior school and then do just that. Naturally, I chose music.

It had been customary to take off our shoes before entering the music room in junior school. It was the same at the senior one, but with a difference. In the younger one, you could bring in playfulness, but in the older one, that had to be left with the shoes. Music was serious business in Mr. Khastagir's castle of instruments tucked away at the rear of the curved red brick school building.

It is safe to say most people in school thought him caustic and either disliked him or feared him and just stayed out of his way. But if you opted for music in MAC then you had no choice but him. He was demanding, quixotic, and a stern teacher. Very much a purist, he always wore white—white *dhoti* and white *kurta*—and was a bachelor. I know all of that is a socially ingrained idea of a socially constructed notion of "purity", and real life is a lot more multi-hued, so perhaps it is better to qualify that statement by saying he was a purist when it came to music. In the very first class, he defined music as "anything that pleases the ear," but the truth is he only had an appreciation for classical forms of music, and even there, he really only knew the Hindustani style.

Music with Mr. Khastagir was supposed to be weekly but from the very first class became daily. He liked me from the moment I stepped into his class, all because I could bow a violin's strings reasonably well. When I told him I had been learning Carnatic music at home for a couple of years, he was even more impressed because he had great regard for South Indian dedication to classical music which he felt was bastardized in the north and other parts of the country.

He wanted me in the school orchestra, which provided accompaniment to the singing of prayer songs in the morning school assembly. There wasn't one song but an entire repertoire, and to learn that, I started going to his music room during the daily 15-minute morning milk break. It took a couple of months to learn all the songs, but just as soon as I had picked up all of them, I became a fixture in the school orchestra playing the prayer songs every morning and his compositions at annual school functions.

His compositions were melodious, and in them, I learnt of the *khali*—a deliberately missed note/beat. If you don't know what *khali* is and search the internet, what comes up is a lot about the Great Khali, an outlandishly big man who is said to be a wrestler, power-lifter, and many other things. If you know Hindi and are searching with music in mind, you'll know that none of that is relevant and what should come up is something about emptiness, for that is what is what *khali* means in Hindi.

I learnt to play Mr. Khastagir's *khali* but had no idea what it was in terms of music theory, so recently, I went looking for information on it. I had always thought it to be an empty note. It turns out *khali* is actually an empty beat. I was never any good at music theory, so I don't know the difference between note and beat. I could listen and play music reasonably well, and for me, the melody was more in the notes than in the beat. That might be why I have always thought of *khali* as an empty note.

Playing the *khali* was a learning experience because you had to imagine a non-extant note (or beat), play it in your head, not in your hands, and then move on to what exists. You can cheat on it by slowing the beat, but then the emptiness is filled, and it's just not the same. I don't remember encountering it in Carnatic music and anything else, but I don't know much about the technical aspects of music, so maybe it is there in other musical traditions. All I know is that Khastagir's *khali* was anything but empty—it was exquisite, and I loved it so.

For four years, he kept me under his wing, and then just as we ascended the throne of high school, that final year called S5 in our school, he and the old guard that was part of the school principal's inner group were gone. I continued to play in the school orchestra that first year of seniority under Mr. Choudhary, who had moved up from junior to senior school. He was nice, and so were his compositions but ... the magic of music was gone.

It might have begun slipping away earlier when Carnatic music had stopped after we had returned from a temporary move to Poona. I am not sure whether that was because Mr. Panchapakesan could not be located, or because adolescence had completely gotten hold of me, or because the long bus and bicycle commutes from Munirka to Barakhamba Road and back left little time for music lessons in the evenings.

Whatever it was, adolescence or the loss of the men in white—one after the other—music slipped away. I was so wrapped up in being 17 that I didn't notice it. When we got to the second year of seniority in school, I gave up playing the violin on a regular basis. I wish I hadn't, but then again, there are many things I did back then that I wish I hadn't, and many things I am glad I did.

I hear Mr. Khastagir went back to Bengal after retiring from school but didn't last much more than a year without the routine of school and composing music. Come '78, or possibly '79, he was gone. When we, or as we used to say "our batch", put out a final edition of Sandesh, the school magazine, the student editors left an empty page to mark his passing. I didn't understand why they had done that and protested, but what was done was done. Could it be that they understood what *khali* really is—a richness of experience the known pattern doesn't capture—and was that why they had deliberately left a page blank to reflect the loss of Khastagir's *khali?* All these years, I have thought that way, but Dev Benegal, one of the editors, told me recently that it was based on something more pragmatic: they would have liked to put in a black page, but the ink cost too much so they left it blank.

I didn't ever pick up the violin again, not in college and not in the faraway lands I moved to after college. *Amma* held on to my violin and kept it safely stored in her Godrej *almirah* amongst her collection of *sarees* and the other precious tidbits that were tucked into their folds. She must have hoped I would return to it. Even I thought about that every now and then, but never did.

She held on to that violin hope for 10 years, and then in 1988, with upcoming retirement and a move out of Delhi imminent quietly asked me if she should sell the violin. Very matter-of-factly, I said yes. It seemed the sensible thing to do. I think she would have liked me to say otherwise. I think the men in white would have concurred. I wish I had.

16

Riffs and alaaps

Music has riffs and licks and all kinds of delightful twinklypicks that sit somewhat separately but not entirely independently of the main composition. Sometimes they appear only at the start, and sometimes they get sprinkled all through the composition. I quite like those preludes, interludes and postludes because they are simpler and purer combinations of fewer notes and, when done well, more melodic. That, of course, is my somewhat simplistic view of these things.

Amongst those simpler combinations, there is nothing quite like an *alaap*—the introduction to a composition in classical Hindustani music. Its beauty lies in … well, so many things that you don't know where to begin and where to end and where to go in between. That is precisely its charm—the variation and potential for improvisation. Formulaic sorts would have a hard time with it, but an *alaap* can accommodate them too. In that sense, it is quintessentially Indian—bending, twisting, adjusting to carry on.

For me, there is another charm in an *alaap*—it often has a lower octave setting which enables hummability. You can hum an *alaap* under your breath, and no one will notice it; for wayward people with open minds, that is a boon. You can keep the windows open for a memory to waft in and keep it humming privately. If you've ever done that, you'll know. If you haven't, maybe now you'll want to have a go.

A movie song, even one inspired by classical Hindustani music, can't really claim to have *alaap*, even when it has a non-instrumental introduction. Songs are short and so are their introductions, but if any movie song can claim to have an *alaap*, then surely the Manna Dey melody, "*Tere nainan talash karen jisse*," can. The way MD extends his vocal cords to stretch out 16 words to 36 seconds is, quite simply, out of this world. The song that follows is a step down, but only because the *alaap* has created unrealistic expectations. It's blending of *sitar, sarod, tabla, ghungroos,* and what sounds like a *sarangi* is beautiful.

Only a genius like SD Burman could have composed something like that, and only Manna Dey could have held a note so cleanly for so long that you feel it would be blasphemy to try and hum along. I can't, and don't. I hear it quietly each time and then try and sing it—in the car with windows closed or in the study at home when no one is around. It is hard to explain the pleasure of wafting on melodies that have words lazing around on notes, each grateful for the pleasure of the other.

All of which begs the question: Where did the memory of this song come from? I am not entirely sure wherefrom it came into my consciousness, but it might have ridden another memory that floated in while reading a brilliant article in The Atlantic magazine on the saxophone riff that leads into "Baker Street," the drifty, somewhat depressing song that made Gerry Rafferty famous.

In the late 80s when I was in graduate school in the US, I used to hear that song quite often on WRDU, "Raleigh's Classic Rock" ra-

dio station in Chapel Hill, North Carolina. I love the haunting saxophone riff which permeates the song, preluding, interluding and
postluding the lyrics. For me, songs were, and still are, mainly about
melody and rhythm, so I am not sure whether I caught on to lyrics
like these that perfectly captured my state of mind and mood in
those days when I was struggling to find direction in my academic
journey:

> "You used to think that it was so easy
> You used to say that it was so easy
> But you're trying, you're trying now
> Another year and then you'd be happy
> Just one more year and then you'd be happy
> But you're crying, you're crying now."

The Atlantic article and the repeated playing of Baker Street on
YouTube and its riff "naturally" led to the *alaap* in SD Burman's
Tere Nainan and had me playing the song ... seventeen hundred and
fifty-five times on YouTube! Don't ask how that is natural; that's
just how my mind works. That, of course, left me wondering why,
quite aside from its beautiful prelude, *Tere Nainan* might hold special meaning. It took a bit of detective work and a bit of luck, but I
now know how it leads back to the second decade of life.

We didn't go to the cinema much in the early 70s, and the
weekly Hindi movie offering on TV on Sundays was invariably
dated, so it is highly unlikely I saw *Talash*, the movie the song is part
of. I most certainly would have heard it on All India Radio, which
played all sorts of music all day long and was the primary source of
entertainment for most of the country's population. Still, I felt there
was something more to the song, some sort of connection. Unable
to consciously find it, and not wanting to force one, I left it alone

thinking … if there was one, it would come, and if there wasn't, there wasn't.

It was several months later, or possibly a year later, when we were in Goa with dear friends from our five years in Bangalore, that the possibility of a link came up. We were in a taxi on the way back from dinner at someplace, and Sridhar was humming the beautiful and whimsical Geeta Dutt song "*Mujhe jaan na kaho meri jaan*" from the movie *Anubhav*. That triggered a memory of the Manna Dey song "*Phir kahin koi phool khila*" which I am very fond of. Could it be that the two Manna Dey songs held special meaning because they were part of another, more specific, memory? Possibly.

At some point in the early 70s, *Amma* decided that our collection of vinyl records had been sitting unplayed for too long and that it was time to buy a new record player. It was a rare spending splurge in the shoestring budget my mother ran the home with, largely on her own university income.

We lived in Bengali Market, and one weekend she and my brother headed out to Berco's, a music store in nearby Connaught place, to buy a record player. Berco's was running a promotion—buy a record player and get three free LPs. I doubt that was the inducement to buy the player; it was just the bonus they came back home with.

One of the three records had a *jugalbandi* of violin and *shehnai* by the great Hindustani classical musicians Pandit VG Jog and Ustad Bismillah Khan, the second was a compilation of Paul Anka's greatest hits, and the third one had a mélange of Hindi film songs.

I am not entirely sure why they chose those three and will never really know, but the third LP, the one with film songs, might have been picked because it had Vani Jairam's masterpiece, "*Bole re papihara*," on it. She was *Amma*'s cousin's wife's sister, and while my simple mother had several connections with "famousity," the musical ones were always special and dear to her heart. She never name-dropped them in the way folks in Delhi often do, but that's no surprise;—she wasn't from there, but from a time and place where genuine relationships, not names and namesakes, mattered.

I am quite sure the two Manna Dey songs, from *Talash* and *Anubhav*, were on that same record and thus got played quite often and lodged themselves into my memory. They are magical in their own unique ways. Both showcase MD's ability to hold notes clearly and cleanly for extended stretches, and both have delightful starts, one with a brief alaap and the other with an even briefer vocal start mixed with distinct *sitar* notes and what sounds like *jaltarang*.

What is distinctive about the *"Phir kahin koi phool khila"* song is the ambiguity in Gulzar's lyrics. They must have meaning in relation to the movie's story, but for those who haven't seen the movie, like me, they are entry points—*alaaps*—into a melodious wander into a different world each time. It must be the reason why I often find myself humming that song more than many others, making something different out of the lyrics each time, or simply floating along on its melody.

17

Yaadon ki Baraat

There are things I know, and things I don't know, and things I will never know. That "don't mean" I am going all Donald Rumsfeld here—with that infamous Iraq war knowns-unknowns obfuscation of his. I'm just saying there are things I know I will eventually get around to, just not how I'll get to them, and there are things I will never figure out. Such was the case with the Bollywood movie classic of 1973, *Yaadon ki Baraat* (marriage procession of memories). I have known for the past 10 years, ever since I started lining up memories to write about, that at some point I would get to YKB. I just didn't know what the trigger would be. It came last year.

For those not in the know, *Yaadon ki Baraat* was "the first masala film, combining elements of the action, drama, romance, musical, crime and thriller genres." So says Wikipedia, that fountain of pointless information that is always worth starting from but never worth ending up with—if you are doing serious work. My little stories aren't really serious, so Wikipedia's "fountainousness" serves as an apt starting point for a story of the trigger to YKB and its memory.

In school, I used to play the violin reasonably well, and while I didn't quite get music theory, I did pick up plenty of "*swar gyan*"—musical note sense. I should have kept at it, but life's dice rolled a certain way, and I stopped playing when I left high school. I did think of picking up the violin again and learning other instruments but never got down to it, forever flirting with the idea but never committing to the relationship.

The good thing is, I am a hoarder—of things and memories—and so the guitar I bought back in 2006 during one of those flirtations stayed. I hadn't planned on buying that guitar, but finding myself in a music shop in Basavanagudi in Bangalore, I went with a whim and bought the beautiful instrument. I tried to get it to twingle a couple of times but found the finger positioning more challenging than that of a violin and gave up. The guitar stayed and travelled from Bangalore to Washington to Wellington, from one home to another, from one closet to another, never once peeking out of the black nylon bag it had come in.

It would have stayed that way, but towards the end of last year, I rode another whim and signed up for a weekly group guitar class at a continuing education centre. The Wednesday evening classes began in the last week of the teaching term, and in the rush to conclude the three courses I was teaching, I forgot about the first class and only got going with the second one. While the strumming was fun, the chord switching was hard to do, and the wrist-twisting was harder than what is required for a violin. Even though the frets provided precise guidance on where to press, there were too many to remember and expectedly the fingertips hurt. I knew that if I persisted, the wrist would align, the fingers would hook the right way, and their tips would get numb and learn to dance on the six strings.

It continued thus for three weeks, a bit of practice every day and then cluelessness in class on Wednesdays. Tired of feeling that way and with the sense that the learning wasn't going anywhere, I stopped going, figuring time would be better spent picking notes on my own. Time agreed.

If it had been another passing flirtation, and I have many to smile about, that would have been it. It wasn't. Class died; music didn't. The three-week stretch gave me what I was looking for—the joy of making music. I've listened to music all along, looping in and out of genres and instruments, but listening to music is one thing, making it is another. It is not about accomplishment, just ... something different that is hard to explain. If you've done it, you get it, if you haven't, you don't. I hadn't done it in 40-odd years but finally found that joy, all because of a whim, a commitment to go along to three classes I didn't really enjoy, and then a willingness to walk away to the sound of a distant drummer.

My guitar playing didn't change much, and two weeks on, I still couldn't switch chords and play the simple chord-combination songs of Bob Marley and Bob Dylan and U2 that were covered in the first three weeks of class. I didn't mind, figuring that someday I'd get there. Or not. I was happy to sit quietly and make up little three-four note combinations, and if I'd get one right, play it over, and over, and over. Not knowing how to read or write music, I wrote them down in my own way—as combinations of string and fret numbers.

It was on the second day of this new fingerpicking direction when the second and third fingers were on the fourth and fifth strings, and the pick rolled from one note to the other and ... my ear started looking for a melody-making third note. One usually comes along, but this time around I sensed that the mind had joined in and was looking ... not just for any note, but a particular one.

A certain rush came on at that point. It is that feeling when you feel that you are on to something, that you are close to something, but not quite there. That's how I felt as I fumbled around looking for the third note without letting go of the two I had found. I knew that if I played those two, again and again, they'd "naturally" lead me to the third. It didn't take long to find it, and just as soon as I had, I knew what had brought the rush—the combination was the initial hook to the title song from *Yaadon ki Baraat*.

The guitar was set aside, YouTube was turned on, "*Yaadon ki Baraat*" got typed into the search box—and the Kishore Kumar-Mohammed Rafi duet was played—again and again. The song is a nice one, and I am sure somewhere along the way, I have sung it to myself, in a motorcycle helmet or in a car. But I am also quite sure that I have never hummed the first three instrumental notes; they make up too short of a riff to get noticed by the conscious mind. Memory, on the other hand, picks up packages of stimuli experienced consciously and nonconsciously and records them with emotional weighting. That must be why I knew the riff without knowing it.

If getting the notes right and lining up a personal experience with stuff I had read in academic journals wasn't worth smiling about, the hook into a particular point in the past sure was. It transported me to the start of the summer of '74. Like every year, the sun had started scorching Delhi by the time final exams for our first year in high school ended in early May. It was the big year in our still-young lives, the year when we had moved from the grey junior school building on Humayun Road to the sprawling red senior school building on Barakhamba Road.

A group of us who had been friends for several years made a plan to see *Yaadon ki Baraat* at the end of final exams. I don't remember if we had ever gone to see a movie together, likely not. The movie had been released in November '73 and was a screaming hit, rivalling Raj Kapoor's *Bobby* which had been released a few months earlier. One was a *masala* movie and the other a teenage romance, and both were defining ones for Hindi cinema. I don't know why we went to see YKB and not Bobby, but it likely had something to do with the fact that one of us was able to use some "connection" to get tickets to one and not to the other. That's how it worked back then.

Sitting in front of the laptop with the three notes of the YKB theme twanging in my ears I ran through the memory of that outing but other than the plot and the songs and some other details, not much else came through other than one question: Which movie theatre had we seen that defining movie in? I knew it was in Connaught Place, which was walking distance from school, and I was pretty sure it wasn't Regal or Rivoli, which meant it was either Odeon or Plaza. Which was it? Substantively, it didn't matter, but just like finding the third note in the sequence, I needed to know. Would the others remember?

I sent messages on WhatsApp and Messenger to see if any of the others in the group remembered. It was a long shot, but I like long shots into memory. Four had either no memory or just a hazy one. Two remembered only the songs, and one, Suhail, only remembered superhot Zeenat Aman. I smiled at that one because if you'd seen the movie in those times, there would be no getting away from the show-stopping long white dress she wore in "*Chura liya hai tumne jo dil ko*" or the short red one in "*Aap ke kamre mein koi rahta hai.*" After being introduced in Dev Anand's movie *Hare Rama Hare Krishna* in 1971, this was her real Bollywood debut. She couldn't act to save her life, but who cared. Her oomph was enough to sear into young adolescent memories and forever stay ready to be brought back by the tiniest of triggers.

I had given up on finding out about the movie theatre, but then the seventh one, Shabi, sent a message saying he remembered every bit of the movie and that we had seen it in Plaza, not Odeon. I had thought so, too but left the door open for memory correction. He also said we had seen it mid-way through the exams, but I am not sure his memory of that is better than mine, quite simply because I doubt our parents would have allowed us to go to a movie mid-way through exams.

Yaadon ki Baraat marked the end of our first year of senior school. I knew I wouldn't be back the following year because my father had retired from university service and taken a job in Uralikanchan near Poona, and we were going to move there for good. That meant moving out of the charming Todarmal Road row house we had rented in Bengali Market and the end of learning two styles of Indian classical music.

I am still playing only three-four notes at a go. If a riff from some song from somewhere comes along and lines up with one of my note combinations again, that would be good. If it triggers another procession of memories (literally, *yaadon ki baarat*)—that would be good too. I figure at some point I will graduate to combinations of a few more notes. If I go no further than that, I am good with that too. Riffraffs like me don't need much more than riffs to be happy.

18

Sholay

"Arrey o Sambha"

That's it. Nothing more needs to be said, for Indians of a certain generation to know exactly what is being talked about. Should their thoughts be occupied with more meaningful things in life, you might just have to add *"kitna inaam rakhe hain sarkar hum par?"* The two pieces together translate to—"O Sambha, what is the bounty the government has placed on my head?" —and make up one of the most memorable dialogues of Hindi cinema. It is from the 1975 movie *Sholay* (embers). I am sure thousands of young boys and men have imagined themselves in dacoit Gabbar Singh's shoes while mimicking the great actor, Amjad Khan, in talent shows, family gatherings and amongst friends. I don't think I ever did, but who knows?

I am no movie critic, so I don't know enough to comment on the movie's significance, but in my simple mind—of then and now—*Sholay* was the definitive Bollywood action movie of the mid-70s. It would be almost blasphemy to pen memories of those times without including a story of *that* movie.

When a memory of *Sholay* floated in sometime back, my initial scribbling was about how many times I saw the movie, and how many of those times it was the "short" 3-hour version, and how many times it was the "long" 5-hour one. The answer to the first question is initially two, but after that ... "I don't know, definitely more." The second question turns out to be entirely incorrect. The more extended version was not five hours long but only 15-20 minutes more, but back in hyperbolic adolescent times, I thought it was two hours longer and have believed that all these years. It took the present and the internet to clear up the fog.

The movie was a serious memory marker at an age when seriousness was nowhere in sight—even though Indian democracy was facing its most serious crisis with the imposition of "Emergency" by the prime minister, Indira Gandhi. I am tempted to detour into talking about how the embers of that fire fizzled out in less than two years when "Madam" called an election and got thrown out of office, and how a very different and larger fire is consuming Indian democracy now, but I'll hold back and get on with this story.

Sholay had a star-studded cast, and with gunslingers and mercenaries, was like a Hollywood Western but with an Indian flavour. It also had an engaging storyline, though the real story—for my friends and I—was how the movie came along into our lives. I had forgotten about that bit till exchanges on Messenger and WhatsApp brought back—our story of *Sholay*.

It was 1975. Our family's adventure of moving to Poona in May of 1974 hadn't worked out. *Amma* was not happy with provincial mindsets in Poona, some that had even pointedly asked her why she had "taken away one of our boys"—in reference to her having married my father, a Maharashtrian and a Shivaji-descendant Maratha at that. So come November, she sent one letter to my school principal asking if I'd be able to come back to school in January and another to her college informing them that the leave-without-pay she had been granted would not be needed beyond December. My father had just started his two-year contract with Manibhai Desai's dynamic Bharatiya Agro Industries Foundation, so he was going to stay on in the two-bedroom flat we had purchased, and we—my mother, us two boys and Lucky, the dog—would return to Delhi.

We had left Delhi on a blazing hot day in May of '74 and returned on a cold and foggy morning in December of the same year. For the first couple of weeks, we stayed with Mani *mama*, *Amma's* cousin, in Vasant Vihar in south Delhi and during that time, my mother looked for an apartment to live in. Going back to Bengali Market was not an option because that place had been rented out to someone else, so *Amma* found an apartment in a new complex of two-bedroom flats built by the Delhi Development Authority in Munirka, which was not far from Vasant Vihar.

The move to Poona had been a big change, but I had settled in quickly in Loyola High School, made the school's junior football team and through that made a bunch of really good friends, somewhat oddly entirely from one class senior to mine. All of this had been greatly facilitated by the purchase of a bicycle, at its core for commuting to school but employed mainly in the service of adolescence and independence. It was on that first bicycle that I started going to see movies on my own, a pattern that continued when we returned to Delhi.

I began commuting to school in central Delhi by bus and bicycle, the latter more often than the former because I often missed the number 680 bus that went from Munirka to Connaught Place and ran only once every hour. Missing it meant walking over to the more established and sprawling government "colony" of RK Puram to catch the 610 or 640 and then another bus to get to school. Multiple bus connections made getting to school on time a bit tricky, and the cost of travel increased, so it was just easier to walk back home after missing number 680 and get on the bicycle and pedal to school. That way, I could make sure to get to school on time and have some spare change from the saved bus fares.

Amma had to travel twice that distance from what was, at that point, the far end of the southside of New Delhi to Delhi University on the northern end. She would take the 'university specials' (public buses earmarked for university students and staff) to go all the way to college, and on the way back, sometimes catch a car ride with one of her colleagues for part of the way, and then take an autorickshaw for the final stretch home. How my diminutive mother possessed the giant spirit and energy needed to do those long commutes, run a household, and still have time for social interactions is something I have always marvelled at.

By the time *Sholay* was released in Delhi in October '75, we had fully settled back into life in Delhi, and I was back together with my school friends—now with the added freedom of two wheels. Having begun our group-watching of movies with *Yaadon ki Baraat* in the previous year, it was natural that when news of *Sholay* started swirling about, we would want to see it. How could we not? It had Dharmendra from *Yaadon ki Baraat* and Amitabh Bachchan from another action movie, *Zanjeer*, that we had either seen together or independently.

As with *Yaadon ki Baraat* the year before, a plan was hatched to see the movie, and someone booked tickets at Plaza cinema in Connaught Place for an afternoon show one weekend or during one of the school holidays. I have tried to dig into our collective memories to figure out exactly when that came about, but no one seems to know. Could it have been the winter holidays of '75? Possibly.

That is my somewhat fuzzy memory of the timing, but Madhav, the central character in "our *Sholay*," doesn't remember sweaters, which would have been necessary for the cold weather that creeps in at the end of the year in Delhi. Was it then, or the summer holidays of '76? Possible, but Madhav's message—"Can't imagine we waited 8 months"—suggests that too is unlikely. Maybe something will come along to clear the fog on the timing, but for now, I'll just go with the Dussehra-Diwali holidays, which came along towards the end of October that year.

The plan was to meet at Hailey's house on Balwant Rai Mehta Lane in the Mandi House area and walk over to CP. Who all were involved in the movie plan is also not entirely clear, but the main characters—Hailey (Suhail), Madhav, Sunny and I—were undoubt-edly part of it. Madhav and Sunny got to Hailey's house early. I was going to get there later because there was no direct bus from Mu-nirka and so I was planning to bike over. I never did.

Before setting out on the bike, I called to finalize plans and was told not to bother coming. There had been an accident, and the movie plan had been called off. It turned out, the three of them had been horsing around—in preparation for the action movie—by en-acting a fight scene and Madhav, who was the toughest of all of us, was showing them "how to kick a knife out of someone's hand." Hailey was holding a pocketknife in his hand, and when Madhav kicked, he instinctively lowered his knife-wielding hand to protect … his proverbial round ones. The knife went into Madhav's thigh. It was a deep gash, and the blood didn't stop flowing till someone tied a tourniquet on his thigh. It ended up requiring 12 stitches. By all accounts, it was a scary scene with—real, not fake, blood—smeared all over the bathroom.

When I heard this on the phone, I was, of course, concerned for my friend, but … I'll be honest—I was also doubly disappointed.

One, I had missed out on the real-life spectacle. I mean, how often does a 15-year-old get to see a fake fight scene with real blood? Second, there would be no *Sholay* to watch that day. At least those guys had made a movie of their own. I had nothing!

Now I don't remember whether I made amends for it right away or the next day by hopping on the bike to cycle through the rough and undulated arid stretch that separated Munirka and Vasant Vihar to see the shorter version of *Sholay* playing at Priya cinema. Either way, *Sholay* did happen, not once but twice at Priya cinema. And I am quite sure that each time I went in and out of the ups and downs of that stretch of the Aravalli hills range on my bicycle, I imagined riding a horse - through terrain similar to that in the Chambal region of the country which was said to be infested with real dacoits.

I'd show you what I am talking about—that stretch where I would often go to ride my bicycle to get the thrills of going in and out of undulations in much the same way mountain bikers and skateboarders do these days—but I can't. That land was levelled a long time back, and the concrete housing built on top has no trace of a 15-year-old on a bicycle imagining dacoit runs on a horse; my memory does.

Did we ever get around to seeing the movie together in Plaza cinema, which was showing the full version, not the cut version of Priya cinema? Quite possibly so. At some point, I did see the full movie, and it likely was at Plaza, and it is highly unlikely that I cycled an hour from Munirka to Connaught Place to see a movie on my own, even one as memorable as *Sholay*. Then again, knowing how I was back then, I wouldn't rule it out.

19

Matchmaker

He just showed up one day. Rang the doorbell, introduced himself and said so-and-so had sent him to meet Mrs Desai because... he wanted to get married, and so-and-so had said my mother might have some ideas. Did she ever? Matchmaking was not her profession, but my mother knew a thing or two about people. She liked the idea of marriage, and all he was asking for was a bit of help. How could she turn him away?

She invited him in and sat him down in the living room she had recently furnished with elegant Scandinavian-style teak furniture that she had purchased from a new store in Vasant Vihar on an instalment plan. They chatted, and she sussed out what he was all about and when she was satisfied that he was a good fella, she asked him if he'd like some tea.

While I struggled to make small talk with him, she went off to fix tea and nibbles while nibbling away at prospective matches for him. Those were the early days of her enamourment with the flavourful and fluffy Gujarati *dhokla*, a savoury snack made of chickpea flour, so he got a bit of that with tea. While he was nibbling on that, she asked him if he had any specific constraints in terms of language, region, caste and whatnot. He had none, which most certainly would have gladdened her heart because she had herself married outside those restrictive settings. Then again, if he had any, I doubt she would have held it against him. She was not like that. She wasn't a chest-beating liberal and didn't have a social transformation agenda; her's was about just getting along and doing the little things that make life social. Once he had indicated that he fit into that structureless mould, she told him there was someone in the neighbourhood who might be right, and she'd talk to her mother and let him know.

When I think back to that day, I realize it was a bit unusual to have a stranger knock on your front door and declare his intentions in such a forthright manner. Usually, these searches and "expressions of interest" were initiated by parents or relatives, or friends of parents and relatives or friends of their friends, and so on and so forth. Instead, here was someone looking out for his own interest!

It was out of the ordinary then but is more normal now with young people doing their own legwork via matrimonial sites. Back then, the only matrimonial service I knew of was advertised on the sides of brick houses along train tracks, and it usually said "*Rishte hi rishte*" (alliances galore!) and provided a contact number in Regarpura, Delhi. Then again, other brick houses along the same train tracks had a painted advertisement for VD (venereal disease), so maybe I have it all mixed up!

The unusuality of the young man's visit didn't faze my mother the least bit because not long before his arrival, she had facilitated a matrimonial alliance when we lived in Bengali Market. During those years, she had befriended a neighbour who taught at a women's college in Delhi University. The young woman was avowedly against the idea of getting married, but when one of my mother's colleagues told her that her brother was in town and might be interested in getting hitched, *Amma* gently said to her young friend: "Why don't you just meet him, for meeting's sake?" Well, they met—for meeting's sake—and hit it off, and the young woman chucked her job, got married, and moved to America.

Back to this matchmaking story, she talked to the neighbour and her daughter, probably over *dhokla* and tea, and there being initial interest, a meeting was arranged. The young fellow came by, and everyone liked everyone, and things moved quickly with talk of engagement and marriage and continental drift, and it would all have gone just fine except ... there was a hitch. He had come all the way from Canada and was in town for just a month and wanted to get married within that month and go back with a bride. That would have been fine too, and it happened and happens aplenty, including my own story, which will have to be told at another time, but there was another hurdle.

The girl's father was in the merchant navy and was out at sea and wasn't expected back on land for another month or two. Naturally, the girl and her mother wanted to wait for him and were not willing to budge. *Amma* tried her best to make it all work out, but she couldn't move oceans and seas, so the almost-there didn't quite get there.

Later, *Amma* said the young man found someone else and got married and went back to Canada, and the neighbour's daughter found someone else and got married, and it all worked out, and everyone lived happily ever after. Actually, I don't know that because we didn't hear anything more from him, and a year later, we moved from Munirka in south Delhi to Lawrence Road in north Delhi and lost contact with our neighbour ... but not before another bit of matchmaking.

Not long after the Canadian immigrant, another young man showed up. This knock wasn't as dramatic. This one had been my mother's student, either in Benaras, Mathura, or Pantnagar; I am not sure, and it isn't particularly relevant to the story. I don't remember if we had a phone by then and whether he called ahead of time or just showed up. Either way, *Amma* knew who he was. In the 40-odd years she taught university students in different places, she didn't ever fail to recognize her students. Nor did they.

He had come by to see a favourite teacher and to pay his respects. He had taken the civil service exam a second time and made it through and been posted to Delhi. He was from the eastern part of UP, and *Amma* had a soft corner for people from that part. It was partly because she had grown up in Benaras and partly because she preferred the somewhat gentler, more civil manner of social interactions in eastern UP. I don't think she ever really got used to the cruder, gruffer nature of interactions in Delhi. When she hit retirement age in Delhi University, she could have easily gotten herself a couple of two-year extensions and stayed on, but she was tired and ready to get out of Delhi and rebuild social life in a smaller, more civil place. Indore wasn't quite Benaras, but it was simpler than Delhi, and it didn't take her long to have a full set of social interactions in the new place.

So there he was, *Amma's* student from an earlier time. Like the bachelor before, he too had tea and *dhokla*, by now a staple of my mother's afternoon teas, and they caught up on the thisandthat of their lives— those shareable bits and pieces we reveal to others in the way we want to. At some point, the conversation most certainly must have come around to his marital status. My mother was always interested in the marital dimension of young people's lives and had this ever-so-gentle way of getting them to share their hopes and aspirations with her.

Somewhere in there, between tea and *dhokla*, or alongside them, he must have either expressed an interest in finding a partner, or she might have planted the idea in his head. I don't remember which one it was, but in the Indian conceptualization of life—in terms of "appropriate" stages at "appropriate" times —marriage fit right where he was in the life cycle. He had a secure job and a desirable career path, so of course, he would be or should be, looking to get married and anchor life even more.

This way of looking at life was somewhat inconsistent with *Amma's* own experiences. She had started teaching at a university at the tender age of 18, then studied in England, married my father, who was older and from another part of the country and had a very different social background and taught in the very progressive environs of the English department of Miranda House in Delhi University. None of that pointed to the traditional way of going about life, at least not in those times, but she was here and there on a lot of things. Aren't we all?

It is hard to say how many visits were needed to get the seed firmly planted in her former student's head, or whether there already was one when he first came to her, but soon enough, the process began.

Amma had recently reconnected with UP friends from way back when, and they lived not so far away. A meeting was arranged, and all seemed to go smoothly, but ... things got complicated when he had their background checked, and they did some background work on him. I don't know what they found in those places, but the foreground got all muddled, and the matter went nowhere. That's how that matchmaking story ended. It didn't dent her relationship with them or him. She was still *Pushpaji* to them and Madam to him, and it all continued just the same.

20

The race run backwards

In today's short-attention-span world, people like soundbites, headlines and, more generally, little morsels of information—to engage with briefly. I must be from another planet because I don't soundbite things, especially not life moments that have meaningful memories. In my worldview, those must be experienced in full, preserved in full, remembered in full. Not sound biting, quite simply, is the reason why I can rewind the tape of life 45 years and live the magic of a great race that I witnessed in person.

Modern School was big on sports. It was that way in junior school when we had a sports class every day, and even more so in senior school when we fielded competitive teams in all imaginable sports and regularly won, what I think was called, the Governor's Shield for overall excellence in high school sports in Delhi. Sports was part of the school principal, Mr. MN Kapur's idea of a wholesome education which included, as equal partners, academics, and extra-curricular activities.

At some point in 1975, Mr. Kapur got it into his head that we must win the All India Public Schools (AIPS) athletic championship.

We had fielded a team the previous year, possibly for the first time, and managed a seventh-place finish. That wasn't good enough for him, not at a time when the school was riding high after celebrating a golden jubilee in 1970 with the Prime Minister, Indira Gandhi, in attendance at Founder's Day, the school's annual function. I am told she was so moved by Mr. Ved Vyas' brilliant docudrama, "*Roopak*," that she asked for a repeat performance and brought her cabinet ministers along to watch.

At that time, we lived in Bengali Market, and even though I was attending junior school, I used to hang around senior school in the evenings and weekends. I remember watching rehearsals of *Roopak* and being mesmerized by the combination of prose, music, and dance in a single show in our uniquely blue school uniforms. I don't know whether the repeat-performance-for-cabinet-ministers story is true, but those were undoubtedly the heydays of the school, so it is plausible.

Given all of that, and the fact that Mr. Kapur had been awarded the Padma Shri, India's highest civilian honour, in 1969, it was entirely understandable that he would be unhappy with Modern School not being on top. In '75, no effort was spared to get a team ready for the competition. The desire to win must have been strong because we hosted the meet at the National Stadium in New Delhi. Hosting was a bold statement of intent, likely used for motivational purposes by the Head of Sports, Mr. Khurana, who was one of the best in getting young sportsmen to outperform their abilities.

We were the youngest of the three classes that made up the senior grouping in sports, and while several from our class would evolve into excellent athletes in the years to come, that year only one of us—Vivek Khanna, aka Baba—was on the team. Baba was a great triple jumper and long jumper at that point, and that year was either groomed into the 110m high hurdles or been pushed into it because SD Mudgil, the captain of the team, was doing the jumps. As good a jumper as Baba was, Mudgil was on a different level—from anyone on that team then and in the years that followed. There is a story illustrating that further along in this collection, so I'll just get on with this one.

National Stadium had an 8-lane cinder track and a grass field on the inside. If you've ever seen a race on a 400m track, you'll know that a track is quasi-oval shaped with two straights and two curves connecting those straights. You can break down the 400m into four 100m stretches, but due to the extra length taken up by the curves, the straights are shorter, somewhere between 80 and 100m.

What that "straights and curves" track means is that the shortest of races, the 100m sprint, is not fully on the 400m track but starts a bit off the curve that leads into the straight section. It's like the lowercase letter b but with the stem chopped off quite a bit. A 110m hurdles race is slightly longer, with 10 hurdles spaced 10m apart and 10m between the last hurdle and the finish line. It starts 10m further back from the starting point of a (flat) 100m race. As a result, it has a longer stem on the lowercase b.

In athletics meets at all levels, it is a sort of a convention that races finish at the same place on the track, that being the end of the main straight, often called the "home straight." Distance-wise, the two straights of a track are the same length, and for the uninitiated, it can be hard to tell which one is the home one and which one the backstretch, but in tracks that sit inside stadia, the main one usually faces the stadium's entrance. It is where the marquee event of all track and field competitions—the 100m sprint—is run, and it is also where the 110m hurdles race is staged.

Of all the events in track and field, nothing compares with the short sprints in terms of the demands on nerves and the success that follows from confidence and downright cockiness. In recent times, we've seen the great Usain Bolt exude that confident cockiness. Back in those days, the same was said about the great Soviet sprinter Valery Borozov who won the 100m and 200m at the Munich Olympics in 1972.

The 110m hurdles is essentially a sprint and thus requires the same attributes as the 100m, but with a measure of calibration. You can't just dash through the distance; you need skill—to rise and split the legs over the hurdles and pull them back in quickly to sprint the distance between them, not once but 10 times.

Baba wasn't cocky, just quietly confident. With his long legs and perfect technique, he didn't run the 110m hurdles as much as glide over them. Still, he was one of the youngest in the competition, so while there were expectations of him winning us points in that event, there were still nerves to contend with—for him and for us. I don't know what he was thinking when he sat down in the starting blocks for that race, but we were nervous as hell. The race was one of the last events of the meet, and while I am not sure where we were in the points tally at that point, I am guessing it was close. All eyes were on the 110m hurdles final.

Normally we would have stood near the finish line, but for this one, we had to switch to the starting point—because the race was run backwards, as in starting from the typical finish and finishing at the typical start. For years I have wondered why the race was run that way. I must have known back then but had forgotten. Recently, I asked Baba about that, and he said it was because there was a strong wind that day and the hurdles kept falling over. Those hurdles didn't have the standard weights that not only hold up the barriers but also slow you down if you hit them. Apparently, when the race was being set up, the wind kept knocking the hurdles over, and the organizers decided to switch the direction of the race.

You can call that—classic "Indian *jugaad*" (innovative improvisation) —but there is nothing particularly Indian about that type of resourcefulness. It is a global phenomenon and reflects human ingenuity and problem-solving skills that people everywhere have in abundance and employ whenever needed. I have seen it in several countries I have worked in, especially amongst the poor. In New Zealand, it is called the "No. 8 wire mentality" for the countless ways in which the Number 8 fencing wire is used.

There must have been a bit of a delay in starting the race because of the need to turn around 80 hurdles, shepherd the runners from one end to the other end, and give them time to set up their starting blocks—at the typical finish line and looking backwards. During all that time, we spectators fidgeted around while moving from the finish line to the start line. Some of us ended up on top of the six-foot-high concrete wall that separated the stands from the usual starting point of the race. Standing on that concrete wall, we had a perfect view of the whole race.

When the gun went off, Baba began his run—that beautiful mix of steps and splits that characterizes the high hurdles. To me, all athletic events are poetry in motion, but the high hurdles is particularly delightful for its mix of grace, speed, and power. I won't make up the details of how the race went and where he was at what point because I don't remember. What I do remember is that somewhere around 70m or so, it became clear that he was in the lead and that if he didn't hit any of the last three hurdles, he would win. It was thrilling beyond belief, and the excitement got such a hold of me that when he glided over the last hurdle and headed to the finish line, I instinctively jumped off the wall to be there to greet him.

I had overlooked the fact that he was in one of the middle lanes, and there were runners coming in on the inside lanes, and I would be in their path. One of them grazed me, but I wasn't fazed. I was more tuned in to hugging my friend and celebrating his victory. It was only after the thrill had subsided that I looked down to see that the graze was more than a brush. I had been "spiked," and my sock and canvas shoe were torn. Removing those, you could see the white flesh through the gash.

Madhav, another great athlete who likely would have been on the team if they had held proper trials for the javelin, had had more sense than me and taken a couple of extra minutes to jump. He saw the tear and insisted we go up to the first aid stand to get the injury looked at. Hobbling up there and getting the wound cleaned and treated took time, and during that stretch, the relay was run, the points tallied up, and it became official—we had won! It was an incredible feeling and resulted in everyone present, team and us supporters, doing a victory lap. I was hobbling in pain at that point but damn, if I would be denied that pleasure! Madhav helped me around the track, and I did the victory lap largely on one leg.

The following year we retained the championship in Gwalior, and then in the two years when we were seniors in the 11th and 12th grades, we won again in Kapurthala and Rai—under Baba's captainship. The details of those victories are hazy, but that very first one which we were witness to is very clear. That might have something to do with a two-inch scar on my left ankle, which is a permanent reminder of the race run backwards and won by one of our classmates.

21

Dinner for champions

If you've seen the movie, "The Curious Case of Benjamin Button," you might remember a three-minute segment that begins with the reverse-ageing Brad Pitt, as Benjamin Button, sitting outside Cate Blanchett's (as Daisy) clinic room. With, "Sometimes we are on a collision course, and we just don't know it," he begins narrating a sequence of events that lead up to Daisy getting her leg crushed in a car accident in Paris. It is a clever and complicated telling of what is called the "butterfly effect"— a series of small events, like the flutter of a butterfly's wings, that cumulate into something significant—in this case, the end of Daisy's aspiration to be a professional dancer.

The butterfly effect belongs to the world of counterfactuals, which abounds in "if-then" connections—*if* this had happened, *then* it would have led to that. For those looking into the past, it holds endless possibilities for passing time, in wistful or dreadful ways. I don't walk that way too often, but once in a while, it is fun.

I was wandering about in that land in September 2019 when I sent a message to my athletics teammates from high school to establish the order of the three All India Public School meets we had all participated in and won in the last three years of our time in high school. I was interested in that small detail, not for itself, but to line up the "butterfly effect" story of a memorable victory dinner at Moti Mahal, one of the most famous Delhi restaurants of that time.

It all began at some point in the second half of 1976 when in the midst of typical jock banter at school, my friend Ricky challenged me to prove my claim that I could run 5000 metres "anytime, anywhere." I used to ride a bicycle back and forth to school, and that was about 25km each day, and I was a very active midfielder on the school's football team, so I knew I had the stamina to do it. More importantly, I was 15 and had an entirely unrealistic sense of my abilities, so the very next day, after football practice, I ran 12 and a half laps of the 400-metre track without stopping.

That run around the track after football training got the attention of the athletics coach, Mr. Chauhan. H added me to the athletics team for the long-distance races and the 4 x 400m relay team for the all-important event on our school's athletics calendar, the All India Public School's athletics meet. We had won the championship the previous year and were preparing to defend the title with another team of great runners, jumpers, and throwers. Unlike the last year when only one member of our class had been on the team, now there were several.

The meet was going to be hosted by The Scindia School in Gwalior in the middle of the country, and getting there required taking one of the southbound trains that left Delhi at night. In the evening, we had gathered in school and were loading up our bags into the school bus parked next to the "tree of secrets." No one might call it that, but the small tree with a knee-high circular concrete base is where generations of Modernites have sat and chatted, knowing their secrets are safe with the tree.

Everyone was there and ready to go except Ricky. The poor fellow had caught the flu and was not going to Gwalior. His replacement was a speedy youngster, Ashim Gujral, who was a year junior to us. If Brad Pitt were telling the butterfly effect story of the Moti Mahal dinner, it would be reasonable for him to begin with the bug that laid Ricky low and ask: What if that hadn't happened?

Luggage had been loaded up, and we were ready to head off to the train station but had to wait for Mr. Kapur, our school principal, to come by and say some inspiring words to send us off in our quest for a repeat title. At some point, he did come by, and in his typical way, say something wise, but I don't remember what it was. What I remember is what followed next ... because that set the butterfly fluttering its wings in a very definitive way.

Ashim's grandfather, Kundan Lal Gujral, had come to drop him off. It will never be known whether it was planned or a spur of the moment thing, but when Mr. Kapur was done with his bit, Mr. Gujral addressed the team and said: "If you come back victorious. I will treat you all to dinner at my restaurant." Those may not have been his exact words, but the invitation was a clearly stated one. He was the proprietor of the famous Moti Mahal restaurant in Darya Ganj, and by some accounts, it was his restaurant that introduced *tandoori* cuisine to India and also invented 'butter chicken,' the dish that is now synonymous with Indian food the world over. I had never eaten at Moti Mahal, but in the days of junior school, our school bus used to pass by that restaurant every day, so I knew about it. I have to guess most everyone on that team, and many beyond were also in the know.

I have no recollection of the meet that year, not even my own contribution in the 4 x 400m relay. All I remember is that we won the championship, thus repeating the first-time feat of the previous year. That was thrilling in its own right, but ... more so for what lay ahead. When we got back to Delhi, a date for the promised victory dinner was lined up, and on that evening, once again, we met at the "tree of secrets" and boarded the school bus to go to the famous restaurant in Darya Ganj.

Moti Mahal was buzzing that night. Live singers were performing in the middle of the open-air dining area, and a long table had been laid out for the team, the coaches, the managers and Mr. Kapur. Mr. Gujral was on hand, said some gracious words, and then gave the order for the "games to begin." Food flowed continuously, and no account was kept of the number of *tandoori* chickens that came along to join the celebration. It is, without doubt, one of the most amazing dinners I have ever had.

The following year we won again, but I don't remember a repeat performance at Moti Mahal. The revenue dent we must have put on Mr. Gujral that first time around must surely have warned him not to be that generous a second time.

That was all more than 40 years ago. I got to thinking about that Moti Mahal feast in September 2019 when I started making travel plans to attend the 4[0]th reunion of our high school class. I thought it would be fun to go back to Moti Mahal and relive the memory. A plan was made, but with few of my teammates remembering the original visit, I started having doubts about the event's occurrence—Did it happen, or did I just imagine it? I needed to know.

I am not in touch with everyone on that team, so my search—for truth—had been limited in scope. Ashim was, quite obviously, the best source, but I wasn't in touch with him, and despite trying a few times, could not get his number from Moti Mahal's website. I had just about given up hope but then took one last shot and asked my friend Rakesh Mathur (aka Babla) for help.

The phone number arrived when I was having dinner at a heavenly Mangalorean restaurant in Bangalore with a dear friend from our five years in that city. I had to excuse myself and step out into the lobby to call Ashim. I wasn't sure he would remember me, but he did. I was even less sure he would remember the evening and his grandfather's promise, but he did. With great enthusiasm, he said: "Yes, I remember. We hogged like crazy that night." I smiled at the sound of that very 70s-80s term—hogging. To us, back then, it meant gorging on food. His confirmation was a great relief. My imagination of that memory was real, after all!

On the night before the 40th reunion, a number of us headed over to Darya Ganj. It was late by the time we got to Moti Mahal on Netaji Subhas Marg. During the day, that road had always been congested, but it used to be less so in the evenings and much less so at night. That's how it was that night, except ... it looked more beat up than it had ever looked before.

I didn't think too much of that because one of the things that gets internalized when you grow up in India is the configuration of urban space—private opulence and order amidst public deprivation and squalor. The disconnect between private and public spaces is unlike anything I have seen anywhere, including all the developing countries I have visited and worked in over 17 years.

When we walked in through the front gate of Moti Mahal, I expected a different world to open up—the way it had that evening in 1976. Instead, what I saw inside those doors was not much different from what was outside. It was drab and worn down, and there were none of the ambiences of the earlier visit—no bright lights, no music, no heaving human activity. It was as if the outside public space had walked in and taken over the inside—"Old Delhi" looked old.

The restaurant was falling apart in much the same way my spirits fell apart when I looked around. I was embarrassed at having made a big deal of the whole evening and collecting so many friends, some of whom I hadn't seen in aeons and others who I saw only once every few years. I desperately hoped the food would make up for the atmosphere; for me, it always does. It was good, but nothing you couldn't have gotten anywhere else in town.

The evening was, quite simply, a disaster. The only thing that made up for it was the company of friends and the laughter and chatter—as it used to be during school years. That bit seemed not to care about the surroundings. I did my best to rise above my disappointment, but I am not very good at hiding my feelings, so I am pretty sure it showed on my face.

I now wish I had left that memory alone. The magic of a moment is always in the moment, and recreating it can tarnish the memory and shorten its smile. I want to say I will remember that lesson and be careful next time, but I doubt it. With memories, as with life, you've got to take chances; sometimes they work, sometimes they don't. That's just the way it is.

22

Bonded in blue

Retrospect is always a mixed bag, and reflecting on the past is tricky business because ... reflection can easily turn to rumination and lead to dwelling on the tragic instead of the magic of times gone by. I wander back in time quite often, and few stretches of life bring smiles quite like those associated with 13 magical years at Modern School, a place that created a very special bond of blue.

Ours was a distinctive school uniform—shirts and tunics in medium blue with interwoven white threading; shorts, skirts and pants of solid blue; and light blue nylon socks with two dark blue lines at the top. Wintry layers were a different shade of blue, but winter was short, and the real deal was the summery blue. No one else in Delhi, and I reckon anywhere else, had that particular mix of blue. The uniform was only available at Mr. Khanna's little tailor shop next to the cricket field at the far end of a line of eucalyptus trees in Senior School on Barakhamba Road in the very heart of New Delhi.

The cloth used for our school uniform was coarse cotton and likely sourced from a single textile mill. Fancier blends of cotton and polyester and whatever else were available, and many of the parents would have been able to afford those, but our uniform was very much 'aam aadmi' (ordinary person). That in no way should delude anyone into thinking that we were in touch with the common person on the street. It was an elite private school that catered to the professional and business classes that occupied the middle to upper strata of society.

All through school years, the blues stayed blue, but sizes grew. Junior school had required black shoes, senior school went flexible, and we could wear whatever shoes we wanted to. I think of them as freedom shoes because, well, because there was a distinctly different and more liberated air about that campus with the red brick building that had gates that swung in and out. Junior school had been all about nurturing; senior school was about maturing.

The size of blue—for us boys—really grew in July of 1977 when shorts gave way to pants to mark our ascent to seniority, a grade called S5 in our school. There was a fresh tingle of excitement in going to Mr. Khanna's tailor shop to get measured for pants, but there was also some apprehension about the transition that lay ahead—something about more than the length of the cloth. An era was about to end, and we would be the ones shepherding in a new one. How would it go? How would blue be blue without the bond that gave it its distinctive hue?

Mr. MN Kapur, our school principal, had been at the helm for 30 years. In junior school we saw him occasionally. Everyone knew who he was and when he was over for a visit. There'd be a hush and excitement when he'd appear in school assembly and speak at length about something or the other. Sitting in neat rows on the dhurries, we'd listen to him, not always sure what he was trying to convey. Still, the difference between his ramblings and those of the staid Headmaster, Mr. RD Goyal, was obvious. It was in Senior

School that he was omnipresent and would speak at greater length at morning assembly. I want to say we understood better what he was trying to convey, but I am not entirely sure.

No other school had a principal like MN Kapur. Sometimes we called him Cooper, sometimes MNK, sometimes Mr. Kapur, but mostly ... he was Bond, as in James Bond. I am not sure when and how he came to be called that, but I think it was because he was the good and stern and stylish and good-looking James Bond of the double-o-seven spy movies. He listened with care, spoke clearly and decisively, and worked hard at experimenting and implementing new ideas. He, very simply, was the father figure you loved because he was caring, but also feared because he was demanding. In developmental psychologist Diana Baumrind's fourfold parenting typology, that would mean the most desirable parenting style—authoritative, not authoritarian, neglectful, or indulgent.

We'd had a taste of Bond's imprint on the institution in junior school, but it was in Senior School where you grasped the full extent of his impact. The institution he had fashioned had a unique mix of academics, music, arts, dance, drama, competitive sports, and a firm grounding in the identity of India—it's ancient past, its freedom struggle, and the 'infancy of independence' years. To that, add in a mix of freedom and voice, and you have the ideal crucible for developing childhood into adolescence and then into confident adulthood. The validation of that assessment came when I got to college and encountered people from various places for whom university was freedom and a breath of fresh air after the confined environment of the schools they had been in. We had already been there, done that—college held no candle to the high school we had been in.

I am not into hagiography and hero-worshipping of any sort, but it is not possible to think of Modern School in those times and not think of Mr. Kapur. People remember their schools for this and that. Those of us who walked through the grey and red buildings of

Junior and Senior School during his time, remember the school for Bond and that shade of blue that bonded us.

I think of those times often—for their innocence, for their wonder, for their blueness. I am aware that looking back at the 70s after so many decades makes for a highly tinted and possibly tainted picture, but I still like to do that. It makes the current Indian reality less crude, less intolerant, less belligerent, less exclusionary. It makes you believe in something better. The Arab proverb Mr. Kapur wove into more than one of his long rambling morning assembly lectures frequently comes to mind:

"I complained that I had no shoes until I met a man with no feet."

It is hard to say what moral he wanted to pitch with that. It likely was about not cribbing and looking out for those who had less. It was apt for those times when poverty was the dominant issue. The dire predictions in Paul Ehrlich's 1968 book, "The Population Bomb," had countries like India in mind, and even Prime Minister Indira Gandhi's 1971 election campaign slogan—"*garibi hatao*" —was about eliminating poverty.

If Bond was at a school assembly now, what story would he pitch? At a time when populism and majoritarianism have created an atmosphere of fear for those who are not in the mainstream and those who disagree, would it be something about standing in others' shoes? He might even have said it then; I don't remember. It wasn't needed then; it is now.

I don't remember at what point we found out he was leaving. It would have had to be in the early months of 1977 when we were in 10th grade, called S4 in our school. There was nothing official, but everyone knew that when we returned in July to begin the year of pants, he wouldn't be there. It didn't seem right, but it was what it was. We still had school to attend and our 10th Board exams to take, and there may just also have been some hope that things would be reversed, and he'd still be there in July.

It must have been our last day in school before the start of study break for the Board exams. I think it was March, but it could have been April. What I am reasonably sure of is that on that day, like me, many held their breath when at morning assembly, Kalpana and Keshwar sang—"To Sir with Love."

I'd heard the Lulu song from the Sidney Poitier movie of the same name on *Yuv Vani* on All India Radio. It is a beautiful song and was just right for the occasion. K&K's rendition was better than Lulu's—a perfect tribute to the man who had steered the Modern School ship for 30 years and was due to leave at the end of the school year. Unlike the movie, where just before the song ends, Sidney Poitier tears up the letter of appointment he has received for a job and decides to stay on at the troubled school he is a temporary teacher at, we knew Mr. Kapur would not return when we did after the summer break. Our journeys in Blue and Bond would end without Bond.

I remember thinking to myself how, for the second time in school, I had been cheated out of something I had wanted so much. First, the Delhi government had redistricted schools and created new zones so we could no longer continue our traditional rivalry with DPS—Delhi Public School, Mathura Road. I had grown up with stories of epic games and contests, them in green shirts and white shorts, and us in blue and white—in our innocent minds, the mirror to India-Pakistan hockey contests of blue and green. They took that away in 1975 when they put DPS in one zone and us in another. Inter-school competitions were never the same after that. Now they had taken away Bond, just when we were ascending to the S5 throne wearing pants and taking on leadership roles—and just when he would have engaged with us as quasi adults, not children. It didn't seem fair, but it was what it was.

I wish I remembered more of that day, but other than that song and a photo reminder of us hoisting him in a white plastic chair and carrying him above our shoulders from the morning assembly to his office, it's a blank.

Life, of course, moved on. It always does. There was studying to do, exams to take, summer NCC camp in the hills, and late adolescence to manage.

When we got back to school in July, there was a new principal—PC Chowdhury—and there was an awkward period of adjustment for him and us. Thankfully, he didn't change the routines and orientation too much, and our schooling continued in much the same way as it had for those who had had Bond all through.

As much fun as those last two years in pants were, and they sure were memorable, there was something missing in them. It wasn't just Bond who was gone, so were the others who had been part of his inner circle who had given Senior school its special flavour. The fortunate part for us was that we had bonded in blue for most of our school years. That fortified us for coping with the Bondless Blues.

Sometimes I think life is like that—about losing, winning, striving, achieving, failing, falling, and somehow just getting up and going on. I just might have learnt that in a place called Modern School a very, very long time ago.

23

Delhi to Agra

Agra is a long way from Delhi—217 km, to be precise. No one in their right mind would think of running that distance, certainly not in August when temperatures are in the 30s (Celsius), the air is thick with monsoon humidity, and running is downright draining. You'd have to be out of your mind to run that distance. Then again, there are plenty of ultra-marathoners and loopy loops who are capable of running that distance, even in August. Punishing bodies to enrich souls gets people doing all kinds of crazy stuff. I would bet good money that if someone were to organize a race from Delhi to Agra, there would be plenty of entrants.

Whether on completing the 217 km the runners would be in any shape to marvel at the Taj Mahal—a monument so exquisite that it can bring you to tears—is another thing. Every time I have gone to the Taj, I have been blown away, not by how huge it is, which it certainly is, but by its sheer delicacy. For a structure so large to look so paper-thin is ... quite simply audacious. No wonder it is one of the seven wonders of the world!

I have done some punishing runs in my time and also been punished by other runs when my internal GPS performed in its typical wayward way and got me lost in the woods and streets of exotic places. But at no point have I been so looped out to contemplate running all the way from Delhi to Agra, not in the month of August, not ever. I did, however, participate in a road relay from Delhi to Agra in August of '77, and while I only ran a 5km stretch of that 217-kilometre distance, the run left its mark on me in more ways than one.

It was the summer I was transitioning from one sport to another. Football had always been my first love, but I saw little potential for making individual progress in a team sport where most others had no interest in working hard. Athletics, on the other hand, offered reward for individual effort, which, for the middle-distance races I ran, required off-season preparation. I wanted to be seriously competitive and was willing to put in the time and effort to improve, so I started going to the National Stadium for off-season training under a proper coach. Football would continue, but on the side, a change enabled by switching from the more physically demanding midfield position to the less physically demanding position of a goalkeeper.

The stadium was in central Delhi, and at that time, we lived in Munirka, in south Delhi. It used to take more than an hour to catch the two-three buses necessary to get to the stadium, but it was summer, and there wasn't much else to do in the evenings, so I didn't mind the long commute.

At first, I stuck out like a sore thumb because I attended an elite school, and there weren't that many from my school or others like it who ran the middle and long distances. Those required long hours of training, and privileged kids from schools like mine preferred to do the explosive sprints, jumps and throws, events where nature seemed to matter more than nurture, especially when the nurturing was sustained punishment over many months and years.

Not long after becoming a regular at the stadium, I encountered another runner who stuck out even more than I first had. He had attended the even more exclusive Doon School up in the hills of Dehradun and then won some sort of scholarship to study at Rugby School in Rugby, Warwickshire, England. I had encountered "Doscos" (those who attend Doon School) at the All India Public School athletics meet, and in typical cross-school competitive mode, thought of them as snobs. Some were, some weren't; he was of the latter sort. He had discovered the joys of running in England and, on being back for the summer holidays, likely found none of his social class much interested in a serious sweat-out on the roads. I reckon that is how he had ended up at the National Stadium.

There is no reason for me to remember all of this except, he was different—not in some prodigious-talent-world-class-potential kind of way—but in the way he ran. His arms had a peculiar circular motion, much like the shaft that moved the wheels of the steam-engine locomotives of those times. They seemed to propel his muscular legs so that he would land on the balls of his feet and bounce off them. His running form was unusual for a distance runner, but it looked very rhythmic and effortless. It might also have been why his upper body was more muscular than most every other distance runner who trained at the stadium and that I had ever seen.

Summer moved along, and evening training continued day after day. I would show up at the stadium and train and see him and exchange pleasantries every now and then. There was a weekly 6.5km road race on Sunday mornings, and I'd show up for those, suffering the stretch—even more so when I'd see him effortlessly bouncing along.

By June's end, monsoon rains arrived, and dry heat transformed into soul-sapping humidity, not the ever-present kind of Southeast

Asia, but in patches—before clouds gathered and after they'd dumped their payload. The cinder track would get flooded after big downpours, and training would switch to running up Rajpath, the long road between the National Stadium and *Rashtrapati Bhawan*, the stunning presidential palace of modern times. There is a small hill on the last stretch, and we'd run up that small incline—over and over again.

I don't remember if he did those hill repeats, locomoting up the hills the same way, but he was still around when the Delhi-Agra Road Relay was announced in early August. It was a Stadium-organized event, and I was thrilled to be one of the two-three school-boys included in the relay team. All excited at being invited to the big event, I had gone over to my friend Sunny's house in Niza-muddin East and announced to all present that I would be partici-pating in that relay. No one paid attention to the small detail that it was a relay, and I would only be running a 5km stretch. What stuck in my friends' minds was 'Delhi to Agra.' Thankfully, most of them have forgotten, except for one, the forever-young Dinesh Dayal (aka DD), who never fails to greet me with some variant of "*Tu Agra se daurh ke aa raha hai?*" (Have you just come running from Agra?).

The relay itself was a full-day affair. Broken up into mainly 10K stretches with some 5Ks thrown in for weak links like me, it was run at each person's top speed. A bus carried the whole squad and food and drinks and would stop at every 10K-5K baton-switching point, picking up the exhausted runner who had just completed his stretch and dropping off a fresh one to carry the baton forward all with just a clock marking time.

There wasn't much to do on the bus but talk, and that is how I got talking to 'locomotive man,' and learnt about where he had been, where he was, and maybe also where he thought he was going. I don't remember much of any of that, quite possibly because my memory is dominated by his running motion.

My 5K baton-carrying stretch was painful. It was hot, it was humid, and I was miserable. In contrast, his was bouncy and looked effortless. I didn't resent it; I just marvelled at it.

They had said we would all run two stretches, and many of the seasoned runners did run twice. Thankfully, I was spared that, quite possibly because I was slowing down the race against time. As a result, when the relay was all done, and we had reached Agra, I could still stand on my feet and marvel at the Taj—for the very first time in my life. You don't have to run from Delhi to Agra for that, but if architecture moves you, then you should visit Agra and see—no, imbibe—that marvel. It'll blow you away. I was only 16 when I first saw it and never forgot that experience.

That summer began a long and fulfilling running life that lasted a good 39 years. The baton passed from school to college to grad school to working life, from one continent and country to another, and from competition to the solitude of long runs on roads and mountain trails. All through those years of running, every time I struggled to find a rhythm, I would imagine the 'locomotive man' and try to get into the spirit of that circular motion—to land and lift off the balls of the feet. Sometimes it worked, sometimes it didn't. When it did, it was heavenly—even though it was never to Agra to see the Taj Mahal, not even in spirit.

24

Golden shoes

When he walked on to the Atlanta Olympics track in 1996, Michael Johnson was dubbed the 'man with the golden shoes.' He was the favourite to win the 200m-400m sprint double, and Nike had custom-designed gold-coloured running shoes (spikes) for him. He thoroughly justified that colour by winning gold in both events and tearing up the Olympics records in each race. The layperson may not fully appreciate the enormity of that accomplishment, but it is a rarity. Most sprinters—necessarily cocked up on testosterone—prefer the 100m and 200m and hate running the 400m, which requires a more sustained uncocking of that lethal chemical. Not only was Michael Johnson able to do that, but he did it by running in a peculiar ramrod stiff way which baffled running experts.

There was no Nike in India during our school and college years. The only international brands we knew were Adidas, Puma and Asics Tiger, but none of those was available or affordable in the closed Indian economy of the 70s and 80s. In any case, none of us was of international standing, so there is no chance we would have merited the attention of big-brand companies. That doesn't mean we didn't have custom-designed shoes—we had Kartar Singh's spikes.

I had begun training at the National Stadium in May of 1977 and, after a couple of months of daily training, was looking forward to the start of the athletics season. One day my coach, the very affable Mr. Tarlok Singh, asked if I had spikes for the season that lay ahead. I told him about the ones I had purchased from Pioneer Sports, or possibly Oberoi Sports, in Connaught Place. One look at them, and he said: "These won't do. You're going to be a serious runner now, and for that, you need a proper pair of running spikes."

He told me to go see Kartar Singh in Karol Bagh. I didn't think much of that suggestion, but Coach had said do, and so I did. I took the piece of paper on which the address was scrawled and went looking in the bylanes of Karol Bagh. I thought I knew that part of town well because the154 and 157 number public buses I took to school passed through there, and I would periodically fetch coffee powder for my mother from a coffee roaster in one of those bylanes.

Coach had warned me that it would take some effort to find Kartar Singh's shop. It sure did. I went looking for a sports store and couldn't find one at the stated address. Instead, what I discovered, after asking for directions multiple times, was a tiny hole-in-the-wall workshop with a few supplies in the corners and a diminutive, unassuming man squatting on the floor working on a piece of leather.

I told Kartar Singh who had sent me. It mattered not to him. He asked me what events I wanted the spikes for, saying that was important to know because the nails for sprint events were longer than those for middle-distance races. I am not entirely sure, but I don't think the standardized stuff sold by Pioneer Sports and Oberoi Sports in Connaught Place made those distinctions. He gave me a stool to sit on, brought out two pieces of paper, traced the outlines of my feet on them, and then told me to come back for the shoes in a few weeks. That was that: no pleasantries, no extra talk, no nothing.

A few weeks later, I went back to the workshop on the appointed day. He sat me down on the same stool and brought out a pair of shoes that looked not entirely different from the ones I already had. At first, I didn't see what was so special about his spikes, but when I started to put my socked feet in them, I couldn't. He urged me to take off the thick 'Bata towel socks' I was wearing and try the shoes bare-footed. It took a bit of wiggling to get the feet in, but once I had managed that and pulled the laces, they fit like a sock—actually better than a sock, like a second skin. I could imagine how running in them would be an entirely different experience compared to the spikes I had worn before.

I couldn't wait to try out the spikes, but the monsoon season wasn't quite over, and the track regularly got flooded, so the spikes had to wait. Track flooding, of course, provided its own entertainment because amongst the regulars at the Stadium were some quirky ones who ran to a very different beat, one that had little regard for rains and flooded tracks. One post-deluge late afternoon when I got to the stadium, I found one of them—a nationally ranked distance runner—out on the track, running laps in spikes. That was somewhat unusual because at that time of the year, we were still in off-season mode and didn't put on spikes. Moreover, most distance runners in those days ran barefoot, so it was very odd to see one running in spikes. What was even more unusual was that—the track was flooded, and he was running laps at race pace!

Several people, including the stadium manager, were watching in amusement. I asked them what that was about and was told that someone had bet him a full *tandoori* chicken that he couldn't run a 10,000m race in those conditions. Quirkiness and challenges being what they are, he was pounding away the sodden cinder for a dead chicken, though I don't think it was about the chicken at all, well-earned and delicious as it surely would have been after 25 laps. It was about a challenge and a normal guy doing quirky stuff. I've done my share of crazy running, but nothing like that 10k race-paced run on a flooded cinder track. Whenever I think of that late afternoon in August of '77, it always brings a smile.

Once the rains subsided and the track returned to its usual self, faster track workouts began, and after one of them, Coach asked me to put on the new spikes and do some strides in them, just to get a feel for them. Crunching the cinder track in those perfectly fitting spikes was a whole new experience and led to a wholly different running year. Instead of just being a competitor, an also-ran, I became a serious runner that year, winning a few races, placing second or third in many more, including the All India Public Schools championships, and eventually going to the National School Games in Nagpur. It wasn't all because of Kartar Singh's "golden shoes," but they had a lot to do with it. They'd provide entertainment of a different kind the following year.

When we got to the final year of high school, we were focused on winning the All India Public Schools championship again—so "we" could be back-to-back champions and the school could have a "three-peat." By then, our sports department had settled into a training structure wherein the athletics team stayed in the hostel for the week and trained together twice a day during the Dussehra-Diwali holidays in October. It was partly for the training, but more so for team bonding.

During that week, I must have pointed out the beauty of Kartar Singh's spikes to the team. The others wanted a piece of that magic, so a trip to Karol Bagh was arranged. The school bus was commissioned, and one morning, after training and breakfast, we piled in to go to the Regarpura part of Karol Bagh. It should have been a simple trip but ... it got a bit of a twist put on it because of something else I said.

During one of the training sessions, I had let slip to the others a wayward thought of getting my head shaved off. I have no idea where that crazy idea came from, but it did. It was a whim, it was attention-seeking, but most of all, it was stupid, simply stupid.

Urban India of those times was a relaxed and free space, but society was still essentially conservative and nowhere near the hair-dying, mohawk-sporting, everything-pierced openness of the West. And even though we attended an elite school, the flexibility afforded by social and economic privilege was still within boundaries.

Moreover, I was a school prefect and meant to be an example-setting role model. What was I thinking? Clearly not a whole lot. Like a lot of our juvenile talk in those times, it could have blown over, but it didn't.

After taking measurements at Kartar Singh's workshop, the bus turned right on Deshbandhu Gupta Road to head back to school. The mindless banter we were engaged in went here and there, and ... somehow came around to what my tongue had let slip. Now I don't know who to lay the blame on, but one of the more forceful ones on the team suggested we look for a barbershop so I could get my head shaved off—because I had said I 'wanted' to. I don't remember if I protested or joined in to show how cool I was or how I reacted. It matters not. A barbershop was spotted, the bus was stopped and in marched the whole team and me with instructions to the barber to shave it all off. If I had been reluctant earlier on, at that point, I wasn't.

While the barber was running his blade (known as 'ustara') over my head and taking off locks, there was much mirth amongst the onlookers, even when it became painful on the top where my hair grows in circles. Jokes were cracked about having the barber leave three Adidas stripes on the side. It was the only international brand that we knew, so why not? That would have been a boundary too far to cross, and the joke remained a joke, but the pate was shaved clean, and training camp continued for what remained of that holiday break.

When I went home after camp, my brother and parents were somewhat surprised at the new look, but there was no admonition. There could have been, because amongst Hindus, grown up boys and men have their heads shaved only when their father dies. My father was very much alive at that point, and while he didn't care much about the rituals of religion, *Amma* did. She could have said something, but she didn't. The whole thing was ignored.

When school reopened, there was plenty of attention directed my way, jokes of this and that, including friends walking up behind me and yelling '*takla*' (bald one) in my ears. I even acquired a new name—'Tuckles' — and two of my dearest friends still call me that.

When the athletics season resumed, I had a new Michael Johnson-Atlanta-Olympics type of look—bald head and custom-built shoes. The shoes may not have been golden, but they were crafted especially for me. Even though I didn't set any new records that year, I recorded a memory that always brings forth a smile, stroking of my now normal-length hair, and a rolling of the eyes ... at what a slip of the tongue wrought a long time ago.

25

Romeo and Juliet

"Romeo wants Juliet as the filings want the magnet; and if no obstacles intervene, he moves towards her by as straight a line as they. But Romeo and Juliet, if a wall be built between them, do not remain idiotically pressing their faces against its opposite sides like the magnet and the filings with the card. Romeo soon finds a circuitous way, by scaling the wall or otherwise, of touching Juliet's lips directly. With the filings the path is fixed; whether it reaches the end depends on accidents. With the lover it is the end which is fixed, the path may be modified indefinitely."

This is an oft-repeated quote from the great American philosopher-psychologist William James' 1890 magnum opus, "The Principles of Psychology." It points to the centrality of goals, desires, and motivations as unwavering drivers of human action. Everyone knows about this and has some experience with it, even though some of us might cynically roll our eyes at Hollywood and ad agencies' "popsiclization" of it with messages like "carpe diem" and "just do it."

If I were to meet James, a century after his passing, I would point out that while what he says about ends and paths and the difference between metallic filings and humans is certainly true, it is also the case that ... the end isn't always fixed.

If Romeo doesn't find Juliet, he doesn't always keep trying and doesn't always fall to pieces. More often than not, he moves on, reconciles himself to the failure, telling himself all sorts of stories—"she wasn't worth it," "it wasn't meant to be," and whatnot. The larger end of survival—biological and psychological—overrides the smaller ones, and we usually carry on with life.

I know a thing or two about this, not just from reading the psychology literature on goals and motivations and having thought about it for some of my research on human behaviour, but also from living it several times over. The earliest incident was in high school, and it is a story worth telling, so here goes.

In May of 1978, my friend Sanjay and I went to see a morning show of the movie Siddhartha in Benaras. The film had caused a stir in India, not because it is a story about Indians and spirituality written by a foreigner—Hermann Hesse— but because there is a scene in the movie where the Indian actress Simi Garewal appears in the nude. That may have been a factor in our decision to seek out the movie theatre—we were 17, after all—but the real reason was to find cooler air-conditioned relief in the blast furnace heat of May.

We had arrived in Benaras that morning on an overnight train from Delhi for the interview phase of the selection process for the National Defence Academy (NDA). Sanjay was interested in NDA because joining the Air Force was the only way to do what he really wanted—fly planes. At that time, the scope for doing that in the private sector was minimal. My interest in NDA was less about flying and more about being an officer in the Air Force. The idea had come along during the few months I had attended school in Poona. The National Defence Academy is based in Khadakvwasla, which is only about 15 kilometres from Poona, and it quite likely inhabits the imaginations of school-going boys in that area more so than other places in the country.

NDA could have remained a flirtation, but it gradually took hold in the 9th and 10th grades of high school when I joined the Air Force wing of the National Cadet Corps (NCC) —the youth wing of the Indian Armed Forces. I liked the order and discipline of the weekly marching practice, the once-a-year rifle shooting, and the annual summer camps run by proper military personnel. The idea gradually took hold, and by the time I came back from the second NCC camp in the summer of '77, I was clear about the road ahead—NDA was going to be my Juliet!

The selection process for the Academy consisted of an initial written exam. If you passed that, you were invited to a four-day interview at one of the different army barracks in the country, and if you made it through that, there was a final medical exam. Those who were interested in the Air Force also had to pass a flight aptitude test during the four-day interview. The written exam and interview were held twice a year, and we were eligible to join the Academy after grade 11 of school.

Sanjay and I had taken the written exam in the winter of our 11th year in school in the hope of making it to the interview the following summer. There was a long time lag between writing the exam and finding out the results. So, like a persistent Romeo, I went ahead and took the written exam a second time in late spring of the following year—just in case I didn't make it through the interview the first time. I was that committed to Juliet!

On the other hand, *Amma* was dead set against the idea of my joining the armed forces. It wasn't because she was a pacifist. She, very simply, was a protective mother who did not want her boys to be risking their lives, never mind how many times I, or any of those who supported my cause, pointed out the infrequency of wars. From the very first time I expressed interest in a military career, she worked hard to dissuade me, getting as much support as she could from others. My increasing resolve to walk that career pathway was alarming to her, even though she had a cousin who had been in the Air Force, and another who had a son who was currently serving. In contrast to her, my father was relatively neutral.

Sanjay and I passed the written exam and either opted for Benaras as the interview site or allocated it because it was the nearest. Either way, when we headed out to the holy city for the interview, I was confident I would get in. I had all the credentials one could possibly have: I had risen to the top of the Air Force wing in NCC, won the Best Cadet award at the annual NCC camp, represented Delhi in the National School Games, done well academically in the 10th class board exams, and was a school prefect. There was, literally, nothing more I could do to enhance my qualifications as a candidate. I did not expect to be back for the final 12th year of school.

After watching Siddhartha and visiting an uncle of mine who was a professor at Benaras Hindu University, we headed over to the army barracks where we had dropped off our bags on arriving that morning. Check-in was that evening, and the interview process began the next morning with all sorts of psychological tests and group exercises that lasted four days. I don't remember the details of those days, but at the end of it all, I felt good about how I had performed.

The results of the interview were to be announced after lunch on the last day. Prior to the announcement, we were instructed to load our luggage onto the two military trucks that had been brought in to transport candidates to the railway station. We were told that the results would be announced after that and those who had been selected were to take their luggage off the truck to do some additional paperwork for scheduling the next stage of the selection process. The rest would just get on the trucks and be driven to the railway station.

The announcement took place in a hall with a dais at one end and an exit door at the other. We had been allotted numbers at the start of the interview process, and one of the officers stood up on the dais to call out the numbers of those who had been selected. He called the numbers one after the other, and selected candidates got up and left the hall through the exit in a continuous stream.

My ears were peeled to his number calling. At first, I was quite relaxed, but as the process went on and the hall thinned out, I started to get worried. With every number called, I thought ... next one will be mine, surely next one will be mine. It continued thus, and then the officer was on the last page, and then ... he was done. My number still had not been called. I was shell-shocked. I sat there stunned, thinking—"this is not possible; there must be a mistake."

On the way out of the exit door, I checked with the orderly who was directing traffic. There was no mistake: I had not been selected. I couldn't believe it, but it was what it was. Before getting into the truck, I stopped to congratulate Sanjay, who had made it through and arranged to meet up with him later to catch the overnight train back to Delhi. On the way to Benaras, Sanjay and I had made a deal that whoever got in would buy a "*paua*" (a quarter bottle) of gin for the train ride back. I had hoped it would be both of us. I was sure it would be me. It wasn't going to be.

The truck dropped us off at the station. There were still a couple of hours before the train's evening departure. It was late afternoon, and the sun was at its hottest. If you grew up in those climes, you took every opportunity to be in the shade at that time of the day. I certainly did, but that day in May of '78, I stood outside the station baking in the sun's blaze, unable to comprehend what had happened.

An hour or so later, Sanjay arrived, and we went to a liquor store near the station so he could make good on our "*paua*" deal. We drank the gin on the way back to Delhi, either slipped into a bottle of cold Limca or in a "*kulhar*" (earthen pottery cup) of hot tea purchased at one of the stations en route. I don't remember what I thought about on the train ride back and the public minibus I took from the Old Delhi railway station back home; I was, quite simply, numbed.

Amma was, of course, greatly relieved at the outcome but didn't say anything. Nor did *Appa*, though I think he might have shared my disappointment. Summer passed, and I got back to school in July. My friends were surprised to find me back in school. My housemaster, Mr. I. S. Arora, who had been one of the NCC supervisors and one of my greatest supporters in school, was shocked that I hadn't been selected. He said he simply didn't understand it. Nor did I, but by then, I had gotten over the disappointment.

The results of the second written exam came a few months later—I had passed and could go for the interview and give it another try. Would I? I don't remember it posing much of a dilemma. By then, I had decided to move on, rationalizing my decision with—"If I wasn't good enough for them the first time, they aren't good enough for me now." I was my kind of Romeo, not the William James' kind.

26

Aerobics

Mrs Sudhindra went to visit her brother in America in the summer of '78. My memory is a bit fuzzy on the timing—it could have been in the shorter "other" seasons of '78, or it could have been in '79. In a way, it doesn't matter, but ... when you've picked up a memory trigger and are lining up things around it and want to be truthful, then it is, sort of, good to get the timing right. In this case, I can't, other than to be very sure that it wasn't the summer of '77 because that's when we moved from Munirka in the southern part of New Delhi to Block B3 on Lawrence Road in north Delhi.

The move came about because the rental lease on the Munirka flat was due to expire at the end of May, and Mr. Dalwani—the owner who had somewhat suspiciously 'furnished' the apartment beyond any reasonable reach of his government salary—had chosen not to renew it. *Amma* could have looked for another flat in Munirka, but by then, she had had enough of the long commute from the southern part of the city to the northern part, which housed Delhi University, where she taught. The move meant she would have a shorter commute, and so would my brother, who was about to start college life at that university.

Lawrence Road was and still is Keshav Puram, but back then, everyone called it Lawrence Road. That sounded somehow more sophisticated than the names of the surrounding neighbour-hoods—Tri Nagar, Ashok Vihar, Punjabi Bagh. The anglicized name lifted it above its pedestrian surroundings. I certainly pre-ferred calling it Lawrence Road. Was I vain? Yes. Was I vainglori-ous? Yes, quite possibly that too. I can blame it on late adolescence, but I won't. That was my view—how others saw it, I don't know.

It is not clear how we got to know the Sudhindras. It must have had something to do with *Amma*. With one foot in her Tamil roots and another in her Benaras shoots, my mother had a unique ability to befriend most anyone, though she did have a preference for Tamilian and eastern-UP women. Wherever we lived, women from those places would find her, and she would find them, and there would be a regular flow of womenfolk in and out of our home. That must have been how Mrs. Sudhindra entered our orbit, though I don't think she was Tamilian, which suggests *Amma's* reach was not exclusive to her roots and shoots.

At some point in that continuous inflow and outflow of people, Mrs Sudhindra went to America to see her brother and returned a few months later. Not long after coming back, she dropped in to see my mother. 'Dropping in' is this lovely and informal way peo-ple in India visit each other—without announcement and without tallying up calendars. It is a social-interaction pattern greatly facili-tated by the proximity of dwellings in apartment complexes like B3 Lawrence Road.

In the few months she had been away, Mrs Sudhindra had changed. There was a little bit of an accent and a good bit more of confidence, not that she was lacking in that department before her trip. The most noticeable change, though, was that she was quite a bit less of herself than before—she had transformed from being "homely" to "shapely."

These days, the homely-shapely description may be grating, especially for people who personalize and relativize everything they see in the world, but back then, it was simpler. Actually, even now, the reality in India is that comments about people's appearance, especially women's—and by women even more so than men—are very much part of the whispers of social interaction. I feel comfortable saying this because I have two daughters and the number of times they have had their appearance commented on—by familiars and unfamiliars —is notable. Thankfully, it does not bother them much.

Of course, body change over the life cycle has some very natural biological and behavioural aspects, so the transformation of what might have been hour glasses and V frames in younger years to the more uniform H frame of middle age is a universal phenomenon. Its Indian variant can be traced to the delicious food that comes fried in *ghee* and oil. Sooner or later, that clogs up the arteries internally and, along with limited physical exertion, pushes out the straight H frame here and there in ... somewhat homely ways. Whether you like it or not, sooner or later, you become "aunty" and "uncle."

Things have changed a good bit, and these days, many people in India make a special effort to put in less and put out more, but there wasn't any of that back then. There were the stray morning walkers and dedicated yoga practitioners, but there were no gyms, and there were no vigorous heart-pounding exercise classes. Body shapes followed their own trajectory, and there was no shame or blame in that.

I don't know how old Mrs Sudhindra was when she went to America, and I didn't pay too much attention to what sort of body frame she had. What I do know is that when she came back, it seemed like she had walked back into an earlier decade of her life cycle—into whatever she may have looked like in her 20s. It was noticeable, and she wore her new form with confidence.

Not long after she returned, she came by to see *Amma*. When my mother, quite naturally, complimented her on how well she looked, she very proudly told her it was all because of "aerobics," the new healthy exercise trend that was sweeping the US. She explained what it was, and *Amma* listened with interest. I am not entirely sure, but maybe my mother also encouraged her to show women in the neighbourhood the wonders of this new thing called aerobics. It would have been completely within her character to suggest these things to younger women who looked up to her for being independent, confident and self-assured.

Whether it was my mother's encouragement, or ideas Mrs Sudhindra already had in her head, or the curiosity of women in the neighbourhood, soon a small group got together in her flat to check out aerobics. I am guessing those sessions played to a cassette tape because those were the days of high import duties on electronics and consumer products, and middle-class neighbourhoods like ours didn't have that many gadgets. Then again, maybe Mrs Sudhindra had managed to slip in a VCR under Indian customs' eagle eyes, so perhaps it was all set to something on video. I don't know. Jane Fonda's workout video was still years away, so if it was video, it would have had to be a less glamourous one, and that too on the black and white TVs that we all had at that time.

Cassette or videocassette, it mattered not. A handful of women would gather in Mrs Sudhindra's living room and try and synchronize body movements to peppy music. It seems easy, but it isn't. We men may scoff at those rhythmic exercise classes, but I have attended one, in times when I was in good running shape and found it very hard to keep up.

How well those "homely" women of B3 performed in those classes is not something I want to visualize. In those days, *kaftans* were in fashion, and how women of whatever shape and size did aerobics in those loose and airy pieces of cloth that went from head to toe with slits for the arms is a question I have no insight into. Then again, they might have just worn a *salwar kameez* for the exercise session or gotten themselves black tights like the ones Mrs Sudhindra wore. Don't ask me how I know that. I have a distinct image of that in my mind, but it might just be my over-active imagination at work!

There is no recorded history of how long those aerobics classes lasted. All I know is that not long after their start, the Sudhindras moved out of the complex, and the classes stopped. Did those aerobics classes start a fitness movement in B3 and beyond? I don't think so, but what do I know? Did Mrs Sudhindra continue the aerobics classes in her new digs? I don't know. We never saw them again. The lives of the 340-odd families who inhabited B3 Lawrence Road moved on. Lives always do.

27

Tears of solidarity

Virmani's daughter got married in the winter months of 1981 in B3 Lawrence Road in northern Delhi. It was just another wedding in our middle-class neighbourhood, a square block of entirely unimaginative boxy two-bedroom flats built by DDA, the Delhi Development Authority. DDA built a lot of affordable housing complexes in the late 70s, and this was one of them.

In the middle of that complex was a rectangular one-storey shopping centre with eight small shops arranged in a squarish C-shape with entrances at each end. When we first moved there, the shopping centre was just a concrete structure with floor, roof, and walls. There were no functioning shops, and for the first few months, we'd buy everything we needed from shops in the more established neighbourhood across the Wazirpur irrigation canal. I would do the daily morning trek to pick up plastic milk packs from the Mother Dairy counter across from Montfort school, and all of us would pick up other stuff from shops in Ashok Vihar. It was only after more families started occupying the flats that the shopping centre came alive.

At one end of the shopping complex was "Goel store," a basic convenience store, what in northern India is called a "*kirane ki dukan*." It stocked all the essential non-perishable foods from wheat and rice of different varieties to other cereals, and sugar and spices and salt and *ghee* and oil. All of that was in open sacks and tins that occupied the entire floor space. Then there were the snacks and toiletries and other essentials of household functioning, which were stacked on the shelves. There was, literally, no space left vacant in that shop.

To an outsider, the shop would have looked chaotic, but to those on the inside, which was Mr. Goel, his teenage son, and a helper, the routes to sacks and tins and shelves were well known. How remains a mystery to me, but that is India for you. You have to be an insider to intuit its chaotic workings; outside working models don't help much.

Goel store was also the ration point for that complex. The Green Revolution had begun to transform Indian agriculture, and the food scarcities of the 60s and early 70s had given way to greater availability of food grains by the late 70s. But ration cards of those earlier times were still in operation, and you could get the monthly allotment of wheat, rice, and sugar from Goel store. The quality of the rationed food grains was not particularly good, and free-market prices of higher quality grains were not a whole lot higher. Like other families in the complex, we didn't take our rations of grains, preferring to buy those at higher prices. Sugar was a different story; it was more expensive in the free market, so we took our monthly allotment of that precious commodity.

The other end of the shopping centre was Virmani's "*chakki*" (flour mill)—for grinding food grains to flour. You could buy wheat and maize grain from Goel store and haul it across to Virmani's *chakki*, and it would be transformed into wheat and maize flour. In between those two ends were other shops which ... sold something that I don't remember very well. Looking back, I can be misty-eyed about that small shopping complex and its occupants, but back then, there was no mist, just flour dust that hung in the air outside Virmani's *chakki*.

Mr. Goel was a typical urban small-shop operator and a long-time Delhi resident. He was friendly, polite, and flexible on payment terms. *Amma* had a running account at his store, so we never paid in cash; she settled it monthly. I don't think she ever checked that account, and I doubt he took advantage of it. Virmani, on the other hand, was another story. He was small-town, not downtown, and crude and loud. I didn't like him much. Unlike Mr. Goel, who didn't live in our complex but came in on a bicycle from somewhere else, Virmani lived there, just not on community terms but his own.

I had had a run-in with him the year before when right during exam time, he had organized a *satsang* (a religious meeting) and set up a loudspeaker to broadcast his piety to everyone. I had gone to him to complain about the noise and pointed out that all the young-sters in the complex had exams coming up, and it was hard to con-centrate with blaring hymns playing all day. His response, in Hindi, was: "*Maine panch soh rupay diye hain, jisko chahoon sunaoonga*" (I have paid 500 rupees for this, and I will broadcast to whoever I like). There wasn't much one could say to that. Luckily, his 500 rupees only bought a day's worth of hoarse singing.

In 1981, in the so-called 'auspicious season' of weddings, Vir-mani's daughter got married. Like the *satsang*, it was a cacophonous affair, and the large *shamiana* tents set up in the main thoroughfare blocked and disrupted everything. How could it not? I am sure he had paid at least a hundred times more for the wedding than the *sat-sang*, so of course, it had to have a hundred-fold effect. Fortunately,

it was in the festive season when people forgive of just about anything, so not much was made of it.

Once the wedding rituals were over, there was the customary
'*bidaai*' moment, that last procession when the bride leaves her par-
ent's home, and things get emotional. The bride and groom and
their entire entourage proceeded to walk out of the complex. We
lived in 23B, a two-bedroom flat on the first floor, not far from Virmani's *chakki* and the flat he and his family lived in. Our front balcony overlooked the exit route. We wouldn't have known of the
procession in normal circumstances, but it was Virmani's daughter's
wedding, so it was hard to miss the sound and fury.

It was late in the evening. I don't know what *Amma* was doing
at that time, but whatever it was, she left it and walked out to
the balcony to watch the procession. She watched the procession
go by, and I watched her in absolute amazement—shedding a few
quiet tears. She wasn't at that wedding, she barely knew his family,
and we had entirely different spheres of interaction, but there she
was—sad in solidarity. I am sure that solidarity was with Virmani's
wife, not him, though I am also quite sure she didn't know her either.

I hugged *Amma* and asked her why she was crying. She didn't say
anything. To her, Mrs Virmani would not have the regular company of her daughter anymore and ... nothing more needed saying. She was like that, my mother. She did the simple things in
her life—teaching, family, music, food and social interaction—simply marvellously, which is why wherever we lived, people knew her
and liked her company. Women in the neighbourhood would come
to her, sometimes for advice, but mostly to be with her. Sometimes
they'd chat and leave, sometimes they'd linger on for tea, and sometimes it would stretch into dinner ... with *Pushpaji*, Aunty, Desai

mami, or just Mrs Desai. That's just the way it was a very long time ago.

28

A musical note

The two Facebook memory notifications arrived three days apart. They referred to events in 2008 that have a bittersweet memory that links Oslo in Norway to Los Angeles in America, with a huge swing back in time to a dear friend and high school years of music, mischief, and adolescence.

The first notification came on the 1st of December and said: "Thank you for your wishes—next time in Simla! (Not)." It was a reply to the birthday greeting I had posted on my high school friend, Ashwani Kapoor's Facebook wall on November 29th. His reply was an inside joke referring to a trip we had made to Simla (India) for dubious reasons; it brought a smile.

The second notification came on the 4th of December and said: "Is looking forward to an early morning run in Oslo." This one referred to a Facebook post I had put up at something like 4:30 am about my intention to head out for a morning run in Oslo, Norway. I had arrived the day before for a two-day workshop on youth in developing countries. Why I was at a workshop on a topic I was only just beginning to get my head around is a story for another time.

The real reason I had agreed to attend that workshop was that I hoped to sneak away and see Bislett Stadium, one of the meccas of athletics. I had read about the Bislett games in college and how world records were regularly broken in the intimate surroundings of a stadium where the packed crowds were so close to the runners that they could almost touch them. Even though it was winter and there were no athletic meetings scheduled at the stadium, I wanted to pay my respects at that temple of track and field.

When I checked into the downtown boutique hotel in the evening, the first thing I asked for was a map of the city and assistance with locating Bislett Stadium on it. The next morning, I was up by 4am and ready to head out for a run to the stadium. The hotel rooms were small and had bathrooms, but not the typical in-room fanfare of hot water kettle, fridge, hot and cold drink sachets and Wi-Fi. That was all available in the lobby, so after putting on winter running gear, I headed down there to grab a coffee and check the news, email and Facebook at one of the two desktop computers available for use by hotel guests. It was then that I put up the post about my intention to head out for a morning run.

By the time I got going, it was 5 am and pitch dark. Oslo is far up north, and in winters, the sun doesn't come out till much later in the day and is only out for about six hours. The stadium was a short distance away, and I was able to run to it in 10-odd minutes. It was locked, which was a bit disappointing, but I still got the satisfaction of going by there and seeing a statue of the great Norwegian (female) runner, Grete Waitz—the first to run the marathon in under two and a half hours, a world record holder at one point, and a nine-time winner of the New York City marathon.

Having satisfied my need to visit a running shrine, I turned around to head back but instead of going straight back and thus getting only a 20-minute run decided to take a few left and right turns to add to the running time. I should have known from past experiences that, with a highly perfected ability to lose my way in the simplest of street configurations, there was a good chance I would get lost. With snow starting to fall and temperature near freezing, that was not a good idea, but fools do what fools do, and so I took a few turns this way and that way and … yup, I got lost. The short version of the long story of that adventure is that, instead of running the intended 30-40 minutes, I ended up being out in the falling snow for an hour and a half!

Thankfully, the workshop had a late start, so I was able to take a shower and catch a short nap before heading down to breakfast. There was still time left after breakfast, so once again, with coffee in hand, I sat down at one of the desktops in the lobby to while away time. It didn't last long. Facebook flashed a message from a friend saying Ashu (Ashwani Kapoor) had passed away rather suddenly. I sat there stunned, not just because we weren't even 50 at that point but also because of the Facebook exchange with him just a few days earlier.

I remember little of what transpired at the workshop that day. My mind was elsewhere. I thought about the time in 2006 when I had gone to LA for a population conference and reconnected with him and his wife Alka, another Modern School friend, and met his lovely daughters. We had driven around the touristy parts of LA and had a fabulous dinner at a Thai restaurant. It was a reunion after 24 years, though really after 27 because we hadn't seen much of each other after "passing out" from Modern School and going on to different colleges in Delhi.

More than the memory of that recent reconnection were memories of high school, of a time in life when we thought we knew more than we really did and believed we owned the world. When I had gotten in touch with Ashu in Los Angeles in 2006, I had run through some of those memories and smiled many times over. At the workshop in Oslo on that dreary December day in 2008, I went through them again, wondering when it all began.

We had been in different sections in junior school and the first two years of senior school and, as a result, had only minimal contact—that being through the school orchestra we were both members of. Was it then, or was it when the class sections were scrambled in 9th grade, and all of us acquired some new friends, and both of us chose to join the Air wing of NCC (National Cadet Corps) and attended weekly marching drills? I am not sure about the timing, so I will hold on to the substantive bits of the memories.

For starters, and this still makes me smile every time, there was that adolescent conversation when we were 15 or 16—of the best way to grow a moustache. Life and luck had landed me a reasonably decent upper lip early on, and I was the envy of all my peers whose voices had cracked but whose moustaches refused to be more than isolated wisps. Ashu's great solution, revealed to us while we were loitering about the old gym in school, was to apply *ghee* (clarified butter). I don't know whether he had tried that strategy himself, but he assured those in attendance that it worked. Did any of the others try? I don't know and won't be asking anyone that question; some things are best left unknown.

Then there were the summer NCC camps. The first one in Dharamshala had been great fun with others of the same mindset, but we were juniors and marched to the orders of those who were a year senior to us in school. It was the second one in the summer of '77, somewhere I don't remember when we were in charge. That one brings many a smile. We, meaning those of us seniors who didn't mind breaching the boundaries of law and order at the camp, had designated one of our tents for late-night gatherings. Some of those involved consumption of *tharra*, the illicit locally brewed hooch, that was purchased with pooled contributions. How did we procure that? I don't know, but I am willing to bet Ashu had a hand in that. Amongst us 16-year-old know-it-alls, he certainly was one of the more worldly ones, so I wouldn't be the least bit surprised if it were his doing.

And then, of course, there was our special bond—music. He played the *sitar*, and I played the violin, and while we were in different sections in the first two years of senior school and didn't attend Mr. Khastagir's classes together, we did play together in the school orchestra—every morning at school assembly, and then at the annual "Founders Day" function. Towards the end of our school years, those annual performances did not have a full orchestra but a trio of guitar, sitar, and violin. In 2006, I had wondered if he remembered the *"pa ni sa, pa ni sa, pa ni sa re ga sa"* note combination the last time we played together but hadn't gotten around to asking him. Sitting in Oslo, I wondered about that while that sequence of notes played out in my head.

The Simla trip that he had referred to in the Facebook post was, of course, another story, but not much of that can be shared in public. It was somewhat on the lines of the many parties of those senior years in school when Boney M and Abba and Saturday Night Fever and all the disco music that was cool in the late 70s played regularly. Often Ashu provided the music and the equipment.

When I had met his daughters in 2006 and seen their interaction with him, I had thought of the Boney M song—Daddy Cool—that used to play quite a bit at those parties and that I'd first heard in his company. I don't remember if the song had any meaningful lyrics other than the repetition of the title again and again, but it seemed just right for him and his daughters.

That day in Oslo passed in a daze. What I had to say the next day was entirely pointless, so it was good to get it over with and get on with going to the Munch Museum and drinking *øl* (beer in Norwegian) and cracking up on various takes on *øl*, none greater than the one stemming from a particular beer brand *Aas*—hence *Aas øl*. It was somewhat like the juvenile *tharra* chatter from NCC days. If Ashu had been there, he would have surely joined in.

I kept thinking of him and our times together on the flight back home and decided, somewhat impulsively, that I would go out to LA to attend his funeral. And so, within a few days of returning, I flew out to LA, rented a car from the airport, went straight to the funeral and then back to the same apartment I had seen him in just two years earlier. An hour or so there, and it was back to the airport to catch the redeye (overnight flight) back to DC. There are many impulsive things that I have done in life, some of which I regret, but not that one-day trip to LA. I am glad I was there to bid farewell to … a musical note.

29

Fortuna's smile

Fortuna, the Roman goddess of luck, is often represented with a blindfold because she knows not whether she will bestow good or bad luck. Her westernized avatar, Lady Luck, is associated primarily with good fortune, which she delivers with a smile, which is why people say, "Lady Luck smiled on ... so and so." I am not sure whether there is an equivalent avatar for misfortune, whether it is male or female, and whether it has a name. For this reason and more, I find it easier to go with the same entity for good and bad luck—Fortuna—and think of what she doles out in terms of her smiles and frowns.

When I got to St Stephen's College in July of 1979, I had decided that I would no longer play football but just do athletics and study economics. I wasn't expecting much out of college athletics but was pleasantly surprised when I won the first college road race—the Thursday 3.2K. The short race started next to the St. Stephen's college gym, went through the main Delhi University campus, and ended at the inside college gate. It was low key but with a big reward—a glass of sweet *nimboo pani* (lemon juice) at Rohtas' *dhaba*, a St. Stephen's institution of sorts. The win was a nice way to start college athletics.

The bigger running buzz came a few weeks later when I anchored the college team in the 4x750m Otto Peltzer Road Relay at the National Stadium to a win, and a new record. That earned me a newspaper headline on a sports page—"Desai helps Stephen's triumph"—and got people's attention in college. In the world beyond, it didn't mean much because it was off-season road racing and a relay. When the athletics season began, it was back to the more typical 2nd and 3rd place finishes of high school years.

With football no longer a distraction, I was taking running more seriously. In the previous year, I had switched to a new coach, SS Rai, but didn't train in front of him because his training ground was in South Delhi at the back of a government school, and most of his trainees were school kids. He would write me a weekly workout for four weeks, and I would go do it on my own, wherever was convenient for me. It was all good, but there was no ongoing monitoring of progress in the arrangement and quite simply—no excitement, no oomph. It was just going along in a ho-hum, hum-drum way.

Things would have probably gone on like that, but then Fortuna came along and smiled one December evening and changed the course of my athletics life. I had known Raghubir Singh from the first summer I started training at the National Stadium. Unlike other coaches, including mine, he actively engaged with his athletes, always talking to them at great length. I had noticed that but not made a connection between his coaching and his athletes' success, even when one of them won the junior national championship in the 800m. I was satisfied with my training arrangement and not looking for a change, but change was looking for me.

That December day in '79, I got to the stadium at the usual training time, but had to wait to begin training because an athletics meet was in progress. During the season, the stadium would regularly be rented out for competitions, and on those occasions, we had to wait for the events to finish and for the track to empty out before we could train. While waiting, I somehow ended up talking to Raghubir and his trainees, some of whom I was friends with. The Delhi State Championships were coming up, and he asked me what events I planned to run, and then said (in Hindi), "Why don't you try the under-19 1500m steeplechase? You'd be good at it." I hadn't thought of that event and wasn't even aware there was no regular (flat) 1500m race in that age category.

For those not in the know, a steeplechase race is run on the same 400m track as all races, but it has four immovable hurdles and a water pit that you must go over. Going over the five barriers, especially the water pit, in all but the first lap of a race, makes a steeplechase race physically more demanding than a race without barriers.

I must have expressed interest because he offered to train me for it, starting that day itself. So instead of going out onto the cinder track after the competitors from the day's athletics meet had departed, I waited till it was dark and only Raghubir and his two-three trainees remained in the stadium. One of his trainees had gotten into a fight earlier in the season and was banned from the stadium, so they trained in the dark when no one was around.

Raghubir showed me how to clear the water pit and ran me through a hard workout of 20 to 25 repetitions of hurdling the immovable barriers and going over the water pit. When that was done, I joined one of his trainees for a set of 250m sprints. It was the hardest workout I had ever done, and I was exhausted but strangely energized with a feeling of accomplishment very different from any I had experienced before.

While I was taking off the spikes and changing into a warm tracksuit, he asked if I did any weight training for building muscle strength. I told him I didn't but had played football in high school and in the 9th and 10th grade regularly biked to school, which was about 25km each day. He smiled and said that must be why I had good leg strength and good push-off from the hurdle over the water pit, abilities important for steeplechasers but not inherent in most competitors who were plain vanilla distance runners.

And then, in typical inspiring-coach mode, he said: "You can be a great steeplechaser. I think that is your natural event." There was a month or so till the state championships, and he said he would train me for that and then for the nationals, but the real work would have to be the following summer when he would completely rework my running form.

It is hard to put in words how excited I was at that point. No one to that date, not one of my coaches, had taken any note of my football and cycling experiences, and no one had pointed to long-term possibilities, let alone say I could be "great."

That winter, I trained in the dark hours after sunset, going harder than I ever had. At the Delhi State Championships, Raghubir insisted I wear spikes in the steeplechase race. It wasn't something runners in India did at that point, believing legitimately or not, that the run through the water would fill up the shoes and slow you down. He said that was a silly notion, especially since I was wearing Kartar Singh's custom-built spikes that fit like a glove. There was no room for water to get into those, though the leather did get wet, and the shoe got marginally heavier. He also insisted I hurdle the barriers, not step over them as most runners did, explaining that, with practice, the hurdling would save vital seconds and not be tiring for me because I had good leg strength.

He trained me for the steeplechase by working on the technique for clearing the water pit and hurdling the barriers, and in the race, the event-specific training showed. I led from start to finish and beat someone who had just come back from winning the 5000m at the National School Games. In a flat race, he might have beaten me, but I was smoother over the hurdles and thus faster. I must have actually gained on the followers at each run through the water pit because I was able to push off from the barrier and gain inches while they had to go over it into the water, lose momentum, and build it back up each time.

When I crossed the finish line, I couldn't believe I had won. I had come close to breaking the state record, but that was a sideshow. It was the feeling of winning a significant event that mattered because I had never won a meaningful race before. There would be races that I would win later that season and in the two years that would follow, and my times would improve quite dramatically, but no other race would ever match that one.

After the race, I was in a different zone and somewhat cockily said to one of the men's runners that I was thinking of running the men's 3000m steeplechase race. It was an outrageous statement because that race was in a couple of hours, and I didn't have the distance training build-up to compete at that distance. It was also very uncharacteristic of me; I had never said anything like that to any competitor. But victory is like that—it makes you think you can do anything. I had experienced disheartening defeats before but never victory this exhilarating.

We prepared for the Inter-State Nationals in Hissar, Haryana, with punishing workouts that alternated with easy recovery days. Going into the nationals, I was full of hope, maybe too full of it. His encouragement was consistent all through, and my journal of that time has two concrete records of that. One says: "No one in India clears the water pit the way you do." Another says: "The question isn't whether you will win the nationals; the question is whether you will break the national record." I could tell he wasn't just saying that to encourage me; he genuinely believed it. At the nationals, he even introduced me to a former middle-distance great by pointing to my abilities and possibilities.

Unfortunately, things didn't turn out that way. I started with the same tactic I had employed in the state championships—going to the lead at the very start. All seemed to go well, but after two laps, a small pack of runners overtook me. I was only two-three steps behind them, but I was surprised by their move. Raghubir and a couple of others were watching, and while he didn't say anything, one of them couldn't help but blurt out: "*Abay, kya kar raha hai?*" (What are you doing?). I heard that, and it took a bit of self-belief out of me. Even though they were running barefoot and stepping over the barriers while I was in spikes and hurdling over the barriers and pushing off the water pit barrier, I wasn't able to make up the ground the rest of the way.

Instead of winning and breaking the national record, I finished sixth. It was very simple —I had choked. Before the meet, he had warned one of his other trainees, the one who had won the 800m at the nationals the year before, that if I won the 1500m, he should watch out for me in the 800m. I was no threat at all. I ran the 800m listlessly, finishing 4th or 5th or worse. I had lost plenty of races before, but this time around, I was devastated. Raghubir was surprised but said I shouldn't worry about it—he had a good sense of why I had lost, and he'd fix it during the off-season.

Things turned around within a week when we got back to Delhi, and I won both the 800m and 1500m at the Delhi University Championship. That eased the pain of the national's loss a little bit, and the pain would ease further when I'd get nominated to be college athletics captain for the following year.

I had come a long way in one year and, for the first time, won some big races, but none of that really mattered. What mattered was that Raghubir had planted—the bug of possibilities—in my head. It would work in its own peculiar ways in the years to come. Fortuna was still smiling when the first year of college ended.

30

Wood without plans

At my workplace, there is a 'morning tea' every Wednesday. It is this nice custom wherein people break from work to have a cup of tea, or coffee, or neither. The admin folks do it every day; the academics join in once a week. I go when I can, but some years back, it used to take place in the common area right outside my office, so I couldn't ignore it. That there were nibbles accompanying tea and coffee (and neither) meant I didn't want to ignore it. I used to look forward to Wednesdays because it was a triple treat: I could skip breakfast, nibble at morning tea, and then continue nibbling on the leftovers—which ended up in the kitchen, which was right across the printer room. On Wednesdays, I invariably had lots to print!

On one of those occasions, after getting a quarter plate of nibbles and a coffee, I found myself next to a colleague who lives in one of the way-out suburbs. Aiming to make small talk, not one of my strengths, I mentioned to her that I had been in her suburb the previous day and had forgotten that it was a good 25-30 km away. She asked me what had taken me there and I told her that I had gone there to buy some very nice Macrocarpa wood. She then asked me what I was going to do with the wood, to which I responded with ... a blank look.

Smart woman that she is, she gauged the real meaning and said, "You don't really have any idea, do you?" Caught in the glare of searching headlights, I admitted I had no idea what I was going to do with it and that I had ended up buying it on Trademe, the New Zealand auction site similar to eBay, because ... it was really good wood, and I had put in a bid on a whim, and no one else had, and that's how I had ended up winning the auction. She just shook her head the way—experienced partners of harmlessly wayward men do.

It reminded me of the time 35 or so years ago when I had spent an entire hot summer morning scouring the streets and alleyways of Chandni Chowk in Delhi looking for a cobbler's awl and cutter. There was no school project or anything that needed those tools of work, just my fascination with the everyday workings of the world around me.

As with all the informal sector workers who greased the functioning of our lives in those times, I was fascinated by the workings of *mochis* (cobblers) who could be found on the streets in every neighbourhood. Every time I'd take a shoe or *chappal* (slipper) to one, I'd watch with great interest how he'd do his thing.

The *mochi* would first wax the thread in preparation for use in stitching and then get the shoe or *chappal* that needed repair ready—by holding it between his feet. That left his two hands free to do the real work. One hand would feed a loop of one end of the thread to the hungry awl that would pierce through the leather/rubber while being held in the other hand. The awl would pull back the thread to the other side to make another loop, and the other end of the thread would be slid through it. The loop would then get pulled back to the other side to secure the stitch. The process would be repeated till the repair was complete. When done, the remaining length of thread would be sliced off with the cutter, the shoe would be placed on the three-way iron stand that all *mochis* had, and the stitching would be hammered in with a short stumpy iron bar.

I enjoyed the experience each time and must have asked one of them where he got his tools, and he must have told me that I could get one in Khari Baoli, which is in the innards of the Chandni Chowk area. I don't remember that interaction but can visualize the *mochi* rolling his eyes and wondering what plans a middle-class boy had with a poor man's tools. He didn't know—I didn't have any plans at all, just a fascination with the tools and how he did his work.

I had gone looking for the *mochi's* tools in the summer of 1980 when I used to go from the northern end of the city where we lived to Okhla in the southern end to run on sand. Summer being the scorcher that it is in India, and sand being an absorber of its burning heat, the only reasonable time to run on the sand was early in the morning—before the sun had come up. To make it all work, I would get up at 5 am, make myself an egg sandwich and head out to catch the very first public bus at 5:45 am. At that hour, the buses were empty, and two connections would get me to Okhla in an hour, leaving just about an hour to run on sand before it became impossible to continue. By the time I'd stop, I'd be covered in sweat and sand and find relief by sitting under a tube-well tap and washing it all off in cool groundwater.

Running done, I would get back on a bus for the long ride back, just around the time officegoers were starting to head out to work. By then, the mercury had climbed, and the buses were crowded. The ride back took longer and would leave me doubly exhausted. It was an ordeal of sorts but worth it because, over time, I could feel the difference sand running made to my running form.

That was the routine for the two months of dry heat that preceded the arrival of the monsoon rains, and it was on one of those days that I had stopped in Chandni Chowk on the way back and gone looking for the awl and cutter—with no idea what I would do with them. That search took me from the Red Fort bus stop to the inner streets our school bus used to wind through, but I didn't find the tools. Eventually, tired and hungry and hot, I gave up. Just as well!

I want to say that that that plan-less wander in Chandni Chowk was on the 23rd of June, but I am not sure. The date sticks in my mind because there was a distinct buzz in the air on the bus ride back from Okhla that day. I couldn't help but overhear what the officegoers were talking about—Sanjay Gandhi, the Prime Minister's son, had died in a plane accident.

He was a very divisive figure, and I don't think many people in Delhi cared for his arrogant ways, especially after the country had resoundingly rejected his mother's authoritarian rule in the elections of 1977. That, and the fact that Sanjay Gandhi had never been elected, not once, rankled people. The rumour in town was that he was the real Prime Minister, not her.

I didn't have strong political views in those days, but his arrogant and dismissive ways were the talk of the town, and his forced sterilisation campaign during the Emergency had touched a nerve amongst young people in Delhi. One of them was my brother, who had been stopped on the street for a potential operation. It didn't come about, but many young men had similar encounters and no one I knew thought much of Sanjay Gandhi.

The bus ride from Okhla to ITO (Income Tax Office) and then on to Ferozeshah Kotla stadium and onwards to Red Fort is the only time I tuned in to people's chatter, and the more I listened, the clearer it got. People felt sorry for a person dying and a mother losing a young son, but the buzz in that bus from Okhla had a distinct sense of relief to it.

The memory trigger from my colleague's remark at the Wednesday morning tea didn't take me to this gruesome story of that summer. It has come along while penning the story of that futile search for a cobbler's awl and cutter in Chandni Chowk the same summer. Good or bad, that is how memory's tickling works—one thing leads to another.

Back to the Wednesday morning tea in Wellington, in much the same way as the Chandni Chowk wander, I had gone looking for the seller of the wood pieces the day before. This time I had a specific address, but that part of town has a lot of small industrial sheds with confusing numbers, and I had not been able to find the seller. Frustrated with the expedition, I was ready to head back when I got a call back from him with clearer directions to where he was. I gave it one more try and was successful and ended up with four square lengths of fine wood with no clear plan for what I would do with them. All of this ran through my head at morning tea, but I didn't tell my colleague any details.

That was all a couple of years ago. Those four-square lengths of Macrocarpa wood are still there in the garage, patiently waiting for a plan. When I see them looking at me in a complaining way, I remind them of the other pieces of wood that have also been chopped and cleaned. Some have a plan whose execution has been interrupted, and some are waiting for a plan. Perhaps the Macrocarpa pieces should feel some empathy for those guys!

As to my fascination with the workings of life and everyday workers, that continues, though there are no street-side workers in New Zealand, so I don't get to see as much stuff. Here, I get by with marvelling at the machinery in use in road works, the wooden framing of houses under construction, and lingering in the aisles of hardware stores. Periodically, that leads to the acquisition of new tools. Some of them serve a very useful purpose and save us a lot of money. Others just sit around waiting for a moment of inspiration, a new plan, something!

31

A victory song

Outcomes of sports competitions often hinge on little things, some real, some imagined. It is said that the great competitors of the world rarely accept defeat as fair beating by a superior opponent. Not taking responsibility allows them to maintain confidence and carry on to the next battle. Victory, on the other hand, is always made out to be—deserved, well-earned, and built on the back of "sweat and tears." How often is it be attributed to a song?

I am not saying a certain song had something to do with our college team winning the Delhi University Athletics Championship in the winter of 1980–81, but ... maybe it did. I happen to remember the song that was playing the evening before the final day of the four-day competition, and maybe, just maybe the song—more than our athletic effort—led to the win.

It was my second year in college, and it was the year I was captain of the athletics team. I had been appointed at the end of the first year, a breakthrough season for me in more ways than one. In school, I had been part of two great championship teams in athletics and one in football, and even though as sports prefect I was in a way in charge of them, they weren't really "my" teams. This was my first chance to lead a team, and I was ready to get going from day one.

The team building had to wait, first for year-end exams to get done and then through the long summer stretch of off-season training. All along, I made notes of who could be roped in for which event and made several hand-drawn designs of what our kit would look like; I still have that notebook, and it always brings a smile. Those were the great England middle distance years of Sebastian Coe and Steve Ovett, and my design of our athletics vest was a replica—two horizontal stripes, one red one blue, on a white background. I still have that vest in a suitcase of track memories.

Once college started, I went about putting together a competitive team for the university championship. The linchpin to that effort was the athlete of athletes—SD Mudgil—who I knew from my school days. I have not known a more versatile athlete than SDM. No one could clean up all of the jumps (long, high, triple and pole vault), win the decathlon, and be a serious threat to win both hurdles' races and even the sprints.

Mudgil could single-handedly win more points than most colleges would score as a team, but I figured that would not be enough to beat our main rivals—PGDAV College, who had won the previous few years. So I went about recruiting anyone who may have competed in high school and could get us an extra point or two and was a slave driver at evening training sessions. I wince at the memory scars those sessions might have left behind on "freshers" (freshmen), but that's how it went that year.

We had a good build-up to the Delhi University Athletics Championship and won the team title in every athletic meet we entered that year. Still, I knew that the upcoming inter-college meet would be different because the team competition was fierce, and our college had not won in quite a few years. The meet didn't start so well for me when I lost the 1500m race on the first day itself. It was my year of emergence as a serious middle-distance runner, and I had trained hard over the off-season, so there was no reason to lose, but I didn't run a smart race and got beat fair and square. It was disappointing, but I quickly got over it because the primary objective at that point was winning the team championship.

The meet was over four days, and by the end of the third day, we were ahead, but just barely. We were all a bit nervous, none more than me. After the day's events were over, I hung around the hostel—known as 'residence' at St Stephen's College—with Mudgil, Kishen Singh, NP and gang. Our talk focused on how many points we had, how many we could expect to get the next day, and whether those would be enough. We knew it would be close.

We were in NP's room in the Allnut North block of residence, and the radio was on, and we were chatting. A song from a recently released Rajesh Khanna-movie, Prem Bandhan, came on air, and Kishoo (Kishen Singh) immediately said, "Turn it off." The song was "*Humain tumse pyar kitna ye hum nahin jante*," roughly translated as—I love you so much, even I don't know.

I didn't understand what Kishoo was fussing about, so I asked him why the radio should be turned off, and he said something about the hero losing the girl in the movie and us not wanting to lose our girl—the team championship. It still didn't make any sense to me, but I was not about to jeopardize the outcome of a year-long quest in any way, and none of the others thought it odd either, so the radio was quickly turned off.

The last day was nerve-racking with us still ahead, but just barely. I managed to lose my second race, the 800m, but again it didn't matter. By that time our lead was secure, and we capped it off with a second-place finish in the 4x400m relay. We knew we had won, but we couldn't celebrate because there was a rumour that a busload of rowdy PGDAV supporters was on the way, and there would be violence. It wasn't just a rumour because if you had been around the high jump pit during that event on the final day, you would have sensed the intimidating atmosphere created by the PG-DAV supporters.

Someone advised us to avoid the closing ceremony and instead head back to college. It would have been nice to be there and strut a bit, but it didn't really matter. We had won after I don't know how many years. I had dreamt of that from the first year in college and then worked on it all through the second, and it had come to be.

Mudgil had won every event he competed in and brought us 42 points, which was huge, but when it ended, we had won by just seven. By my calculation, that difference was the sum total of points my recruits in the high jump, 20km walk, triple jump and rag-tag events had earned. I was very proud of that. I had lost both my races but won the big one.

A specific song just might have had something to do with our victory, but there is no way to prove that. I remember the song, and I remember the win, and that imagined connection endears and endures. It would have been nice to have a photographic record to go along with the victory song, and there could have been one, and there is, but... well, I might as well tell that story too.

When it was all over, and the sports calendar had ended, and our team had deservedly won the "best team award" at the annual college function, there was the college sports dinner to look forward to. It was a yearly affair, a formal one with a jacket and tie for men and *sarees* and *salwar kameezes* for women. All who had played on college sports teams were invited, along with a handful of selected sports alumni. There was a seated three-course dinner, always with a clever menu that brought attention to notable achievements and achievers of the year, and there were speeches by the principal and a couple of others.

I had been to the dinner in my first year, but this one was going to be special because of our victory and being judged the best team in college. I was informed that I would be seated at the head table with the principal, the Reverend William Rajpal, the Head of Games and a former Olympian, Ranjit Bhatia, and the Vice President of Games, our very own SD Mudgil.

The sports dinner was an evening to look forward to, but it also happened to be during study break for the final exams when there were no classes, so we didn't go to college every day. It was also during the Holi festive season—and on the day Holi was being celebrated in residence. In the previous year I had been in college on that day and had been dunked into the mud pit, which was dug up every year and filled with water.

Holi is my favourite Indian festival, and celebrating it in college the previous year had been fun, and I didn't mind the dunk in mud. But I didn't want to go through that experience again, so I had decided not to go to college during the day and just show up for the sports dinner in the evening. When Mudgil and Kishoo called me up around lunchtime and asked me to come earlier because—they had arranged a photographer to take a team photo—I thought they were looking to trick me into coming to college so they could dunk me in the mud pit. I wasn't buying that. Despite their pleas, which included getting another teammate to vouch for the event, I refused to go. I just showed up later in the evening—a bit earlier than the formal time to go through the ritual of pre-dinner alcohol consumption.

At some point, "drinks" were done, and we tottered over to the dining area, somehow going by the sports notice board. I had enjoyed putting up notices of practices on that board all through the year, always getting a little kick from signing them with "Captain." That evening there weren't many notices, only some team photographs. There, smack in front of me was a photo of the athletics team—without me! I couldn't believe my eyes. Mudgil and Kishoo's pleas had been genuine, and they clearly had not been trying to trick me into a dunk in the mud pit ... or maybe that was also on their minds. It didn't matter. The end result was that I wasn't in the photo of a team that I had put together. I wish I had played along. It would have been nice to have that concrete image. In its place, I have a story of a song and the victory that it might have brought along. It is not optimal, but I can live with that.

32

Fortuna's frown

"Remember Red, hope is a good thing, maybe the best of things, and no good thing ever dies."

Someone, somewhere with a lot of time on their hands, must keep tabs on the most quoted lines from movies. If they do, I'll bet this line from the movie "Shawshank Redemption" is one of the most-quoted ones. I certainly have used it a lot, so much so that I know it by heart. Still, every time I use it, I feel the need to go to YouTube and watch a clip of the letter-reading scene where it is delivered. The simplicity of the message, delivered in Tim Robbins' voice against the background sounds of crickets and birds chirping in a field and the gradual appearance of orchestral music, is pure magic. It gets me every time. The movie and its core message, delivered in that one-minute scene, resonates with people. It sure did for me in the first half of 1980.

At the end of my first year in college, I was full of hope about my running prospects and looking forward to the coming summer and the year beyond that. My new coach, Raghubir Singh, had planted the bug of possibilities in my head and got me dreaming and hoping of great things on the track. What I didn't know was that reality was about to throw in a wrinkle, what in baseball lingo is called a "curveball."

Fortuna had smiled at me in December 1979. In April 1980, she frowned. I first heard it from my friend and running buddy Virat, and then Raghubir confirmed it—he was leaving and for good. His friend had a restaurant in Innsbruck, Austria, and he was going there to work with him, or for him, I don't quite remember. He had a family to support, and his modest job at Maidens Hotel in Old Delhi wasn't working out. Even though this move would mean giving up the thing he clearly loved doing, "a man's gotta do what he's gotta do."

It wasn't as if producing a string of national champions would have changed his life in India. I seriously doubt anyone in the athletics establishment even noticed that two years later, at the Asian Games in Delhi, two of his trainees won medals in the 110m hurdles and the 1500m. Indian athletics had a rigid structure, and moving up the ranks of officialdom wasn't based on results. Given all of that, who could begrudge him for being practical and walking away?

His departure was a huge loss, one I didn't fully comprehend back then and for many years after. I look at my training diary of that time and smile at the somewhat hyperbolic and immature description of his departure as "tragic," but my entry was quite perceptive and prescient. Only now, on looking back and reflecting on things with a degree of clarity and honesty not possible earlier, do I realize the significance of that loss.

Every athlete has strengths and weaknesses, things they may not be fully aware of, things that an observant coach can pick up on and work with. I had an insatiable appetite for hard work, good core strength from years of football and cycling, and a desire to excel. But I was weak-willed at crunch times, ran races too cautiously, had no real sense of race tactics, and lacked a killer instinct. Looking at my notes in the training diary for that year and the letters Raghubir wrote to me—that year and the following year—I sense that he had a good read on those weaknesses. He had that unique mix of skills great running coaches have—careful observation, individually tailored workouts, and highly personalized coaching. They can drive you to exhaustion, to the point you hate them, but also inspire you to go beyond yourself in ways you can't manage on your own, no matter how driven and ambitious you are.

Life, of course, had to go on. I now had a dream, and I was going to chase it. I went back to my earlier coach, SS Rai, and worked hard that summer of 1980, alternating long-distance runs along the Wazirpur irrigation canal with sand running in Okhla in the mornings and evening workouts on the track. It was, as it always is, very hot that summer, and my body wasn't used to that punishment. It would break down periodically, and those breakdowns, in particular one bout of malaria at the time of the college cross-country competition, tested my resolve. They never managed to break it. That bug of possibilities Raghubir had planted, it was resilient. Each time the system broke down, I'd rest for a few days and then keep going.

I didn't win a big race like the year before, but there was a huge improvement in my running times, and I could legitimately say that I had arrived on the men's running scene in Delhi. There was even a fourth-place finish in the national inter-university championship in Gwalior, a story worth recounting at some point—for its athletic angle, team camaraderie, and late adolescence buffoonery. I was heartbroken at the 4th place finish, but I had been beaten fair and square by the top two finishers who broke the national universities record in the event, and even the third one who overtook me in the last lap. An interesting bit about the result was that, technically, it was a bronze medal finish because the second-place runner, who had beaten me in the Delhi University championship, was later found to be ineligible and—retrospectively disqualified. That bit didn't come to light till the following year, with more serious consequences than just a medal.

In the grand scheme of things, the year was a good one. I had made great strides in my running and captained the college team to a university championship, but ... it wasn't enough. I wanted more and was ready to work for it.

Prodded by Raghubir's letters from Austria and my coach in Delhi, Mr. SS Rai, I set higher goals for myself and trained even harder the next summer, micromanaging every bit of my regimen not to have the breakdowns of the previous year. I didn't, but that might have also led to overtraining and burnout. There were some good race outcomes, and while my race times were more consistent than the year before, there wasn't any big improvement on the previous year.

I held on to hope till the very end of the season, confident that I could improve on the previous year's 4th-place finish at the (national) inter-university championships. It didn't come to be. Done with the Delhi University competition, I had started preparation for the inter-university meet but was then informed that the university would not be sending a team to the competition—because the whole team had been disqualified for fielding an ineligible runner the previous year, the same one who had beaten me and won the silver in the 1500m. That finally broke my resolve to keep going, and I buckled down for the final-year exams.

The rough plan at that point was to complete the bachelor's degree, get back to off-season training in the summer, and continue with a master's (in economics) and keep competing, but ... the dice rolled differently. I applied for a one-year exchange scholarship to Davidson College in the US, and when I got it, I took it. I could have and should have continued with running, but I gave up—on my dream. Hope had taken a big hit that year and slowly died in the months leading up to the final-year exams.

I have often wondered if what happened with running in the last two years of college was because I was not good enough or whether I lost the right coach at the wrong time. There probably is some truth to the former. In reflecting and researching a book on health, I have picked up on peculiarities that might have been physical barriers. Maybe those would have held me back from reaching my goals. The bigger truth, though, is in the latter.

I needed a coach like Raghubir—a motivator tuned in to my particular strengths and weaknesses. He got me going, but I couldn't do it on my own. I am sure that if he had been around at the end of the third year of college, he would have explained that two years of hard training is nothing more than a start for middle and long-distance running and that several more are needed to realize one's potential. Realistically, given my family background and academic abilities and aspirations, I doubt I would have given the "several more" needed to go the distance. But I am also reasonably sure that a good talk with him would have brought me back for at least two more years. What would have come of that? I don't know. I believe that I went to him too late and that if I had spent even one full year with him, it would have been a different story.

My assessment of all of that is best captured in one line from the Hollywood sports fantasy movie 'Field of Dreams.' There is a story of that movie further along in this collection but here is the gist of it—to set the stage for the relevant dialogue. The film is about a corn farmer in Iowa, Ray Kinsella, who hears a voice in the sky—"If you build it, he will come." It leads him to mow down a part of his cornfield and build a baseball field for great past players to come and play. They have been dead and gone for a long time, but their ghosts return—to play baseball. The story then has him driving from Iowa in the American Midwest to Fenway Park in Boston on the east coast and then to Chisholm in Minnesota to track down Archie (Moonlight) Graham, a baseball player who made it to the major league in American baseball, but never got to bat, and gave up baseball to become a doctor.

In a classic Hollywood scene heavy on sentimentality, Kevin Costner, as Ray Kinsella, encounters Moonlight Graham on a foggy midnight walk, accompanies him to his office, and in there asks him about not getting to bat in the major league: "So, what was that like?" Burt Lancaster, as Moonlight Graham, delivers the response that perfectly captures how I think of my journey: "It was like coming this close to your dreams, and then watch them brush past you like a stranger in a crowd."

Those words have played out in my field of dreams many times, especially the three times I tried to get back in shape and chase the dream again. When in 2006, at the age of 45, I finally gave up, it was with some satisfaction—at least I had tried. It was also with a smile at the good fortune of meeting a coach like Raghubir and a wink at Fortuna … for frowning a little too soon.

33

Nikhil Banerjee

Amma was right, not always, not about everything, but my mother was always a good bet when it came to food and music. She liked playing the *sitar*, teaching others to pluck its strings, and listening to the masters play it. How she found the time and energy to do all of that while raising two boys by herself and holding down a teaching job at the university is a bit of a mystery to me, but that's how she was.

For her, the globalized Ravi Shankar was good, but the localized ones who played the concerts and *mehfils* and *baithaks* were better. There were two of note at that time: the flamboyant Vilayat Khan and the bespectacled Nikhil Banerjee who looked more like a statistics professor than a musician par excellence. As maestros, they had titles in keeping with their religious affiliation—one Ustad, the other Pandit. I am not sure these are real titles or just what people call highly accomplished musicians, but that's how it was, and that's how it still is.

Amma said Ustad Vilayat Khan was brilliant, but the real genius was Pandit Nikhil Banerjee. They were both melodious and gifted and could play so fast, their fingers were a blur, but the latter's *alaap*, that introductory phase of a classical Hindustani music composition, was ethereal. He could play an entire octave on one bridge, and the sound of those multiple notes would pull on the heartstrings till they were ready to cry. She didn't really say that; I am just making it up because that's how I feel when I listen to him.

If I didn't already have a special place in *Amma's* heart, I earned one when I bought her a Nikhil Banerjee LP with the few hundred rupees I made by going for a final interview for a job I wasn't really interested in. That was in 1982 during the year-end 'prep leave' we got to study for exams. At that time of the year, private sector companies used to post advertisements for management trainee positions on the college notice board. I wasn't interested in a management career but followed the herd, applied, had an on-campus interview, and got shortlisted for a final interview. None of us who were shortlisted were willing to spare the time away from studying for final-year exams, so the company offered to pay for round-trip airfare to their head office in Calcutta. All the others flew. I took the train, studying on it all the way there and back, and pocketed the difference in fares. I had bought her the LP from that money, and she loved the fact that I had remembered who Nikhil Banerjee was, what he meant to her, and had taken the time to buy her a recording of his.

I don't remember what *ragas* were on that album, but it is unlikely it had *Raga Jhinjoti.* I wouldn't have known anyway, because even though I had learnt to play a couple of classical *raga*s on the violin, I didn't have much of a head for theory and couldn't be bothered with *aaroh* and *avroh*, and *vadi* and *samvadi*, and *tal* and *gat,* and all the bits that make up the structure of a classical Hindustani music composition. I could play what was asked of me by my teachers, the men in white (earlier story), and that was that. That those frameworks for improvisation are built on selections of notes that go one way on the ascent and another way on the descent and have a main note and a secondary one, and all of that gets played to a particular beat and more was in my ear, not in my head. More importantly, I had never heard of the playful *Raga Jhinjoti* ... till December 2018.

It came about like a lot of things these days—quasi-randomly. It is entirely related to how I periodically end up in a free-floating state of mind where a welcome mat is laid for all sorts of triggers, what psychologists call stimuli. Set things up that way and let 'em play, and they'll lead the mind "hereandthere" —as opposed to here and there. Some may say it is time-wasting, and sometimes I might even agree with that characterization, but many a time it is a highly productive "time pass" of joyous wanderings.

That is how it came to be that I was lolling around on the internet one evening and ended up on YouTube, that magical resurrector of melodic memories, connector to other bits of thisandthat, and instigator of new ones. Somehow, and I don't know how and at what point in the lolling, I took one of the baits YouTube laid out and ended up at a one-hour recording of Ustad Rashid Khan.

I had no idea who he was, but within a minute of listening to him, it was clear I wasn't going anywhere. I had never heard anyone with a voice like that and sat in the study chair transfixed, for once paying attention to the *raga*s he sang. Somewhere in that one-hour collection was *Raga Jhinjoti*. I played that portion again and again and later found a separate recording of just that *raga*. If your ears and heart are tuned to Hindustani classical music, the "*tanana nana tana dere na dani dani*" in the *Tarana* segment is quite simply magical.

That one recording began an obsessive streak. It might be a mild form of obsessive-compulsive disorder, but—fortunately, or unfortunately—it only applies to music. If I like something, I am liable to listen to it again and again, and then again. In years past, it entailed rewinding tapes. These days it involves hitting the double back-arrow button to go to the start of a track or clicking the circular Replay symbol to play the piece repeatedly.

YouTube's algorithms offer relief of sorts from repeated playing of the same piece by offering suggestions and links to related recordings. I got suggestions for recordings of *Raga Jhinjoti* played by different musicians on *sitar*, *sarod*, *bansuri*, *santoor*, violin and more. I played them all and copied the links to a page so I could play them whenever I wanted. The beauty of YouTube is that new recordings keep getting added to the platform, so the list continued to grow. After a while, I had settled on a few favourites and didn't tire of listening to them again and again.

The shrink in my head would have known that sooner or later, I would ask the umbilical question: "Did Nikhil Banerjee ever play *Raga Jhinjoti?*" In the past, one would have had to ask the knowledgeable ones. Now you put that into the search box of YouTube and see what comes up. The answer isn't definitive because it depends entirely on whether someone has a recording and has bothered to upload it to YouTube—so others can share the pleasure.

At first, my search on YouTube yielded nothing, but then one day, up popped two-three recordings of *Raga Jhinjoti* by Nikhil Banerjee. There was no video of him playing, just audio. The sound quality wasn't great, but the magic was unmistakable. Ravi Shankar's *Jhinjoti* is ok, Shahid Pervez's is beautiful, but Nikhil Banerjee's is simply sublime. *Amma* was right after all!

34

Waheeda Rehman

It was early one Friday morning, at something like 6:30 am, and I was driving my daughters to the gym. They would have taken the bus, but it was dark and cold, and they would have had to walk to the bus stop, and I was already up and am their father and ... that's a good enough reason for me. I figured I'd drop them off and come back and work at home; these are the small perks of an academic job.

We were sitting at the traffic light on Salamanca Road, waiting to turn right on to The Terrace, a major stretch of tar in downtown Wellington. I am calling it 'a stretch of tar' because I am not sure where it falls in terms of the hierarchy of surfaced pathways (motorway, avenue, boulevard, road, street, lane, drive, etc.), and it has no identifying name. It is just—"The Terrace." A little odd, in my opinion, but it is what it is.

Anyway, we were sitting there waiting for the light to turn green, and out of the blue, in popped the words of a Hindi movie song from long ago: "*Ye nayan dare dare, ye jaam bhare bhare.*" It's not anthemic like Lennon's Imagine or Aretha's rendering of Otis

Redding's R.E.S.P.E.C.T., but in my heart, it sits about where those two songs sit in my head. It is this slow and incredibly melodic romantic song by Hemant Kumar, one of the great playback singers of the 60s and 70s. It's about fearful eyes and full lips and wanting to drink from those lips and live a little and … oh, what's the point of even trying to translate these things?

When the song popped into my head, I had an inkling it would hook into my "Radiohead" days of the late 70s and very early 80s when I used to listen to movie songs on All India Radio all day long. We had a record player but not much of a collection of records, and while there was also a tape player that *Amma* had purchased to record classical music from the radio when she was doing a master's in music, there were no tapes for me to play. Radio was it.

You could say I lived in "Radio Ga Ga" land, though what Roger Taylor and the British rock band, Queen, had in mind in that chart-busting song of 1984 isn't how I interpret my "Radiohead" days. Their song was about television and music videos and visuals taking over from the aural experience of radio in the Western world. In contrast, my experiences in those times were almost entirely aural. There was black and white TV in the evenings, and while it did offer *Chitrahaar*—a half hour melange of video clips of Hindi movie songs—on Wednesdays and Hindi movies (with songs) on Sundays, they were no more than blips in the daily morning-to-night offerings of radio.

Given how tuned I was to radio, I am certain I heard—"*Ye nayan dare dare, ye jaam bhare bhare*"—several times during those years, so much so that I knew the lyrics from start to finish. After dropping the girls, I sang to myself in the echo chamber of the car all the way back home with a big smile because … I had the sense that there was more to the song than its melody and memories of radio times.

When I got home, I typed in *"Ye nayan dare dare"* in YouTube's search box and clicked on the first suggested link and listened to the song and watched the movie clip and the smile grew bigger because … there *she* was—Waheeda Rehman. To me, she was the most beautiful woman in the world. There was another goddess, Madhubala, the one with mischief and twinkle in her eyes, the one whose ethereal beauty makes her look-alike Ingrid Bergman seem somewhat photoshopped, but she was a bit before my time, and my monotheistic eyes only worshipped WR.

I watched the video clip to see if my memory of Waheeda Rehman (and me) was rose-tinted. It wasn't. There she was, as beautiful as I recalled, flitting through flowing white curtains while the hero, Biswajit, crooned away. For a metrosexual type of guy, he looks ridiculous in the movie, with a pencil moustache and a twirly lock of hair pasted on his forehead. Then again, maybe I am just jealous of him.

Watching Waheeda Rehman had made the smile grow bigger; watching the video clip and reading its movie citation—*Kohra* (fog) —added a chuckle when I thought of when and how I saw the movie.

The acquisition of a bicycle in 1974 had led to periodic solo movie watching in theatres, and while that was not a regular feature of life, it did fill in time gaps here and there and when I had spare change. It was, therefore, not that unusual that in the summer of '82, when I was getting ready to head off to America to Davidson College, I showed up at a decrepit *Filmistan* theatre in the very innards of old Delhi to watch a movie by myself—not on a bicycle, but a public bus. It was a cheap morning show, and it was a movie I knew nothing about, other than the fact that it had Waheeda Rehman. That was the only reason I had hopped on to one bus, and then another, and then more with the unlimited-rides student bus pass that I still had even though I had graduated from university.

Sitting in front of the laptop, I tried to recall the movie's storyline but couldn't. Playing the video clip again and again didn't help, but it highlighted Waheeda Rehman's dark and burdened eyes. Naturally, that led to looking for information on the story. Wikipedia and IMDB's entries were brief and didn't help with remembering the whole story, but they did help in understanding how the lyrics of the song line up with the essence of the—dark—story. That got me thinking of the other black and white movies she has featured in and the other great Hemant Kumar songs associated with them.

A list of those songs and B&W movies would surely have at its very top, "*Tum pukar lo, tumhara intezaar hai*" the super-melodious song from the 1969 classic, *Khamoshi*. People say Waheeda Rehman's portrayal of a nurse in a psychiatric ward in that movie is her best performance ever. I suppose yes, but the truth is … I have no ability to make any judgement of any sort about her. She was and still is, faultless.

All of that thinking put me in a rather familiar dreamy state of mind. The welcome memory mat had once again become a magic carpet! The nostalgic ride to that summer of '82 was disrupted when I recalled the theatre I had seen the movie in. It was thoroughly beaten up with no air conditioning and only big fans whirring along the walls. Delhi heat in May/June is usually suffocating, but that summer, the rains had come early, and it was unusually mild, so it was tolerable. What was less bearable was the sight of a huge rat scurrying about. The movie cost hardly anything, so I could have left right then, but … she was on the screen, and I was there to watch her, so how could I? I just picked up my feet and watched the rest of the movie squatting in the seat. There wasn't much of an audience in the theatre, but those who were there looked to be ordinary folk, informal sector workers who lived hard lives on the streets and lightened them for a couple of hours with Bollywood movie entertainment. They were sitting the way they usually did on the streets—on their haunches—and I fit right in.

It was my last summer in Delhi before leaving for the US. Having given up on running, I wasn't caught up with training twice a day, so I had lots of time and that free bus pass. Every morning I would check the inside cover page of the newspaper for morning shows of movies that were invariably from yesteryear and had heavily discounted ticket prices. If there was one even remotely interesting, I would figure out the bus combinations needed to get to the theatre and go. I saw quite a few movies that summer but don't remember any, other than those with Waheeda Rehman or those with magical music.

You could psychoanalyze that, and the fact that when home I would record movie songs from the radio on cassettes to take with me to America, and say that … I was pocketing the past for imagining it's memory in the future. I won't disagree entirely, but that is way more perspective than I had at that age. In simpler, more real terms, I was just enjoying the freedom I had given up in previous summers when I'd run in the morning and in the evenings and try and catch my breath in between.

I had forgotten about that carefree summer. A song with a movie actress I worshipped had wafted in at a three-way traffic light on The Terrace and opened up the *Kohra* (fog) of times gone by. What more could one ask for from a dark and cold Friday morning?

35

Summer of '82

When summer comes along in New Zealand, it begins with strawberries and the promise of peaches, plums, apricots, nectarines, cantaloupes and watermelons to follow. In much the same way I used to know the sequencing of mango varieties in India, from the early dry-heat ones to those that came in the final monsoon months, I know the sequence of fruits in New Zealand and look forward to it every summer.

Something must have worked right last summer because it was a bumper crop with strawberries everywhere and at prices lower than years before. I had invited the tutors who help me teach undergraduate courses for an Ethiopian dinner at home and figured the strawberries would be the perfect finale to a delicious but heavy dinner of *enjera* and *doro wat* and more.

In my excitement at getting strawberries at a great price, I didn't notice that several had gooey dimples deeper than the naturally occurring achenes on their skin. Not one to throw away food unless it is absolutely necessary, I salvaged as much as I could and ... very naturally followed the memory trigger leading to nectarines in a neighbourhood convenience store in Geneva, Switzerland and the large-hearted aunt who landed me there in the summer of '82.

I had graduated from St Stephen's College and was headed to Davidson College in North Carolina in the US for a year. The year before, or possibly the one before that, I had been introduced to Ayn Rand and being at the age where values and convictions were still being formed, found her advocacy of individualism and rationality, in The Fountainhead and Atlas Shrugged, appealing. Exposure to other ideas and reflection would alter things in the years to come, and the process of figuring out the right mix of ideality and reality—the "ought" and the "is"—would become a lifelong pursuit, but at that point, her thinking had made an impression.

I must have conveyed my admiration of those ideas and a desire to work with my "bare hands" to *Paddu chitti*, my mother's youngest sister who lived in Geneva, and she must have remembered. When the Davidson plan became final, not only did she rally her other siblings to pool together the money for my plane ticket, but she also arranged a six-week job alongside my cousin, Rajeev, in a neighbourhood convenience store.

The proprietor of that store, Jackie Steiner, had not met me, likely knew that I spoke no French, but hired me anyway. Gino, his Italian helper who did all the heavy lifting, was going on his annual month-long leave, and he needed a replacement. Lifting and shifting don't need much speaking, not in English, French or any other language, so he hired me.

Rajeev and I would get up early in the morning and go down to the store to start work. It was before anyone else was up, and we would sit in the kitchen and have cereal for breakfast. I was used to eating cornflakes with warm milk, but the first morning I sat at the kitchen table, I was taken aback by the different boxes of cereals to choose from and the cold milk to have them with. It was all very different but all very easy to get used to—at that age of flexibility.

For the first two weeks, I worked alongside Gino, and he showed me all the things that needed to be done with as few words as possible. He was a bit gruff and impatient at the beginning, but not so once he figured out that I had energy and wasn't averse to expending it on all that he wanted me to do. After two weeks, he left, and I took over as the mover and shaker of products.

I had shadowed Gino and knew the routine—of unloading trays from delivery trucks, moving new produce in and overripe ones out to the back for disposal, arranging things in the storage room and then moving them on to the shelves. There was a simple rule for shelf placement— the fresher produce went to the back, and the soon-to-expire stuff was moved to the front. I learnt that rule in Jackie's store on the supply side and then applied it on the demand side as a consumer all through graduate school.

Steiner's neighbourhood store had to compete with the lower prices at Migros, the supermarket chain in Switzerland. He managed that well by being convenient for those who lived close by, adhering to his simple rule of product placement on shelves and by ensuring that what he sold was top quality. He would tirelessly monitor the produce for signs of wear and tear and move anything that showed unwarranted dimples and pimples off the shelves. The rejected pieces, even those with the smallest sign of over-ripeness would end up on trays at the back and would get tossed. It killed me to see perfectly good food, or almost perfectly good food, being thrown away, but it was his quality control regimen and I followed it—except once, and then a couple of times.

It was the thick of summer in the northern hemisphere, and Steiner's store had all sorts of fruit, some I knew, some I didn't. I'd never encountered a peach or a nectarine before, had no idea what they tasted like, but would periodically move the damaged ones to the backroom for their final journey to the dumpster. Curiosity being what it is and having been a friend of mine from early on in life, I wanted to know their taste.

One day, while catching a break in the back room, I saw the barely dimpled and soon-to-be-dumped nectarines and peaches looking at me longingly. They were about to be tossed, so I reasoned with myself that if I took something that was going to be thrown away, I wasn't really stealing. I had seen Gino do it, so there was precedent. Of course, if I had been challenged about that action and my reasoning, I am not sure how I would have explained myself in French.

Whipping out the small box knife I had been given for opening packages, I cut out the dented part of one of the nectarines and took a bite. The sweet and mildly tangy taste was lovely and unlike anything I had encountered before. I had the rest of it and then did the same with a peach which had a slightly different taste.

There weren't that many tasting opportunities after that because Steiner was very picky with the produce he bought and also very good at aligning his purchases with the flow of sales. The farmers market strawberries I had purchased for dinner last summer wouldn't have passed Steiner's eagle eyes.

That was my first job ever, and I worked hard and earned Steiner's trust, so much so that he took me along on one of his produce-purchase trips across the border into France. I didn't have a visa, but he wasn't about to be put off by that little technicality. He asked me to bring along my passport and, at the border, sweet-talked the immigration officer into letting me in. At the wholesale market, all I had to do was follow him and move the crates of the stuff he purchased. All of that was done quickly so we could be back in time for the store to open in the morning. It was quite an adventure—for him to have a Gino substitute do the heavy lifting and for me to watch the workings of a fresh produce wholesale market in France.

That's how it went those four weeks that I functioned as Gino in Jackie Steiner's convenience store. In between all that work were family outings with my aunt and her family and much else that could make for a book of stories on its own. The first time of anything is always memorable, and those six weeks in Geneva, my first time outside India, sure were.

Before I knew it, six weeks were almost over, and I was looking forward to the onward journey to America and getting on with life. One final adventure remained. Steiner must have been happy with my work because he decided to take Rajeev and me on a long road trip to the 'top of Europe'—Jungfraujoch—on the last day of my stay in Geneva. We had made family weekend trips to Gruyere and other places, but this was a little further and during the week when he would have normally been managing his store.

It was an unbelievable experience. To drive to Interlaken and then take the metre-gauge train up to the highest railway station in Europe, have lunch at the restaurant on top, and then drive back, all in one day meant leaving very early in the morning, driving fast and managing time with Swiss clockwork precision. Despite getting a hefty speeding ticket on the way, Steiner managed all of that and paid for everything. His generosity topped the amazing feeling of being at the top of a mountain and seeing and feeling snow for the first time.

Did he know it was my 21st birthday? I am not sure. My aunt surely did. She made a special dinner for the occasion, and at the end of it insisted that I have 21 of the *gulab jamuns* she had made—from scratch. Those were not ready-mix powder days, and to make them, she must have taken time off from working on the next edition of Geneva News and International Report, the English language news magazine she had started a few years back. It was my last evening in Geneva, my first birthday away from home, and she made it memorable in her own way.

She was like that, of sharp intellect and an unbounded spirit of generosity. When the pandemic got her last year, I shed a quiet tear thinking of those 21 *gulab jamuns*, those six weeks in Geneva, and the many spirited discussions and arguments I had with her. I would have liked to send her a copy of this book, but I will have to make do by thinking of her signature *"Arrey bhai"* greeting that she always had ready for me. I might just have a *gulab jamun* to remind me of the 21 from that summer of '82.

36

Funk van

Maurice White died on the 4th of February 2016. Truth be told, and what good is it if it isn't, when I read news of his passing and his links to funk, I didn't know who he was. I had heard 'Earth, Wind and Fire,' the band Maurice White was founder and leader of, but not often enough to make the connection with him. I did, however, know about funk music because I heard it aplenty on the 'funk van' at Davidson College in the fall of '82.

In the summer, I had graduated from St Stephen's College in Delhi University and won a one-year exchange scholarship to Davidson College in Davidson, North Carolina. Actually, I didn't win the scholarship, and there really was no exchange because at that time, no one from Davidson College came to St Stephen's; the traffic was one way. I had applied for the scholarship only because at that stage in college life, one applied for all things remotely of interest. My plan at that point was to continue with a master's in economics at the Delhi School of Economics and take it from there. But I applied, placed second, and then got awarded the scholarship because the fellow who won it got into one of the Indian Institutes of

Management and decided to not "waste" a year. That is what a lot of my high-achieving contemporaries in St. Stephen's thought of the Davidson scholarship—a waste of time and "a paid holiday." What a shame. For me, it was quite possibly the most important year of formal education.

After six weeks of working in a grocery store in Geneva, Switzerland, I showed up at Davidson at the very end of August. I can roll the (movie) tape of that stretch of time and clearly see all the pieces of that trip—the flight to JFK, a couple of days in Manhattan at my friend Madhav's parents' Waterside apartment, the Greyhound bus ride to Washington DC, a few days with my uncle and his wife Pat, the 11-hour Greyhound bus ride to Charlotte, the pickup at the bus station by my host family, the very warm and friendly Baggets, the few days with them, and then the move into the 3rd floor shared room in Sentelle Hall. Someday those pieces will ask for detailed accounting, and I will gladly give them that. For now, I'll continue with funk music.

When I got to Davidson, I thought my running days were over, but then I got back to training with the cross-country team, just for fun. At the orientation for international students, one of the senior Davidson students who had been overseas in the school's junior-year-abroad program made a friendly suggestion about cross-country, and out of sheer curiosity, I went along to a training session. It was a fun and chatty outing, and I ended up going back the next day, and then again and again, quite simply because ... the college provided the kit, washed and dried it every day, and the people who came to training were lovely. This was back in the early 80s, and I am quite sure none of them had met an Indian, but it made no difference at all. They were friendly, welcoming, curious, respectful and all the things that make for an inclusive environment. It really was that simple.

I had been used to twice-a-day slogs in blistering heat, so the once-a-day trainings were easy. In my college years, I had trained alone. Here everyone trained together, and the warm-up and cool-down runs through the handful of streets of Davidson were chatty. There were some adjustments to make, like training at 3 pm when it was hottest, communal showers, and early dinners by Indian standards—but all in all, it was a great way to settle in.

Training went on for a couple of weeks, and then one weekend, there was a selection trial, and I made the team. That, quite honestly, didn't say much because the Davidson men's cross-country team was a cellar dweller, and except for one serious runner who was very, very good and another very competitive runner who also did well at the cross-country meets, the rest were just there for fun. The women's team, on the other hand, had more competitive runners and did much better.

Once the season began, there was a cross-country meet every weekend, and the men's and women's teams would travel in two vans—not segregated by sex but by studious intent. One was the 'nerd van', and the other was the 'funk van'. If you wanted to study, you travelled in the first. If you wanted to chill, you went in the second.

Logic would have dictated that I go in the first one because on my way to Davidson, I had decided that instead of doing a master's in economics, I was going to do a PhD and use that year at Davidson to apply to doctoral programs in economics. Even though I already had a bachelor's degree (a BA honours in first-class as they say), I was determined to do the best I could at Davidson and strengthen my applications.

International exchange students, and there were a handful from France, Germany, Spain, and Japan, were not required to take a full load of three courses per quarter, but only five courses spread out over three quarters. When Sue Ross, the international student advisor, suggested I go easy and settle in with one or two courses in the first quarter, I informed her of my intention to apply to graduate school and insisted on taking a full load of three courses in the first quarter—to prove that I could perform in US academic settings. I wanted to take only economics courses, but she gently suggested I do at least one other course, and so I agreed to take a course in international politics.

With three senior courses in the first quarter and an academic structure that required regular engagement, not the end-of-year cramming I was used to in India, there was lots of regular studying to do. It would, therefore, have made sense to go in the nerd van where everyone studied on the two to three-hour ride to meets or to a motel for an overnight stay before a morning race on Saturday.

Logic should have ruled, but I got along best with a guy who would have nothing to do with burying his nose in books on a Friday afternoon, so I went in the funk van. I had no idea of what funk was, but when I heard "You dropped a bomb on me" and "Play that funky music" and "Get down on it" and "Superfreak" and several others like it, I had the sense I had made the right choice. That's not to say people didn't study on the funk van; they did, but with music and less stress.

I was only at Davidson for a year and can't be entirely sure about this, but in that short time, I had the sense that the college as a whole was a bit like the cross-country travel vans—nerd and funk—though much more of the former than the latter. I had no idea about Davidson's academic reputation when I showed up in that small town. All I knew was the description I had read in a reference book at the United States Information Service office on Kasturba Gandhi Marg in New Delhi, and whatever little I was able to gather from those who had received the scholarship in previous years.

At that time, people in India only knew of the Ivy League institutions and some other big universities; small liberal arts colleges were largely unknown. It was only when I got to America that I found out that Davidson was highly regarded, and the academic workload at the college was heavy and steady—not something you could leave to the end of the year as we did in India. Students did have fun, but that was not Davidson's reputation, as it was and still is with several large universities which have the reputation of being "party schools."

I didn't get enough of a sense of Davidson's funky side in the year I was there. For two of the three quarters, I was in a nerdy frame of mind wanting to prove myself and get into graduate school. It was only when those applications were in that I eased up by taking only two courses in the final (spring) quarter and going ... academically funky. The two courses, one in social and political philosophy and the other in American literature since 1870, were very different from all the economics I had studied till that point. Having to think about things I had never thought about before in Dr Beatty's very unique discourse-oriented philosophy course and then having to write original essays on Huckleberry Finn and The Great Gatsby in Randy Nelson's American literature course were eye-openers. In many ways, *that* was the real education I got in that first year in America. I didn't appreciate it as much then as I did later and do now.

The lighter academic load, the spring weather, and the decision to not run track in the spring season allowed me to have some fun and engage with Davidson's lighter side. Even though it was the equivalent of a "Bud Light" and not the real "Budweiser" (beer), it gave me the sense that there was more funk in the academically pressured liberal arts college than just the funk van. When I think of those lighter moments and the friends I made in that first year in America, several of whom I am still friends with after 40 years, it brings many a smile and tickles many a memory to pick up and write about ... at some point.

37

A different kind of worker

He was different. Not in any distinctive way, but in those little ways which make all of us distinctive, if only we bother to look. I must have looked, which must be why almost four decades later, with only a few months of life-overlap, I still remember him—for advice, his quirkiness and the pickle it landed someone else in.

When I got to Davidson College, I was told that visa regulations restricted paid work to 20 hours on campus. Permission to work off-campus wouldn't have counted for much anyway because the town population was not much more than 4000, and there were only a handful of establishments that might have needed extra hands. Furthermore, I had no means to go to Charlotte, the big city 20 miles away.

Those who had come on the same scholarship before had worked in the library and administrative offices, but that year there were no openings in those places, and the only real working option was with the catering service. So I signed up for my first paid job—serving food at mealtimes at the large cafeteria called Commons. The job paid minimum wage, which back then was $3.35 an hour. I was on a scholarship, had no unmet needs, few wants, so that minimum was maximum for me.

I worked whatever hours I could pick up at the Commons, including special events when you had to wear a white shirt, dark trousers, and a tie, and serve fancy food to invited guests, always serving from the left and clearing from the right. On a couple of extra-special occasions, like when classical music maestro Zubin Mehta visited the college, we even wore white gloves.

The catering network included the café in the student union building. There was an 11-hour shift there on Saturdays that no one wanted to work, so I was able to pick that up and thus have a good chunk of earnings each week. The café opened at 1 pm and closed at midnight, and I would be there for the entire duration. A couple of other students would come in for shorter stretches, but I was the only one there from opening to closing. In that café job, I was a short-order cook—flipping burgers, making pizzas, scrambling eggs, fixing bagels and hoagies and whatever else was on the menu. Except for some crunch times when it got hectic and started to look like the diners you see in movies, it was easy work, and I was able to do my class readings behind the counter.

The worker bees of the catering system—all Davidson students—were paid minimum wage and wore white T-shirts with three red stripes on the sleeve. Supervisors, who were the more experienced workers, were paid 15 cents more and wore white T-shirts with three blue stripes. They managed the work shifts, deciding who did what. Sitting on the top of that work pyramid was one student manager. She did not have to wear any stripes and was paid more; how much more, I don't know.

John was one of the supervisors—skinny, bespectacled and easy going. We worked several shifts together, which is how I got to know him. Many of those must have been at special events where you had to wait for the guests to finish one course before serving another. During those breaks, we'd sit around and, as they say, "shoot the breeze." I must say *they*, whoever they are, do come up with the zaniest of ways of saying ordinary things.

It was at one of those events during the spring quarter, after I had been accepted to the PhD program at UNC, that we were chatting between meal courses. I must have voiced my concerns about managing life on the monthly stipend I was going to get as a research assistant. When I left home, I had decided I would make do on my own, and this was going to be the first go at doing that. The year at Davidson didn't really count because I was on a scholarship, and everything was paid for.

John told me how he lived on very little by following simple rules: he always cooked his own meals, did not eat out, paid attention to sales prices at the grocery stores, ate only what fit his budget, and if need be, skipped a meal. I had just finished reading Gandhi's autobiography, "The Story of My Experiments with Truth," and there were parallels in how the great man had managed in his barrister-training years in England and how this guy was managing his life in small-town North Carolina. My mother and father, both of whom studied abroad and lived on little, must have also told me about their frugality, but that was a very long time ago in the 40s and early 50s. My co-worker's account was closer in time and more real.

What John said and what Gandhi did, were not things I didn't already know. I had always been careful about money, but it was going to be different now. Up until then, survival hadn't depended on being careful; from then on, it would. In graduate school, I did follow those simple rules, tweaking them just so for cold college beers and occasional cheap-eats outings with friends, balancing income flow with expenditure and still managing to save enough to head home every two years.

The world is filled with all kinds of prescriptions and proscriptions on how people should live their lives, and there are plenty who are willing to dispense that advice to the willing and unwilling. I don't have many rules, and I sure as heck try not to dispense whatever I have, but I do live by the simple rule of living within my means and always being aware of who I am and where I stand. It just might be one reason why despite innumerable stumbles, I am still on my feet.

During that frugality conversation or perhaps another, it came out that the student manager was a bit of a bully and relations between him and her were chilly. Never one to know, then and even now, what is going on around me, I was surprised. She was stern as managers are and have to be, but she was perfectly nice to me. Given what John had told me about having limited means and living on little, I figured he'd just bear with it and ride out the term. He didn't.

One evening, when he was scheduled to supervise a special event, he didn't show up. He didn't call; he didn't send along an excuse or explanation; he just didn't come. I was on that work shift, and it was tense and awkward. The student manager tried to get one of the other supervisors to fill in, but it being spring term with all that spring does to college life in America, she couldn't find a replacement and had to manage that shift herself.

She was furious and said she would give him an earful next time and might even fire him. It didn't matter. He didn't come back, not even to pick up his last paycheck. I didn't run into him the rest of the term, so I have no idea why he didn't come or what became of him. I can guess the former but have no idea of the latter.

I am not sure why I remember him and the pickle he landed the student manager in. It might be because I have always valued people standing up—for themselves, for others and for what they believe in—not just when it is convenient and fashionable, but particularly when they have something to lose from taking a stand. Or maybe, it is because it was so quirky and different. It doesn't really matter; what matters is that the memory is indelibly associated with that first year in America at a small college in a small town.

38

LL Bean

Randy was enamoured with the fact that I wore custom-tailored shirts. I am not entirely sure how much of that had to do with the custom tailoring and how much to do with the fact that the shirts were—always—crisply starched and ironed and always looked sharp. I had nothing to do with that. It was because my scholarship at Davidson College included laundry service and they would send back the shirts and my white *khadi kurtas* looking that way. Whatever it was, custom tailoring or sharp lines, Randy liked my shirts—enough to offer me a trade at the end of the academic year, one that I couldn't refuse and one that would have long term implications.

The scholarship also covered meals, which were to be had at the Commons, the large eating hall where I also had a part-time job in the catering service. All freshmen were required to eat at the Commons, and Randy was one of them. That is how I met him, other freshmen, and several others with whom I would regularly have meals and long chats. In the year I spent at Davidson I got to know more freshmen and seniors than sophomores and juniors because I ate at the Commons and because most of the courses I took were advanced courses taken by seniors.

When Randy first expressed his admiration for the shirts, I explained to him quite matter-of-factly that custom tailoring didn't mean anything special in India. Everyone wore custom-tailored shirts and pants because it was the norm and the result of a labour-abundant economy operating at low-income levels. I had become aware of the fact that the norm in the US was standardized factory-made sizes and that only the rich and very successful got their clothes tailored. I hadn't encountered any, so I have to guess that bit of information was provided by Randy.

His curiosity about my clothes wasn't unusual at all. There was general curiosity about me and the country I had come from. It was the early 80s, and Davidson was a small liberal arts college in a small town in North Carolina, and it was entirely normal for young people like Randy to not know much about a land far away. People would ask me all sorts of questions, and I would provide all sorts of details, often pointing to the huge differences I had started observing since arriving in August of that year.

At some point in our various conversations, I must have commented on a Grandfather Mountain marathon T-shirt and another red striped Polo T-shirt that he wore quite frequently. He told me that the marathon T-shirt was from a 10K that he had run in the mountains of North Carolina. The T-shirt was a standard round neck one that wasn't unique, but for the marathon logo on it. The Polo, on the other hand, was a very nice piece of clothing, and I must have complimented him on it more than once. That led him to tell me that it was made by LL Bean in Maine, and what was unique about the company was that it offered a lifetime guarantee on its products—even clothing. That caught my attention and stuck in my head, more for the unique quality assurance provided by the company than any sort of aspiration to acquire something like it one day.

As the academic year at Davidson drew to a close, I got busy picking up extra work shifts to save up money for the financially independent life that lay ahead. That meant shorter mealtimes and less frequent encounters with the people I used to have meals with at the Commons. It was in that quick-meals period that one day I ran into Randy, and he surprised me.

I must have had one of the starched and ironed shirts on, and he must have had the red Polo on. He asked me if I would be interested in trading my two custom-tailored shirts for his—standardized—T-shirt. At some point, he must have told me what it cost, so I knew that in monetary terms, it was a fair trade, but it would leave me with one less piece of clothing, so I was hesitant. He really wanted my shirts, so he upped the offer by including the Grandfather Mountain marathon T-shirt in the trade. I couldn't say no, partly because the balance of pieces of clothing in my wardrobe would be restored, and partly because after a year in America, I had gotten used to the casual dress code of students and no longer felt the need to wear ironed shirts.

The trade was made, and Randy was happy with his acquisition, and so was I. What he did with those shirts and how long he stayed enamoured with their custom tailoring, I don't know. I didn't see him again after that year at Davidson. For me, the acquisition of those T-shirts and the loss of formal shirts was very opportune because that summer was spent at boys' camps in the mountains, and in those places, there was no reason to wear anything but T-shirts. Graduate school after that was much the same in terms of dress code, and casual wear came in handy.

There was, of course, more to that trade than just shirts for T-shirts—I got introduced to the catalogue shopping culture of America, and soon LL Bean would acquire a loyal customer. During that trade or before it, I must have asked Randy where he had purchased that red polo T-shirt, and he must have told me that his family got a catalogue that listed all the things that LL Bean sold. He gave me the label from one of the catalogues, and just as soon as I had an address in Chapel Hill, I sent LL Bean a note requesting a catalogue. They replied very promptly and thus began a regular stream of catalogues that would appear in the mailbox every few months.

When the first LL Bean catalogue arrived in the post, I wasn't exactly surprised by the prices listed in it. The trade with Randy had already made me aware of what they charged for a Polo, and it was evident that the clothes and shoes advertised in the catalogue were not within reach of my graduate school stipend. But the beauty of those catalogues was that there were always things on sale—at heavy discounts of anything from 30 to 50%, sometimes even more. That put the sale items within my reach. Then, of course, there was the—undiscounted—lifetime guarantee.

Over the next six and a half years in Chapel Hill, I bought a few things from them, none possibly more important than the very first purchase—an oversized green and blue backpack. That bag doubled up as a book bag and a good-sized grocery bag to carry purchases back home on the bicycle and later on a motorcycle. It was an integral part of my life in Chapel Hill and even beyond that.

LL Bean and I were good friends all through those years in Chapel Hill —but only through their sales, never full prices. It was when I got back to Davidson in 1990, this time to teach and with a real income, that, for the first time, I bought a black cotton ribbed round neck sweater and a pair of "chukka" boots from the LL Bean catalogue—at full price. The two pieces of apparel were stylish, and I was mighty pleased with my purchase ... partly for the style and partly for being able to go full price.

Thereafter, our relationship continued, with more of a full-sale price balance, but still only when I needed something, not when they tempted me with pretty pictures and deep discounts. One of those occasions of need was when I went back to India in November 1993 to get married and bring back Sumi to Washington, DC, where I was working and living at that time. We were going to arrive in DC in January, and to help her handle the initial shock of a cold east coast winter, I bought her a winter jacket—quite naturally from an LL Bean catalogue and at full price. How long she wore the maroon-coloured jacket before transitioning to others, from clothing brands, she was already aware of before coming to America—and I wasn't after 11 years—I don't know and … don't really want to know.

LL Bean and I parted company after we moved to New Zealand. The shipping cost is too high to justify continuing with those purchases, even on sale items. But our relationship hasn't ended entirely. I still have the two turtlenecks I bought from them around the time I bought Sumi her one and only LL Bean jacket, and I still have the cotton jacket and lined canvas shirt that she bought me as a birthday present in the first year of marriage. The four pieces of clothing are a bit worn and fraying, but 25 plus years on are still going. I suppose I could check whether LL Bean's lifetime warranty still holds, but … I won't be doing that. I have no desire to replace them, even if that is possible. The memories they trigger have a warranty of their own.

39

Last Dance, First Song

It happens every year, without fail and without a plan. While teaching, somehow or the other, I manage to slip in a reference to Michael Jordan—about how my first year in graduate school at the University of North Carolina at Chapel Hill was his last year as an amateur, and how I got to watch him live in a small stadium, and before he became the god of basketball and conquered the imagination of sports lovers all over the world. I joke that it is my claim to fame. Those who know something about MJ smile; those who don't likely roll their eyes and wonder what a basketball anecdote has to do with a course in public policy.

In those random references to "His Airness," I don't tell the students how I first encountered Jordan, but for as long as I have been recording these memories, I have known that at some point, I will come around to that first encounter and tell its story. What I had not known—until last year— is what would get me there. I was waiting for a trigger. It came during the pandemic lockdown when Netflix streamed the miniseries—The Last Dance.

News of the miniseries had us all excited. Everyone in our family knows that I am a bit of a nutjob when it comes to Carolina basketball. Sumi was introduced to the nuttiness within two months of our marriage at a bar in San Diego in 1994, and the girls witnessed my screaming and jumping in front of the TV in Bangalore when the Tar Heels won the national championship in 2005, and in Washington, DC when they won again in 2009. I am sure I have told them about Jordan and his connection to North Carolina and how I got to see him play live, but it is unlikely that I have said anything about his years in professional basketball. I don't follow it until the very end of the season, and then too only the final series, so there couldn't have been much conversation about Jordan and the Chicago Bulls.

On the appointed day of Netflix's streaming of the miniseries, we all sat down to watch and just as soon as the first episode got going—with footage of Jordan's Tar Heel years—I knew what the trigger was. It wasn't any of Jordan's games that I got to see in Carmichael Auditorium, a 10,000-seat facility where you could almost reach out and touch the players. And it wasn't this very clear image I have of a home game when the University of Maryland team was up by three points with 17 seconds to go and Lefty Driessel, their coach, was pacing the sideline with his shirttails hanging out—salivating at the prospect of beating a hated rival on their home court and then looking dejected on losing the game. It was Z-man's words in January of 1983 at Davidson College: "You gotta watch this guy."

Growing up, I didn't play basketball, but I liked watching the game. Our high school and college teams were very good, and their games were competitive, but the thrill aspect of those competitions was much the same as that in other sports. It was only when I got to Davidson that I had a taste of how thrilling basketball can be. I had never seen slam dunks, and alley-oops, and nothing-but-net jump shots before, and I had never experienced the excitement of watching the last seconds of a close game.

From the very first game I saw in Davidson's small gym, I was hooked. When the Davidson men's team, known as the Wildcats, played home games during the week, I would make sure to be there in the small gym early and watch the whole game. I couldn't watch their Saturday games because I worked an 11-hour shift at the café in the student union building. Not wanting to miss out entirely, I'd hoard up the 15-minute breaks I was entitled to every couple of hours and run over to the gym across campus and watch as much as I could, and then run back. It was a bit crazy but totally worth it.

According to 'Quips and Cranks,' the school's yearbook—a copy of which I still have—but for a notable win against Notre Dame on national TV, "the 1982-83 men's basketball season was disappointing." Not so for me. To my untrained eye, the Davidson Wildcats were fantastic, and Kenny Wilson was simply unbelievable. When he'd break away for a dunk, the crowd in the small gym, including one nutty Indian, would go bananas.

I couldn't stop talking about Kenny Wilson, which must be how I got around to mentioning it to Z-man, who had been on the cross-country team with me. He was what I'd call a bit of a renegade runner because he never came to team practice, only to the weekend cross-country meets. The team had some runners who weren't always at practices, but that was because they had classes or science laboratory sessions during practice time. I don't think that was the case with Z-man. He just didn't come. Coach Sterling didn't mind because he knew that Z-man trained every day, preferring to run the trails with his beautiful Irish setter dog. I only saw him when we travelled to the meets, and I am reasonably sure he rode the "funk van" with us (earlier story). That's how I became friends with him and liked running into him on campus even after cross-country season had ended.

It must have been one of those run-ins in January, likely soon after a Davidson basketball game, when I was excitedly blabbering about Kenny Wilson and the Wildcats. I don't remember much of our conversation, so I don't know how he received my excitement, how he grounded my superlatives with the reality of play of better players and teams in the country, and what he told me about the Carolina Tar Heels who had won the national championship the year before. All I remember is him saying, "You gotta watch this guy."

Z-man was, of course, referring to Michael Jordan, who, as a freshman, had hit the winning shot for the University of North Carolina in the national championship game the year before. Chapel Hill is only two hours from Davidson, and stories of the crowd on Franklin Street, the main drag through town, and the buckets of Carolina blue paint that flowed after the victory were the talk of the town that year. I had heard about that and wouldn't be the least bit surprised if Z-man and several Davidson students had made the trek up to Chapel Hill and got doused in blue paint.

To make his point about MJ, Z-man invited me to watch a North Carolina game with him on the large TV in the student union building. I used to walk by the TV room on the way to work in the café and had seen students watch MTV over there, but not paid much attention. On Thursday, February 10, 1983, I met up with Z-man in the evening and watched Michael Jordan for the first time.

I know this sounds hyperbolic, but for me, at that point in time, it was, quite simply, an out-of-this-world experience. I knew next to nothing about North Carolina and Michael Jordan and Sam Perkins and Dean Smith, and even less about Virginia and Ralph Sampson and Terry Holland. Listening to the TV commentators, I quickly learned how the Tarheels were ranked number one in the country and were playing at home against the number three ranked team and how the rivalry between the two teams had been intense in recent years.

Carolina trailed most of that game but then came from behind to win by one point— with two last-minute shots by Jordan, including a steal and a spectacular dunk. Davidson's games had been super thrilling, but this was a completely different level. And Jordan, well, I could see what Z-man had meant—MJ was on song in that game, especially in the last two minutes when it mattered most.

From that point on, I was thoroughly hooked to college basketball and watched as many college games as I could on that same TV in the student union building. I don't remember the details of all but two of those games. One was the Tar Heels heartbreaking loss to Georgia in the regional finals of the national tournament, and the other was North Carolina State's improbable last-second win over Houston in the final. The image of their coach, Jimmy Valvano, running around at the end looking for someone to hug is firmly imprinted in my mind, but even more than that is Z-man's words and that first song—of Michael Jordan in a North Carolina jersey.

40

Wild Turkey

It is highly unlikely that Mahendra Kapoor—the forgotten sixth of the six great male playback singers of Hindi films in the 60s and 70s—knew of wicked Wild Turkey, that Kentucky straight bourbon which can make flightless young men flutter and flitter about. Then again, Bollywood dances to a different hooch, so who knows.

It was the summer of '83. I was making the transition from Davidson College to the University of North Carolina at Chapel Hill and working at a camp in the mountains of North Carolina. I had met Sumner Williams, the director of Camp High Rocks when he had come to Davidson to recruit camp counsellors for his five-week-long boys camp. The pay wasn't great, but room and board were free, and he also arranged a second five-week job for me at Camp Arrowhead. The two camps would cover most of the summer break and give me some spare change to begin independent life as a graduate student.

Camp High Rocks turned out to be a job, adventure, and education rolled into one. I was a camp counsellor in the junior-most age group and lived in one of the cabins by the lake with five boys who were between six and eight years of age. Some had been to camp before and were used to being away from home for that long; others had emerged from their homely cocoons for the first time. I hadn't worked at a camp before or managed young kids, but I was at an age when nothing fazed me, so I thought nothing of being in an entirely new setting with new responsibilities. During the day, I helped out in the craft shop, and in the late afternoons, I organized soccer games for the boys.

Five weeks at a camp in the mountains of North Carolina with limited off-camp options makes for a lot of stories—of me picking up on bits and bobs of Americana, and the others picking up on bits of Indian life, like 'gulli danda'. It would be fun to work through the details of those, but it is time for me to move on to the first encounter with the wicked hooch.

Camp had just concluded, and excited young boys, homesick after five weeks away, had been picked up by their parents. The campsite was empty. Some counsellors had also left, and the rest, including me, were going to head out the next day. Someone came up with the idea of a party with previously forbidden alcohol, and before you knew it, those who had vehicles had hopped in to go procure some from nearby Brevard. A couple of cases of beer made their way to camp, and so did a bottle of Wild Turkey which was pulled out at some point and got passed around. It must have passed my way a little too often because I had a lick too many.

Soon the beer was gone, and another procurement trip was organized, and I found myself in the passenger seat of a pickup truck. For reasons unknown, I had a song on my lips that I started humming under my breath. When Betsy, who was driving, asked me if I cared to share the song, I did what I would typically have shied away from—I belted out the Mahendra Kapoor song composed by OP Nayyar, "Lakhon hain yahaan dil waalley, par pyaar nahin milta.

Aankhon mein kisi ki wafah ka ikrar nahin milta" (there are many here with heart, but I haven't found love, and no indication of it in their eyes). The song is a sort of lament about looking for love and not finding it. I don't know whether that had anything to do with five weeks at a boys-only camp, or the Wild Turkey, or something more, but there I was, brazenly singing a Hindi song about love in a pick-up truck on the backroads of western North Carolina.

I had a special affection for OP Nayyar's music, not just because it was magical with its clippity-clop sounds of horses pulling a *tonga* (horse carriage), but because I associated it with it my dear Ambi *mama* (maternal uncle). He was a man of exquisite taste and social flair but a look on life so impractical that it frustrated practical people. Of all of my mother's siblings, I had spent the most time with him and was very fond of him.

All self-respecting Tamilian families have an Ambi, which is probably a short form for *Tambi* (younger brother), but how many young boys have Ambi *mamas*? I had one, and at one point, he had been in Bombay and had Bollywood connections, and that is how OP Nayyar had come along. He was my stopping point in America, and I had come to camp just after spending a few days in his rented flat on North Park Avenue in Chevy Chase, so maybe that was what had triggered the Mahendra Kapoor song.

I am not sure Betsy grasped any of the melody or the meaning of that song. It didn't matter. I was somewhere else singing that song, and the next day ended up somewhere I didn't ever want to go again—when I had dry heaves and the worst hangover I have ever experienced. I swore never to tangle with that tipple again, and but for one memorable slip after that first one, have stayed true all these years.

The slip of a sip came about not too long after the first one. On getting over with the next five-week gig at Camp Arrowhead,

I headed out to Chapel Hill to begin graduate school. I had a room in Craig Residence Hall, the high-rise dormitory for graduate students, but didn't see how the shared kitchen arrangement, one for a whole floor, would let me implement my living-within-stipend plan. I am sure I could have made it work if I had to, but then I ran into three graduate students at the International Center—from India, Indonesia and Tunisia—and we decided to rent a two-bedroom pad in Kingswood Apartments on 54 Bypass, a four-lane highway that wraps around the southern part of town.

The day we could move in was a Wednesday, and it turned out to be a day with many days within it. It was the day we wrapped up two and a half days of a preparatory math course that the economics department had organized for incoming PhD students. It was the day we were introduced to 'He's Not Here,' a college town bar that would go on to bookmark many memories in the years to come (and be a story in this collection). And it was my birthday, the first one when I was going to be entirely and truly independent. It was a day to celebrate.

The woman who had graciously put me up in her apartment for a couple of days drove me to Kingswood Apartments, so I could drop my bags there. She then took me to Craig dorm so I could meet up with Jehan, my classmate and new friend. We then went downtown to celebrate on Franklin Street, the main street with bars and restaurants that, for some undergraduates, is likely the only university they attend in Chapel Hill.

Fall term was about to get going in a few days, and students were heading back to town, so Franklin Street was heaving with activity. How many bars we visited and how many cold beers slipped down thirsty throats on that hot and steamy August night is anybody's guess. I wasn't counting, but I was also aware that at some point, I needed to find my way to my new home for the year.

It was getting close to midnight, and I was about to call it a day and figure out the way to Kingswood Apartments when we ran into a group of new graduate students who Jehan had befriended in Craig dorm. They were heading to Papagayo's, a restaurant tucked into the inside part of the main building stretch on Franklin Street and invited us to join them for one last drink. Naturally, we went along. It turned out, one of them was also marking her birthday that day, and she insisted that we join in for a family tradition—a shot of Wild Turkey.

Memories of dry heaves were still fresh, and I was wary of the hooch, but it was a special way to celebrate a special day, so I couldn't possibly say no. If a bottle had been passed around, things might have gotten out of hand again, but this time around it was at a bar, and I was mindful of costs, so I didn't have more than the one celebratory shot. I don't think any of the others did either.

That was the end of the first night on Franklin Street. Everyone in that group was staying at Craig dorm and knew where to go and how to go. I only had a general idea of my sleeping quarters which I had only visited twice. But I had a map and the confidence of youth, and that was enough.

I walked back with them to their dorm and then opened up the map under a streetlight and figured out how to get from Manning Drive to South Columbia Street and from there to the 54 Bypass, walking that last highway stretch through overgrown grass on the side, singing to myself—quite possibly the same song Wild Turkey had accompanied only a few weeks earlier.

41

Eyes without a face

In the winter of 2008, I'd regularly run to work along the Capital Crescent Trail in the Washington DC area and listen to music on a pencil-shaped Sony MP3 player that I had purchased the year before. It didn't have a specially created 'running' playlist, just an assortment of peppy rock, pop and bhangra albums that I had copied from my laptop. Some of the pieces were strollers more suited to the early warm-up phase of a run, and some had the perfect beat to align with strides when they were in full flow.

Of all the albums that got played on those hour-long runs from home to work, the most fun was Billy Idol's Greatest Hits, but only if it aligned with the second half of the run when I'd be in full stride. When it did, and the sixth song also lined up with the final coasting along G Street, I'd bet good—"Mony, Mony" —I had a smile on my face thinking of the time I first met Billy Idol.

It was the summer of '84, two years into my journey through Americana, and the second one working at Camp High Rocks. I had decided that, unlike the previous year when I had worked at two camps, I would only do the boys camp at High Rocks and then head back to Chapel Hill to study for the first round of doctoral exams. I needed the money from the camp job because, during the summer months, there was no stipend from the economics department, but I also could not afford to ignore studying for the exam. Doing only one camp instead of two was a good compromise.

I knew the camp routine from the previous year, in particular the fact that "lights out" for the campers was relatively early in the evening, and after that, it was possible to squeeze out a couple of hours of studying. With that in mind, I had purchased a battery-operated booklight from Brendle's, a store on the outskirts of Chapel Hill. Every night, I would turn it on in bed, put on the headphones from a Walkman and get some studying done. It was not ideal, but better than nothing.

Sumner Williams, the camp director, had asked me for help in recruiting camp counsellors, and I had suggested my friend Jorge with whom I had played on a recreation soccer team in my first year in Chapel Hill. As he had done for me in the previous year, Sumner arranged a job for Jorge at a second camp so he would be able to get a 10-week stretch. Not surprisingly, Sumner and his wife Jane fell in love with Jorge, and Jane offered him a job in the girls camp that she ran after the boys camp, and Jorge stayed on at High Rocks instead of going to the other camp.

High Rocks was somewhat counterculture in that it took kids out of the commercialized and hyper-competitive world they lived in and put them in a bucolic surrounding with a huge one-acre lake. Except for one day when the camp was split into two teams, and the teams competed against each other all day long, all activities were non-competitive. In the prevailing cultural context of the country, this was an anomaly, but it appealed to some parents who wanted their kids to have a break from constant competition in school. It did present challenges to counsellors who could not use individual competition to motivate the boys and had to figure out other ways to get them to engage in activities.

The other break from mainstream culture was that candy and chewing gum were not permitted in camp. The kids yearned for those but knew that it was contraband and constantly pleaded with counsellors to bring back some from their day off. Gum, in particular, was not permitted in the dining area because, in previous years, there had been instances of boys sticking chewed gum under the serving trays while eating meals and forgetting to take them out. The trays were fed into a large commercial dishwashing machine, and the heat would melt the gum and spread it on the tray, and it would harden up and not come off. I was told they had to freeze those trays and use a chisel and hammer to chip off the hardened gum. That's when gum became verboten.

Neither Jorge nor I did the core camp activities at High Rocks—outdoorsy things like hiking, canoeing, kayaking, rock climbing and horse riding. Jorge helped out where help was needed on camp while I spent the day in the craft shop with Rex, who, during the year, taught math and woodwork at a high school in Virginia. The craft shop was bare-bones and oriented as a filler between the outdoorsy stuff the camp was focussed on, and my involvement was in the clay modelling area. I didn't have any special skills, just whatever I remembered from Mr. Mawasi Ram's clay modelling room back in Junior Modern School in India.

On their in-camp rest days, the boys hung around camp and occasionally showed up in the craft room—just to chat or chat while trying to make something. The atmosphere was somewhat like what I had experienced in junior school, but there was one big difference. In our school clay room, you had to have something to show at the end of the class when Mawasi Ram would come around to check each person's work. That often led to hilarious last-minute concoctions of some 'objet d'art' that was explained as an object or animal, but looked very much like the lump of clay it had been fashioned from in a couple of frantic minutes. In contrast, there was no such completion requirement in the craft shop at High Rocks, so the boys just hung around chatting and whiling away time. Every now and then, though, there was genuine art produced in that place.

Two of the regular attendees were a pair of 13-year-old twins. Like the others, they'd chat, but they also paid attention to what their hands were doing, and those were very good at sculpting with clay. The small pieces they made were very creative, as were their entreaties to bring them back candy on our days off.

I wasn't about to break the rules, but just for fun, I made a transactional deal with one of them—in exchange for making a small clay bust of me, I would get him a big bag of M&Ms on my day off and even let him work with the more exclusive white clay that others did not get to use. I didn't expect him to take that offer seriously. I thought he would start and then get distracted by something else. Little did I know the value of that inducement in a candy-deprived environment.

He got going right away and worked at it that day and the following days, skipping whatever other activity he had signed up for. As he progressed on the sculpture, it started becoming clear that it was going to be really good. His twin brother felt a bit aggrieved that he was going to miss out on a bag of candy, so I suggested to Jorge that he strike a similar deal with the twin. He did.

In a week or so, both busts—about the size of a fist each—were ready. Along with the ragtag misshapen pieces other boys had made, I fired them up in the kiln so they would harden and not chip easily. The two busts were uncannily accurate renditions of our faces. I was amazed at what teenagers, with a bit of inducement, could do. I kept my bust carefully wrapped in old socks and still have it after wanderings through four continents. Jorge, with whom I have reconnected after 30-odd years, doesn't and is not too happy about that.

The two fist-sized busts were beautiful, but there was one big difference—mine had eyes closed, and Jorge's had his open. In the several hours the twins spent in the clay room, I remember saying something to them to the effect that—"eyes are too beautiful to be sculpted." The one who sculpted me faithfully closed mine. Jorge said no such thing, and his bust had eyes open.

I didn't listen to hard rock at that time and had no idea who Billy Idol was, but his "Eyes Without a Face" reigned the airwaves that summer, broadcasting from radio stations that my Walkman radio stopped at. I now wonder if that had anything to do with what I said to the young sculptor.

Cute as the subconscious connection is, it is unlikely the real one. A more likely explanation is that I quite liked Greek statues of men with beards and flowing robes and none of them had clearly defined eyes. An even more likely reason is that I didn't have the skills needed to do the careful work eyes require and had left out the eyes in a figure I had sculpted to show the boys how to work with clay. When asked why there were no eyes, I must have come up with that explanation on the fly.

Over time my musical tastes widened. While they never extended to hard rock and metal and whatever else young people think of as music, they did take me to Billy Idol and to purchasing his Greatest Hits album.

'Eyes Without a Face' is the sixth song on that album and is the perfect one to coast on after 'Dancing with Myself' through 'Rebel Yell' have got the running stride into a rhythmic turnover. I don't run anymore, but I can still imagine myself during morning rush hour on G street in downtown DC—layered and covered from head to toe in freezing temperatures, soaked in sweat and coasting along on 'Eyes Without a Face'. There is a smile on my face. I am sure of that.

42

Sumner Williams

I think of him quite often these days. Every time I am on the bean bag and my little furry friend, Beanoo, the rabbit, comes by and waits patiently for my hand to drop and stroke her, I dial back the years and think of Sumner Williams.

It was September of 2000, about the time leaves start changing colour on the eastern seaboard of the US and magic unfolds. It is a sight to behold, year after year, after year. Back then, we lived in Washington DC. My father had passed early in the year, and my younger daughter Anushka's arrival was still a year away, so the 'we' was just three—me, my wife Sumi, and two-year-old Tishya. Heidi, a friend from DC and UNC days, had invited us to her wedding in the mountains of North Carolina, and the prospect of attending her wedding and taking a road trip through the mountains in the fall was not to be passed up.

I hadn't been back in the Brevard-Asheville part of North Carolina in 11 odd years. The closest had been a motorcycle ride along the Skyline Drive through the Shenandoah National Park in the spring of '89 after attending the Population Association Meeting in

Baltimore. Even then, I hadn't gone all the way to Asheville but cut off earlier to head east to Chapel Hill. Of all the road trips I have been on in all the places in the world, that bike ride surely ranks amongst the best.

You can drive along the windy roads of beautiful mountains in a car and "ooh" and "aah" at the scenery, but there is simply nothing like being on two wheels. The delight cannot be shared with anyone from inside a helmet, but the tilting and bending along the curves of windy roads and the experience of being one with the vehicle holds a thrill of its own. I'd say it is metaphysical, maybe even the Zen of motorcycle—riding, not maintenance—but I am no writer-philosopher like Robert Pirsig.

The trees hadn't fully turned on their colour show that September, but the drive through the Shenandoah National Park was still delightful. We got to the lakeside resort venue by late afternoon and had a day to ourselves before the Sunday wedding, so I figured we'd drive along the windy roads to Brevard and see if we could find our way to the two-mile stretch of gravel that led to Camp High Rocks. I wanted to show Sumi and Tishya where I had spent parts of three lovely summers in the early 80s.

What I also wanted to do was meet Sumner Williams, the man who had hired me as a camp counsellor in the summer of '83, and then promoted me to head counsellor for the youngest age group the next summer because ... he said, "I liked the way the kids looked up to you, and how you were able to hold their attention." It flattered me a bit, but what really flattered me was the somewhat higher pay I got that second summer. He might have also mistaken their fascination with a foreigner and a foreign accent for something more, but I didn't say anything to counter his compliment.

Those two summers were supposed to be it for me at High Rocks, but then the following summer, he called and said he needed me to help him out of a bit of a pickle that had resulted from the firing of a counsellor for inappropriate behaviour. I was in the midst of teaching a summer statistics course and couldn't just up and go, but I couldn't say no to him either, so I told him that I'd come as soon as the course was done. "I'll take anything," he said and flew down his two-seater plane to Horace Williams airport, the little runway for non-commercial planes in Chapel Hill, and waited several hours for me to finish marking the final exam and hand in grades before whisking me off to camp.

I wanted to see him again, not because of that plane ride into the mountains, which matched the adventure of biking through them, but because of who he was—honest, straight-talking, hardworking and understated. I haven't thought about it this way till now, but maybe that trip was about wanting to see again the father I had lost earlier in the year.

My navigational skills being what they are, I am sure it took a while to find highway 276 and the narrow gravel path off it right across from the Sherwood Forest Golf course, but once we were on it, I knew exactly where we were. I had run up and down that stretch almost every day those three summers in the 80s and knew every drop and climb and flat section of that single-lane road.

When we got to the top, and I parked the car and walked into the tiny office, I didn't really expect to find Sumner or Jane there. Even back in the 80s, they didn't sit around in the office. They were always out doing something—there was always something to fix, something to arrange, just something out of the confines of four walls. It was no surprise they weren't there. It turned out they had retired, and the camp was now run by their youngest daughter, Townsend, and her husband, Hank. Over the three summers in the 80s, I had become friends with the whole family but didn't remember meeting Townsend. It didn't seem to matter; she was warm and friendly like her siblings and parents.

I said I had come by to show my family the camp and also meet Sumner and Jane. Would that be possible? Camp yes, Sumner and Jane, potentially difficult because they didn't live on the campsite anymore. I must have shown my disappointment because they offered to call Jane so I could talk to her. I wasn't too sure she would remember who I was. After all, I had worked the boys camp Sumner ran, not the girls camp Jane managed, and even though I had met and talked to her many times, that was a long time ago, and surely hundreds of counsellors would have passed through High Rocks in that time. Why would she remember me?

Jane was straight-talking like Sumner, or maybe Sumner was like Jane. Either way, when she said on the phone, "Of course I remember you," I knew it was genuine. She said she would like to see us and if I could wait an hour, she would come by.

We were road-tripping through a beautiful fall day in the mountains and had time, and time insisted, so we were happy to wait and walk around camp. I showed Sumi and Tishya the beautiful one-acre lake, the cabins I had stayed in, the places in camp I had worked at, and Hank showed us the rock-climbing wall he had built to add a new activity to the camp's repertoire of outdoorsy stuff. There were minor changes here and there, but it was very much like what it had been years ago. I must have had a stupid smile on my face—remembering the campers, the activities, and other bits and bobs of magical summers during an age of innocence; I have one on right now.

By the time we had walked around camp, and I had wandered back into the past, Jane arrived, and we sat down to a cup of tea in the house they used to live in. After the basics of catching up and talking about who was doing what, the conversation got around to what I was really there for— Sumner.

I asked if I could see him. She said that was not possible because he had Alzheimer's and lived in an assisted-care facility, and while she visited him often, he didn't remember much, so he likely wouldn't remember me. It was disappointing not to be able to see him but sadder to hear of his condition.

She also said that Sumner spent the day stroking his dog, who would sit by him faithfully. I don't remember if she meant at the facility or before he moved there, but that bit—about the stroking—stuck in my mind because I remember imagining his big hands gently stroking the dog.

If you've paid attention to the differences between the manicured delicate hands of city folk and the thicker fingers of those who work on the land and in the mountains—digging holes for fence posts, clearing and hauling brush and whatever else nature requires—you'll know what I mean.

My hands aren't big, and my fingers aren't calloused. The skin on my hands is wrinkled, but it is not from working outdoors; it has always been that way. I like being outside and doing things with my hands, but I am no farmhand. I am a city boy. I marvel at the majesty of mountains and admire the ruggedness of those who live there, but I don't idealize or idolize any of it. In short, I have little reason to feel any connection to any of that. I just happen to remember Sumner Williams, a mountain of a man, every time little Beanoo comes by the bean bag and waits for me to stroke her.

43

Carolina in my mind

It was 1984. Jim Hunt was running for the Senate against Jesse Helms, and James Taylor was on tour with a concert in Raleigh in late September. If you had political leanings and leant to the left, then Hunt was your man, but if you leant to the right and liked Reagan and Thatcher, then Helms was the one. It was the 80s, and that's how it was back then in the southeastern state of North Carolina in America.

I had never been to a big concert, so when my friend Adrian asked if I wanted to go, I jumped at the offer. As a graduate student, I didn't have much money, but enough for the 17-odd dollars needed for the ticket. We drove from Chapel Hill to Reynolds Coliseum in Raleigh in his maroon-coloured Buick along North Carolina Highway 54, were late getting there and couldn't find the entrance to the section our seats were in. In a rush to get in, we ended up going through the nearest door, and that landed us bang next to the stage ... just as JT had started teasing the crowd with the first notes of "Carolina in my mind."

I'd heard the song before in many places, including a beautiful rendition by a Davidson College alumnus at Camp High Rocks in the summer of '83. He had a baritone voice eerily similar to James Taylor and was headed to graduate school in music. He regularly led the singing at the morning and evening meetings at camp and was regularly urged to go JT. The one and only time he obliged—with "Carolina in my mind"—was a time to remember. Everyone in the room sat in stunned silence, taking in the pure sound of his voice and the strumming of his guitar.

I love that song for its simple melody and lyrics, but I also know why it tickles my toes more than any other song. It is because it hooks into a Carolina blue sky in Chapel Hill, North Carolina and quite possibly, the most formative years of my life.

Chapel Hill wasn't supposed to happen in 1983, in much the same way Davidson wasn't supposed to happen in 1982. Davidson had come about because the guy who won the exchange scholarship didn't take it, and it came my way instead. Chapel Hill wouldn't have happened if Peter Hess, my economics professor at Davidson College, hadn't chased up my application which then resulted in an offer of admission and financial assistance to the doctoral program in economics. If either of those had not happened, I would have attended Delhi School of Economics, which might have made me a better economist, but quite possibly less broadly educated in the social sciences—and in innocence and idealism.

The ride into Davidson in late August of '82 had been on a Greyhound bus from Washington DC. The ride into Chapel Hill in late August of '83 was in a pickup truck from Tuxedo, North Carolina. After working at Camp High Rocks for five weeks, I had done another five-week stretch at Camp Arrowhead and then caught a ride in a pick-up truck with another camp counsellor, a short, muscular ex-army guy with a handlebar moustache. He was driving to Virginia Beach and was going to drop me off at the closest gas station near Chapel Hill on I-85, from where I hoped to hitch a ride into Chapel Hill. But it was 3 am by the time we got to Durham, and he decided to drive me into Chapel Hill and drop me off at the first motel in sight.

The first one we saw as we drove in on US Route 15-501 was the Tar Heel motel. I had stayed at a few motels during Davidson College cross-country team travels but never had any interactions with their management, so I had no idea what to expect. When the proprietor of the Tar Heel motel turned out to be an Indian, not American as I might have expected, I could only smile at the fact that the very first person I was meeting in Chapel Hill was Indian. He might well have been from one of the immigrant families who owned and operated motels across America, the type depicted in the Mira Nair movie, 'Mississippi Masala.' The hour being the hour it was, there wasn't much of an exchange with him, just cash for room keys.

After the cooler air of the mountains, the air in Chapel Hill felt hotter and more humid than it really was, even at 3 am. It didn't matter that much because the sparse room had a functioning air conditioner, and even though it made a rattling sound, it wasn't loud enough to prevent me from sinking in and drifting off to sleep.

My plan was to go into campus the next day and see when I could move into the graduate dormitory where I had a room. I figured I would likely need to stay in the motel for a couple of days. I knew nothing about the town, hadn't bothered to visit the campus even though it was only two hours away from Davidson, and didn't know a soul. None of that concerned me one bit. I was walking into a new chapter of life, sure of who I was and what I wanted, and had gumption galore. What more did I need to know?

One of the camp counsellors at High Rocks, a Davidson alumnus, had given me his mother's phone number in Chapel Hill. When I got up the following day, I slipped in a quarter into the payphone and decided to call her—just to touch base—before heading out to the International Students Office.

A year in North Carolina had introduced me to southern warmth and hospitality, but I was still surprised when she offered to pick me up in an hour and put me up in her two-bedroom apartment for a night till I figured things out. I had never met her before, her son was not much more than an acquaintance at Davidson and then at camp, but here she was—ready to take in a stranger into her home. I still shake my head when I think of that morning in Chapel Hill. Then again, my mother wasn't that different and had taken in barely known youngsters more than once, but those were all young women. This was a bit beyond that. I was supposed to stay with her only for a day but ended up staying four.

The original plan to stay in the graduate dorm was ditched, and instead, I moved into a two-bedroom apartment with three international graduate students—none of whom I had met before or had any connection with. I had been in America a year, but they had just gotten off the proverbial boat. We didn't have any furniture, pots, pans, or any of the things needed to live in an apartment, but we figured we'd work that out in the days ahead. And we did. With the help of the "Village Advocate," an advertising supplement of the local newspaper, we went to yard sales and called up people selling used things and little by little furnished that apartment.

The furnishing of our minds would come about more slowly in the liberal air of Chapel Hill, the university town William Meade Prince called the "southern part of heaven." He coined that phrase in a memoir of his time growing up in Chapel Hill. I haven't read the memoir, but several websites point to a part of the book in which, when asked by a local resident what heaven might be like, a minister says, "I believe Heaven must be a lot like Chapel Hill in the spring." I couldn't agree more.

The James Taylor concert came about a year after arrival in Chapel Hill and was in support of Jim Hunt's unsuccessful run for the Senate. After the initial song, arguably the most popular one, JT played all of his big hits and then some. I'd heard some of those on the radio and then some more on the 'Funk van' that we rode to cross-country meets in Davidson. Listening on devices was one thing but listening to him sing live was quite something else. I'd hear him and others live in concert in the years to come, and each would etch a memory, but the first concert and first song will always be special.

My Chapel Hill journey was supposed to last four years. Together with the first year at Davidson, that should have meant five years in North Carolina, but life's dice would roll differently, and I'd end up spending six and a half years in Chapel Hill and then one more in Davidson, this time teaching economics and working on my doctoral thesis. By the time I rode out of North Carolina on a 650cc motorcycle on the Fourth-of-July weekend in the summer of '91, I had spent nine years there—seven powder-blue UNC ones bookended by two red-and-black ones at Davidson College.

It was a time wrapped in innocence and idealism. People say you lose innocence in your 20s. I feel I grew into it in those years. Maybe that's why it's been so hard to have it slip away in the years since, always grudgingly, always with an element of self-blame.

I did return to Chapel Hill with family in 2001, thinking we'd settle down there and let the southern part of heaven infuse the girls with the 'i&i'—innocence and idealism—I had picked up in the 80s. It was a good plan, and we even bought an idyllic house in a cul-de-sac with a creek on one side and open woods at the back. That was to be it, but … that dice wasn't done rolling. After less than two years, we'd end up leaving for Bangalore, India. The move was supposed to be a temporary one for just one year, but one would become two, and then two was to be permanent, except ... permanent didn't seem to have permanence at that time in life.

Five years into the move to lovely Bangalore, we'd move again, first back to Washington, DC for a year, and then to Wellington, New Zealand. The last move was a big gamble. We had never been to New Zealand, let alone Wellington, and while it was the internet age and we were able to pick up all kinds of information on the city and the country, and while all of that sounded good, you have to spend time in a place to see if it works for you. No amount of information can give you that feel.

I couldn't possibly have known at that time that this cute little capital city in the southern hemisphere would be as close to the southern part of heaven as I could possibly find. I couldn't have imagined that it would be the ideal place—with i&i—for the girls to grow up in. I got lucky; we got lucky, very, very lucky.

Life sure has meandered about quite a bit in these sixty years, and I am no longer as innocent and idealistic as I was back in those Chapel Hill days. I am more of a realist now and quite like wearing a realist lens when looking at the world. It makes the world more understandable, not necessarily more bearable. The truth is ... reality bites, and when it bites hard, I like going back to i&i and ensuring that the barcode of my life never loses its lines of white. I suppose Carolina will always be in my mind!

44

Headlining despair

"Oh well!"

That was the headline in the Daily Tar Heel, the student newspaper at the University of North Carolina at Chapel Hill, on March 23, 1984. Everyone knew that what they really wanted to say was "Oh hell!" but couldn't because you can't say those things in student newspapers in America.

The occasion was absolute despair at the men's basketball team (Tar Heels) losing to Indiana University in the national collegiate (NCAA) basketball tournament the night before. The Tar Heels had been ranked #1 for all but one week that year and were the overwhelming favourites to win it all. They had two All Americans, a flashy point guard, a towering centre, and a reliable defensive player to round out the starting five. One of the two All Americans was Michael Jordan, the national player of the year that year; he would, of course, go on to become, arguably, the greatest basketball player of all time.

College towns, like Chapel Hill, have a unique feel to them when the university football or basketball team is nationally competitive. It is hard to describe the feeling to those who haven't experienced it. Cities with professional teams likely have a similar energy, but cities are big, and not everyone is into sports, and even those who are, have jobs to go to, families to raise and ... lives to live. There are other things going on in college towns, but during 'the season', everything gets overridden by the passion generated by the sport in play—football in the fall and basketball in winter and spring. In colder parts of the country, there is also ice hockey in winter, but it is not in play in warmer places like Chapel Hill.

That year Carolina had a decent football team that did reasonably well in the fall season, but everyone—even us newbies—knew that the main game in town was basketball. Saturday football games were fun but, in Chapel Hill, they were only a warmup act for the main show.

When the season began in November with the Tar Heels ranked #1, and the two All Americans, Michael Jordan and Sam Perkins, on the cover of Sports Illustrated's "College Basketball Preview," the atmosphere turned decidedly electric.

It was my first year in Chapel Hill. I had already got hooked on Jordan and the Tar Heels the previous year at Davidson and watched some of their games on TV. Now I was eager to see them live. Our student fees made us eligible to get free tickets to football and basketball games, and we grabbed every opportunity to watch Jordan and the Heels up close in the 10,000-capacity Carmichael Auditorium.

The season progressed as expected, and despite a disruption in team chemistry resulting from a wrist injury to the point guard, Kenny Smith, and two losses following that injury, the Heels entered the national tournament in March heavy favourites. Expectations in Chapel Hill were sky-high. You could sense it. There was no getting away from it, not even for graduate students buried in books, papers, and research.

Of course, all followers of sports know that in serious competitions, there are no guarantees. The Tar Heels were supposed to beat the Hoosiers of Indiana University, but they lost. Some blame Coach Dean Smith for benching Jordan with two fouls in the first half, others credit Indiana's volatile genius Bobby Knight's coaching. Get those two sets of armchair critics together and you'll get a never-ending, never-conceding argument. It doesn't matter who is right and who is wrong. Fact is—the Heels lost, and the Daily Tar Heel captured the morning-after feeling perfectly.

I remember the occasion well because the next morning, we had a dreaded mid-term exam in Michael Salemi's required macroeconomics course. Studying was suspended for a couple of hours to watch the game and then had to be resumed with deflated spirits. Over the years, there would be other deflations but none quite like that one.

The nice thing about sports is that you can rue a loss for some time, but there is always another season, another contest. Even though March 23rd felt like the end of the world, it passed. Jordan and Perkins were gone to the pros the next year, but Carolina was still strong, year after year. That first year of following the Tar Heels so locked me in that for the next six years that I stayed in Chapel Hill, I followed every bit of them and continued to do so after moving on with life.

There is a load of quirky memories of those times that, at some point, will be dusted off and told, but that '84 loss and the spirit of deflation it produced will always be one of the clearest ones. Even more than the loss was the newspaper headline the day after—it came to encapsulate deflating outcomes of all types of contests, none more than the results of the Indian elections in 2014 and 2019.

When I was in graduate school, I followed the broad workings of Indian democracy and continued to do so after those years. Subscription to the magazine 'India Today' and coverage of India in international newspapers was the basis for staying informed on what was going on in the country. That scanty information base exploded when the internet came along, and newspapers went online. By the time we moved to Bangalore in 2003, I was fully tuned into Indian democracy—not so much into the details of who was in power where, or who was looking to dismantle whom, but the big picture.

I had watched the rise of the BJP and its divisive, exclusionary views with considerable uneasiness. I didn't and still don't, have a problem with their economic policy orientation. India's economy desperately needs further unshackling to realize the potential of a continent-sized market and great entrepreneurial spirit. What was worrisome was their social divisiveness and sabre-rattling.

I didn't care much for the obsequious Congress party, forever beholden to the Gandhi family. Like others, I was disgusted by the astounding levels of corruption and misgovernance it exhibited in its second stint in power (from 2009-2014). Still, the secular fig leaf it held up was better than the exclusivist and majoritarian religious orientation of the BJP, especially that of the more hard-core faction within it.

My uneasiness with right-wing rhetoric and the support it seemed to garner turned to alarm before the 2014 elections. I found that several of my friends were so desperate for decisive leadership, they were willing to look past the social divisiveness of the BJP, the Godhra pogrom of 2002, and the ghettoization of Muslims in Gujarat. In classic Indian ways, they offered assurance in the form of—"*kuch nahin hoga*" (don't worry, nothing bad will happen). It was not reassuring.

The evening of May 16th, 2014, I sat in the study on a bean bag with a Jack Daniels in hand, watching the election results come in on the internet. As the hours went by, it felt like the second half of the UNC-Indiana game on March 22nd, 1984—despair and disbelief at how the election game was unfolding. As the hours progressed and the results became clear, it felt like that evening in Chapel Hill. My reaction that evening, and in the days that followed, was not the euphemistic Daily Tar Heel headline, "Oh well!", but an outright— "Oh hell!"

The same story unfolded five years later, in 2019, but with a larger parliamentary majority for the party of exclusivity. That this came along despite all that had occurred in the previous five years—demonetization, lynchings, undermining of institutions, and the rise of authoritarianism—was beyond despair and disbelief. It brought a sense of resignation and loss of hope for which "Oh, hell" didn't suffice; it had to be—"Oh bloody hell!"

45

He walked on water

It was a blisteringly hot summer day in '77 when my school friend Bharat Rana and I made a plan to go watch a movie at the theatre in Chanakyapuri. I was at my home in Lawrence Road, and he was at his in Chanakyapuri when the plan was hatched. His place was a short walk to the theatre, mine a good hour and a half by bus.

Back in the late 70s, if you travelled by public bus—the green and yellow ones of the Delhi Transport Corporation, or the maroon/brown ones of private contractors—it took an hour and a half, at best. If, like me, you had the Rs 12.50 unlimited rides bus pass and had learnt the skills of hopping off and on running buses as they slowed around sharp bends, you could have shaved off 10-15 minutes from the long journey, but not much more than that.

Bharat was eating lunch when we finished talking on the phone. I am guessing I had already eaten or couldn't be bothered. After hanging up, I walked out into the hot sun and got on the first bus, knowing well that regardless of whether I went left on number 154 or right on numbers 912 or 913, there were two more connections to make to get to his place. It was a weekend, so the buses were relatively empty, and I was able to get to his place in an hour and a half. Bharat was still eating lunch.

Aunty, his mother, offered me a plate, and I joined him … and watched in absolute amazement as a spoon would be filled, lifted towards his mouth, and then stay suspended somewhere en route while he talked and listened. It continued like that for a while. After a little while, I was done eating. He was still at it. Eventually, he finished, just in time for us to catch the 3 pm show. I have no recollection of the movie, but for some reason, I remember the prelude to it, and it brings a smile.

There are several other stories of him, of things we did together, and things he did in ways only he could have. I have some, and I am sure the others—Sunny and Shabi and Sonit and the rest—have more. If we were to sit together and tell those stories, I have the feeling that we would have a hard time stopping, but an easy time agreeing that he was unique and quite possibly unlike anyone we have encountered since.

Some people are like that. When they've touched you once, you never forget them, especially not when Facebook pops up a memory on a particular day in the year, and you remember exactly where you were and what you were doing when the story ended.

It was another summer—the summer of '85. Our lives had moved on from high school, and we had gone to different colleges and walked different pathways through them. After college, Bharat had moved to Bombay and was figuring out his life, and I had moved to the US and just finished the second year of graduate school in economics.

Summer is slower in university towns in the US, with a mass exodus of undergraduates who make up the large proportion of the student body. Some stick around to take summer courses that are shorter in duration but more intense with daily lectures that are longer and attempt to pack in a three-month-long learning experience into five weeks. That summer, I was teaching one of those summer courses in statistics for economics and getting ready for a final set of written exams in the doctoral program at the end of the summer. It was a busy time.

I was living with two friends, also graduate students, in a two-bedroom, two-storey apartment on Greene Street. Actually, it was one bedroom and a small study on the upper level and the kitchen and living room on the ground level. The company managing those apartments had rented it to the three of us, and we had set things up, so two shared the large bedroom, and one person had the study. Since none of us had much money and we split rent equally, we rotated sole occupancy of the study every four months. That summer, it was my turn to have the smaller space—a perfect spot to seclude myself on the weekends and burrow through all that I had learnt in courses on development and population economics.

It was a typically hot and humid Saturday afternoon that first of June. I was in my room studying when the phone rang downstairs, and I went down to answer it. Madhav was on the line from New York and had bad news—Bharat had died in a freak car accident. It was a short call. After I hung up, I tried to go back up the stairs to my room to continue studying, but I couldn't. I had to sit down.

I hadn't seen Bharat or talked to him or exchanged any communication in the three years since I had dropped him off at New Delhi railway station in the summer of '82, not long after which I had headed out to the US. I had just expected that someday we would catch up. Madhav's phone call meant we wouldn't.

I don't remember if I cried; I probably did. All I remember is sitting on those steps, recalling all the things we'd done together, his walk, his languorous ways, and that gentle manner. I am sure that made me smile, as it has every time I have thought of him through all these years.

When I was finally able to get on my feet, I called Sunny in Texas and broke the news to him. We talked about him. Sunny told me about the year he had spent with Bharat in Bombay, how things had gone and where he thought they were going. I remember the details of all of that, and some of that made it all a bit heavier to bear at that time; I don't know if I got any studying done that day.

Time, of course, moves along, and you move with it. Many years have passed since that summer of '85. Some memories of him have faded, and some have only gotten sharper. The line between what is real and what is imagined, always somewhat fuzzy, is fuzzier now, and I am well aware that we tend to be generous with remembrances of those who have passed, especially those who have moved on too early.

I have often wondered if my memory of Bharat is airbrushed; maybe it is. But there is no doubt in my mind that in all these years, I have never met anyone quite like him—no one who walked that way, no one who did things at that pace, no one who talked the way he did, just simply no one like him.

What I wrote in memoriam on Facebook some years back still rings true:

There are some
You always remember
With a special smile
And feel lucky
To have walked with a little while
He was such
Oh, how he walked on water!

46

Yoon

Some say there is only one road to heaven; some say there are many. I don't know much about heaven, but I do know that the southern part of it—Chapel Hill, North Carolina—has three roads going in but only two going through. Yoon lived on one of those through-heaven roads in Ridgewood apartments on Jones Ferry Road, just before Jones Ferry crosses the 54 Bypass and wanders off into obscurity. Like many of heaven's temporary residents who come in and go out with the academic tide of degrees and programs, he was unique in ways you might not expect, especially if you think of all Asian students as faceless workaholics. If you had encountered him, you wouldn't have forgotten him.

He was in my PhD batch, and we took a lot of classes together in the first two years of graduate school and interspersed those with easy time in the downtown environs of Chapel Hill, or what the conservative senator of North Carolina, Jesse Helms, once called a zoo. To Helms, the liberal town was a zoo to be fenced in and kept separate from the conservative backwater that elected him to the US Senate five times. Of course, what he dumped on the world as a conservative anti-communist would make you think he, not Chapel Hill, needed a fence.

All of us liked Yoon. Unlike the other Korean students who would stay to themselves in their offices in the far-right corner of the windowless fourth floor of Gardner Hall, home of the economics department, Yoon mingled with us. It had a little something to do with being confident with English, but a whole lot more to do with ... just being Yoon.

He had a quiet confidence about him, was a bit roly-poly, smoked, drank, and smiled all the time. He even played a couple of games on our recreational soccer team in the first year, smoking on the sidelines while awaiting his turn to play, or as one of the others in my class remembers ... even while playing. How could you not like a guy like that? Even now, after all these years, I smile when I think of him.

Besides being supremely amicable, Yoon was also good with numbers and loved to gamble. He'd take any bet you wanted on the Saturday football games, saying that he always came out ahead over multiple weekends. He wasn't the only one who liked gambling. He and his Korean friends would periodically road-trip up to Atlantic City to have a go at what was on offer there. How often, I don't know.

That whole group, which included PhD students from other departments, also had a classic collective set up for handling the parking meters, which would only take up to four quarters at a time. They would come together in a couple of cars, park them near the student union building, and have a clearly defined rotation schedule for sliding in the coins and staying legally parked.

I doubt Indian students—or for that matter, any other international students—had such a cooperative working style. That might have a lot to do with Korea's development success, but try telling mainstream development economists that culture matters, and you are likely to get some nonsense about the invisible hand of markets and the mystical way in which multiple individuals acting in self-interested ways produce magic.

In our first year in the program, all of us were research assistants and had windowless offices on the fourth floor of Gardner Hall. In the second year, most of us transitioned to teaching assistant roles and moved to offices in Hanes Hall, which was better for interactions with students. Unlike the 4th floor of Gardner Hall, which was reserved for PhD students and had a common area with a couch, there was no such space on the office floor of Hanes Hall. Our offices had desks, and that was about it.

We saw less of Yoon in the second year because he stayed on as a research assistant with an office in Gardner Hall. In that year, sometime in the fall semester, Yoon asked us to help him move. He said he was moving to an independent apartment because he was going home to Korea to get married and would be coming back with a wife.

So one weekend, some of us showed up at Ridgewood apartments to help him load his stuff in a U-Haul truck. I don't remember Yoon doing much lifting—he was smoking, smiling, and directing us. I know memory is faulty, and I might be wrong, but that image fits and I am going with that.

When we got around to picking up his pull-out living room couch, he said not to bother loading it into the truck but to leave it by the dumpster. It was a long couch with check fabric and in good condition, but he was just throwing it away ... because it had one broken leg. I suppose he didn't want his new wife to encounter broken pieces of his past.

We asked him if it was okay to take the pull-out couch to our office in Hanes Hall. He was okay with that, so Jehan and I took the couch to the office we were sharing in Hanes Hall, and instead of fixing the one broken leg or propping up that end with bricks, broke the other three, so it was all level.

It was a comfortable long convertible couch that came in very handy for lounging about, chatting with fellow students, and ... for the afternoon naps I liked to take. Those days I used to pack two sandwiches for work—one with lettuce, tomato, sandwich meat and cheese, and the other with basic peanut butter and jelly. The plan was to have the meat sandwich for lunch and the peanut butter one with afternoon tea, but I rarely stuck to that plan. I'd have the meat one and then go on to the peanut butter and jelly one. The combination would drag down the eyelids, and I would give up and 'horizontate' on Yoon's legless couch.

After Yoon returned with a wife, we saw less of him. That declined further after we got done with coursework by the end of our second year in the program. The other graduate students still met up with him at the economics department, but I had been awarded a fellowship at the Carolina Population Center and had an office there, so I didn't go by the economics department that often. As a result, I saw even less of him and eventually lost touch ... but not completely.

In two years of regular contact, in classes and in office chats, I picked up a bit of Yoon that has stayed with me all these years and pops up every now and then when I am in pointless meetings with people wanting to make their own point. That's when I sit back and 'do' Yoon, which is this spinning of a pen on the tip of the middle finger, aided by the fourth and pinkie held together, and the forefinger and the thumb held out a bit. It's not a continuous spin, but one spin at a time and takes a bit of practice to become automatic. I suppose wanting to—be Yoon—I picked it up, and it has stayed.

Learning to 'do' Yoon and then doing it is a form of social mimicry that all humans engage in— unintentionally and nonconsciously. It is called the chameleon effect, and the great Yale psychologist John Bargh and his students have done a good bit of experimental work on that and other forms of what is more generally called automaticity. Mimicking is how children learn and how we do a lot of things—a point entirely lost on fools who theorize that all human actions are based on rational thinking with careful consideration of their potential consequences.

In the early years of mimicking Yoon, I must have realized I was copying him, so wanting to retain a bit of me, I developed a variation. It is a twirling of the pen between the middle three fingers, kind of like a cheerleader twirling a baton. It is not as smooth and elegant as "The Yoon," but it is distinctive because it doesn't have to stop after one go around; it can go on continuously—if you become good at it.

Years of practice has brought me to the point where now I can slip into either form of automaticity in a meeting. Still, I avoid doing my twirl because … if I miss, the pen is likely to fly off into the air and catch attention and disrupt the pointless swirl of the meeting. By contrast, "The Yoon" just falls nearby and disrupts nothing.

Not too long after I lost touch with Yoon, I found an Indian student of mine at North Carolina State University, a precocious high schooler taking advanced placement courses, trying to do "The Yoon" and fumbling with the action during a one-hour exam he had finished in 30 minutes. I wondered if he had, unintentionally or intentionally, picked it up from me—for I seriously doubt he had had the good fortune of meeting Mr. Yoon.

47

Patsy Cline

The other day Sumi was getting ready for a Diwali party and, for reasons unknown, was listening to Patsy Cline croon, "I fall to pieces." When that song ended, something jazzy came on to break the country swoon, and I switched off because ... my brain follows a music logic that says you can go from country to pop or soul or maybe bluegrass, but not to rock or jazz or classical.

I am no musicologist, so I can't and won't defend the logic of that; it's just how the twingles and twangles of country music align with other genres in my head. When the playlist led back to "Sweet Dreams," I felt relieved and smiled at where the two songs were leading me—to a January morning in 1986 when Patsy Cline hung musical notes in cold hungover air in a house with ... seven rooms and seven hundred stories.

After two years of sharing a room in an apartment, I wanted a room to myself but did not have the money to get an apartment on my own or a separate room in a shared apartment. A group house was the only option, and college towns have scores of those. They tend to be of varying condition and configuration, some with rooms formally advertised, others through word of mouth. Not long after I put the word out that I was looking for a room, I heard about 122 Mallette Street, a red brick house walking from campus.

Like every summer, the house was going through a complete turnover, and several rooms were available. I was one of the first ones to come looking, and so I was able to get a room of my choice. The one I picked was quite possibly the oddest one in that house. It was more beat up than the others, was one of the smaller ones, but while all the other rooms had the standard four-walls and a ceiling configuration, mine was ... a suite, a room within a room.

The main room was small and had a hole in one wall, which I covered up with a large poster of Jungfraujoch, the mountaintop in Switzerland I had visited on my 21st birthday. It was airy with large windows that brought in the morning sunlight, but the best part of it was the wash sink at one end; that was a luxury of sorts in a group house with one bathroom per floor.

The even better of that room was the room within—a large walk-in closet with a peekaboo window that faced the street, a small built-in desk, and space enough to hold a rack of clothes and more. I set that space up with a waist-high fridge, a two-coil electric stove, a toaster, and an electric kettle, all picked up at yard sales and through the Village Advocate, the local newspaper's advertising supplement.

The room-within-a-room configuration meant I could keep all my food in the room-within, cook all my meals in that space, and clean up in the wash sink in the main room. That meant I did not have to deal with the common kitchen downstairs, which had all the problems of common spaces in group houses. The only common facility I needed to use was the adjacent bathroom which was tiny but entirely functional. I was mighty pleased with the fact that I had managed to gain the independence I wanted for a fraction of the cost in an apartment setting.

I did not know any of the occupants when I moved in, but it mattered not. For the first few weeks, I was hardly ever in the house, spending days and sometimes even nights in my office in Hanes Hall studying for the second-year written exams in August. It was only when those were done and a memorable beach trip to Hilton Head had been taken that I tuned in to the red brick house on Mallette Street—and a new set of housemates. It didn't take much more than a few nights and a few more beers to get going with the laughter and warmth of new friendships. That it all began with my cooking the others an Indian dinner on my birthday, and my new friends providing dessert—a half bottle of vodka poured into a watermelon—brings a smile and a chuckle.

The house and room may not have had much—materially—but it had more soul than material can get you and fit right into the southern part of heaven. I inhabited that room for two years, and that room and house led to the most thorough immersion in Americana possible. I couldn't have known that when I moved into that house. All I had wanted was a room to myself; what I got was more, much more.

Patsy Cline came around in that house one morning after a winter house party. The occasion was the Superbowl—American professional football's season finale event, with half-time performances by big-name entertainers. It is said that a 30-second TV spot on Superbowl night is the highest price for a TV advertisement anywhere in the world, and ticket prices to the actual game are also some of the highest anywhere.

It was late January of 1986, and it was the Superbowl in which the Chicago Bears crushed the New England Patriots. In the two years leading up to that football season, I hadn't paid that much attention to American professional football, occasionally watching games on TV, but only when friends were watching.

College football had been of greater interest, quite simply because the Saturday games in Kenan Stadium, with 50,000 in attendance and pre-and post-game activities, were spectacles in more ways than one. There was the game on the field, which I didn't really understand beyond the basics. Then there was the hoopla around the game with drums and marching band and cheerleaders and ... the cheers. How could you not pay attention to something like, "If you lean to the left and you lean to the right, and you peel your banana and you "unh" take a bite. Go bananas, go, go bananas."

It was easy to focus on all of that and not the game because there was so much movement and stoppage in the game. There were downs and time-outs that stopped and started plays. Those weren't that hard to figure out, but what was, at first, very confusing was entire teams running off the field and being replaced with new ones—from the same side. The concept of dedicated offensive and defensive, and kicking teams (within the same team) who were only on the field for parts of the game was new to me and very hard to follow. I hadn't watched football at Davidson College, thankfully, some would say, and so it took a few games to get a grip on all the movement on the field.

Then, of course, there was the social spectacle in the stands. In Chapel Hill, and I am told more generally in the southern part of the country, football games are occasions for undergraduates from fraternities and sororities (social organizations at the university) to dress up formally——to see and be seen. I never went to the pre-and post-game parties where that activity occurred in small settings, but in the stadium, it took place on a gigantic stage with young men and women strutting up and down the stands, many with little interest in the game.

That social game in the stands must have been irritating for diehard football fans, but for village idiots like me who had never been to a sports event of that scale, it was ... how should I put this—sensory overload. Football being very much of a stop-and-go game, you could watch the game on the field and the one in the stands, and sometimes not know which one to pay attention to.

I went to quite a few games with my graduate school friends but didn't tune in to football beyond those Saturdays, definitely not to the professional football that came on TV on Sundays. It was only when I moved into that group house on Mallette Street, and became good friends with Mike, who was from Chicago and a lifelong Bears fan, that football-watching became serious stuff.

We watched Bears games on the TV in our living room on Sundays in earnest. Not only was the team very good, it was also very entertaining—what, with the cockiness of the quarterback Jim McMahon, the rap song "The Superbowl Shuffle" the team recorded, and the sight of the 350-plus pound William "The Refrigerator" Perry playing fullback and, in one play, carrying McMahon over into the end zone.

The Bears had been a dominant team all season long and were expected to win hands down. Their opponents, the New England Patriots, didn't have a chance. Mike was charged up about the game and organized a party in the house.

As would be expected of late January, the night of the Superbowl party was a cold one, and according to records in the Old Farmer's Almanac, the temperature was somewhere in the mid-30s (F). The house had an inefficient oil-based heating system which was very expensive to run, and so the only affordable option was the wood fireplace in the small living room. That is what we used through the winter, and on that cold January night, it had a rip-roaring fire all through the Superbowl with 20-odd people crowded around the TV moving in and out of that space and the adjacent dining room which held the beer keg.

I don't remember anything of the game other than the fact that the Bears crushed the Patriots, and the game was essentially over at half time. By then, the beer keg Mike had bought was nearly empty, and the attendees, many of whom were from the women's field hockey team that we had supported full-throatedly in the fall, proceeded with Tequila shots—in youthful ways. I also have no memory of how the party ended and what time I walked up to my unheated room and into the warm comforter.

The only memory I have is waking up the next morning and coming down to clean the aftermath of the party and hearing Patsy Cline's beautiful voice. The living room fire had died out in the night, and winter had crept back in that morning. Someone in the house had a record player, and they had put on one of her LPs, and there she was … hanging melodic notes in hungover air. In some ways, there was nothing to the moment; in other ways, there was everything to it. It must be why I remember it 30 plus years later.

I was no country music fan, only having heard Kenny Rogers on All India Radio's *Yuv Vani* program in college days. It was when I got to Davidson that I became aware of music genres and how, in the minds of uptown folks like those at liberal arts colleges, country music was downtown. Did I conform and therefore not listen to country, or was it just that I wasn't actively exploring other genres at that time? I am not sure. The truth is, I didn't turn the dial to radio stations that played country. Even when I joined the Columbia Record Club, which sent a catalogue every month with listings from multiple genres, I didn't ever buy a country tape from it, not even of Kenny Rogers.

Patsy Cline was the first country singer I listened to in full. She didn't turn me on to country, though later that year, I bought a cassette of hers and watched Jessica Lange's brilliant portrayal of her in the movie, Sweet Dreams. In the years since then, I have tuned in to country only two times—once to listen to Leann Rimes sing "Blue," or rather ... Blueoouoouoou (the way she stretches out blue), and the other time to listen to Taylor Swift twingle "Love Story."

I like Taylor Swift's Romeo and Juliet love song, especially its starting riff. In years past, whenever it came to mind, and the girls were in the car, I'd ask them to play it on their phones. They'd always oblige, always with an indulgent look. Now that they have moved on with their own lives, I play it when the thought wafts in. It's still lovely but nothing compared with Patsy Cline's "I fall to pieces"—not just because her voice is ethereal, but because it reminds me of how it hung in the cold air of a Carolina winter morning a very long time ago.

48

No one is to blame

She was Dutch. He was American. I don't know the details of their relationship and whether Taylor Swift would have written a love song about them. All I know is that in the summer of '86, there was a Howard Jones song that repeatedly played on his boom box in the tiny bedroom he rented in our group house on Mallette Street in Chapel Hill. The first catchy notes of that song have stuck in my head for years, and what can I say... if there is a song in my head for so long, there is usually a story to go along.

I had moved into 122 Mallette Street in August of '85, and by the time the summer of '86 came along, I had been in that house for 10 months and become friends with my housemates, some of whom were graduate students who had undergraduate friends who then became my friends. College towns are like that—you make friends become friends with their friends, and the social circle expands before you know it. Of course, that is if you choose to be social in that way, or happen to get plonked into a setting that naturally lends itself to expansion.

One of the Mallette Street housemates I had become friends with was Mike, and he was friends with Claire and others on the women's field hockey team. As a result, I watched a lot of Carolina field hockey games in the fall of '85.

She was a top-notch hockey player on that team and an All American in one of her three playing years. There were a lot of very talented players on that team, but her game was different—it had a bit more of the Indian dribbling flair, which, growing up in India, I naturally liked. That it also carried European-style discipline and team orientation lifted it a few notches beyond the individual dribble. It is something I have grown to appreciate over time, especially in my short stint as a girls' football coach. In my mind, that difference—individual within team—is the hallmark of European teams, be they football or hockey. It is a style Asians, Africans, and even South Americans find tough to compete against.

Hockey skills weren't all of it. She was also beautiful, not in a typical Carolina way, but in a very confident, athletic way. She wore those looks not as a crown but as a casual, breezy summer dress. I bet there was many a heart that fluttered in her presence.

He was a lacrosse player on Carolina's perennially competitive team. I am guessing he was from one of the New Jersey–New York high school stud farms that supplied Carolina's thoroughbred soccer and lacrosse teams. I didn't know much about lacrosse, so I don't know how good his collecting, twirling, checking, attacking skills were, and whether he was an All American, or even what notch he occupied within that team. I rarely saw him, other than at lacrosse games, and then too in a helmet, so I don't remember what he looked like or what he was like. In my mind, his identity was entirely in relation to her.

I didn't see much of her till the beginning of summer when he started renting one of the rooms on the ground floor for the summer months, and she came by frequently. His room was the first one to the right of the corridor that ran from the living room to the stairs that led up to my room, so there was no avoiding it.

Summers are slower in college towns when most undergraduates are gone, and there are only locals, graduate students and some identity-searching stragglers. If that drop in population doesn't slow the pace, the heat and humidity of North Carolina sure do. Unlike the previous two summers when I had caught a break from the heat while working for a few weeks at Camp High Rocks in the mountains of western North Carolina, the summer of '86 was a long uninterrupted haul through the oppressive humidity. It seemed even longer because I was writing my thesis proposal. That might seem like a focussed activity, but it really isn't because you are never sure whether what makes sense to you is sensible to others or plain gobbledygook.

During the day, I would flit in and out of the house to the cooler temperatures of the university library or my office at the Carolina Population Center. In the evening, I would stick a box fan in the window to suck in the cooler outside air. It would cool down the small room and make it bearable by bedtime. Having grown up in the stifling heat of northern India, I had a great appreciation for the value of circulating air, even if it was hot. It seemed to be less of a concern for Americans who went with either the cooler but motionless feel of air conditioning or nothing at all. I didn't understand that at all.

During the two-three summer months that he was there, we saw a good bit of her. I don't remember if I ever talked to him, but I remember chatting with her on the wooden swing we had bought for the house. I must admit, at first, it was hard to engage in a conversation with her—she was so beautiful, it was easy to admire her looks and ignore the content of the conversation. I am not being sexist here, just stating the reality of life. Thankfully, she wasn't vain and self-absorbed, just confident and relaxed, and soon enough, conversations became easier.

Her confidence was such that she could ask for anything, and you wouldn't blink an eye handing it over. I had heard of her walking up to complete strangers in a restaurant and asking to try their French fries or something else and them not refusing. I hadn't believed that story, but one of those summer days, I had on a nice black T-shirt that I had picked up at some sale. She complimented me on it, and without thinking twice, I asked her if she wanted it. When she said yes, I just walked up to my room, changed out of it, came down and handed it to her.

It was her last summer in Chapel Hill. She had decided to forgo her senior year and return to Holland. I don't know what had prompted that decision, but he was pretty distraught. The day she was to leave, or the day before, he had covered his bed with little bits of paper with something written on them. What it was, I don't know; I didn't go in to check. I just happened to walk by his room and saw the scattered bits of paper as Howard Jones sang, "No one is to blame."

The song ruled the airwaves at that time, and I'd heard it many times—for its catchy start and lovely melody. I hadn't paid any attention to the lyrics and had no idea what they meant to him, her, or them. I still don't. All I knew then, and even now, is that there was a song that played at what seemed to be the end of "their" story. That, in my head, is now a "li'l ditty" from that summer of '86.

49

Air India

"Wow, you are doing a PhD!"

Thinking it was a compliment, I smiled. So did *Amma,* who was happy that I had headed down the academic path that she was still on, and not so long ago had walked in dual mode—as teacher and student. Her re-entry into student mode came about when, after more than 30 years of teaching English literature and into her 50s, she decided that the gold medal she had won on graduating from Benaras Hindu University with a degree in English and Music at only 18 had sat lonely for too long. It needed some company, so she decided to do a master's in music. There was no professional reason for it. It was because ... she wanted to do it, and that was about all the reason she needed. I am tempted to go on and recount the full story of that endeavour, but I'll leave it for another time.

The "Wow" line was followed up with, "You boys were so rowdy. I thought nothing would come of you." I knew just what she was talking about. My smile grew wider as I tried to think about where and what stage of our wildness she had encountered. *Amma's* faded quickly. She didn't like that, but she didn't say anything; confrontation was not her style.

It was January of 1988, and *Amma* had taken me to the Air India office in Janpath to see if her Miranda House student from years back could help with my return flight back to Chapel Hill. It was my third trip back home after leaving in 1982 and had come about somewhat last minute with one of my classmates, the ever-resourceful Mr. Yoon, arranging a ticket on Korean Airlines through Seoul, with a layover in Bangkok, and the final stretch on Air India.

My India trips came about in those graduate school days when I had saved up enough money to buy a plane ticket. That was every two years and always during the winter break. Each of those trips was a homecoming, but invariably turned into an adventure because something or the other always happened. In the very first one, I had forgotten my passport at the bank counter at the airport and had to get a new one and then go to the US embassy to get a new student visa stamped on it. Both bits had caused all sorts of headaches. The second one had involved a long layover in Rome airport. I had gotten stiffed by a waiter at the airport restaurant in Rome and then been harassed by Indian customs officials at the airport in Delhi. This was the third trip, and it was following the same script.

When I had purchased the ticket on Korean Airlines, I hadn't paid attention to the details, so when I landed in Bangkok, I was surprised to find that there was no connecting flight to Delhi till the next evening. It was a last-minute booking, and I could be excused for that oversight but … that would be letting myself off the hook easy. The truth is, I have never been careful about the minutiae of life, and that has landed me in quite a few pickles along the way, stressful in the moment but fun to recall and write about later.

The nice thing about being young and resourceful is that nothing fazes you. There was a tourist counter at the Bangkok airport, so I walked over and asked for suggestions. They gave me a map of the city and helped in identifying a cheap youth hostel. I left my suitcase in the left-luggage storage at the airport and caught a public bus to the youth hostel. It was in a residential neighbourhood, and there was nothing much around, other than a couple of eating places for locals. The one I walked into had a laminated menu in Thai, which I quite obviously couldn't make head or tail off. Thankfully, there were pictures, and so I ordered a couple of dishes by pointing to them. I had no idea what I had ordered, but it turned out to be delicious. That was my first Thai dinner, and it so tickled the papillae that Thai is now my default go-to food when eating out and the only non-Indian food I like to cook. I get a hard time from my family for that, but it is what it is.

After a night in the youth hostel dormitory, I wandered about the city the next day, had more Thai street food and then headed back to the airport to catch the Air India flight to Delhi. The whole Bangkok adventure cost less than 10 dollars.

The return flight to Chapel Hill had the same routing and the same carriers, but then Air India called the evening of my departure to inform me that the flight had been cancelled and I would be rescheduled on the next available flight—which might be in two or three days. On enquiring, we found out that it was because Prime Minister Rajiv Gandhi was travelling to the US to see Ronald Reagan and needed to keep a plane on standby. I guess he needed two jumbo jets for his trip ... so he could pose in cool shades and a black *bandhgala* (closed neck) coat with the Gipper! I am not entirely sure how true that is, but that is what I heard, and that is what I remember.

Amma's former student did get me on a flight out the next day, but again there was a day-long layover in Bangkok, this time because of their rescheduling, not my oversight. Air India said their local office would arrange a hotel for the day, but when I got there early the next morning, there was no one to arrange anything. I was a graduate student and had only 20 dollars in my pocket, so I stayed in the airport till much later in the day when an Air India official came by to give me a voucher for a hotel.

I vowed never to fly Air India again and held on to that for almost 30 years, breaking it only three years ago when they offered a fare substantially lower than other carriers. Their customer service seemed to have improved a little bit, but then two years ago, when I had to fly them again from Mumbai to Bangalore, it seemed like not much had changed. Oh, well. At least I had finished the PhD and wasn't a poor graduate student anymore and had more than 20 dollars in my pocket. I could, and did, buy a ticket on another airline and keep going.

I have heard that the airline has finally been privatized and been taken over by Tata Sons, the conglomerate known to run efficient businesses. Hopefully, that will get the airline out of the financial mess it has been in for years and improve passenger service. That second part should be a bit easier these days, given that now there is a designated plane (Air India One) to ferry the prime minister around, and flights don't have to be cancelled—because someone wants to prance and preen in cool shades or personalized pinstriped suits. All signs seem to be pointing in the right direction for the Air India Maharajah to start delivering. I sure hope he does.

50

Art of teaching

Art was a piece of art. Short, colourfully dressed, with a clean-shaven head well before it became fashionable—he had energy somewhat unusual for an economics professor. If you like hyperbole and knew Art Benavie, you might say, "he was a force of nature," but I am not hyperbolic, so I won't go that way. Actually, none of that was the real art.

The real art was how he could hold an auditorium full of 300 students in the palm of his hand with nothing more than a piece of chalk. Semester after semester, he'd repeat the same basic introductory economics material, but week after week, he would deliver it like new with electric energy and enthusiasm only great teachers have. His ability to extract an economics concept from "news just the other day" and excite students about abstractions and models and their power to explain the world around them was quite simply remarkable.

He never told them they wouldn't encounter economics concepts like demand and supply curves and market equilibrium in their dorms and fraternity and sorority parties. But I'll bet that by the time they were done with ECON 10 if they had encountered one of the said abstractions in the middle of a drunken party, they would have wrapped an arm around it and offered it a cold beer.

I didn't know Art, personally or as a student. I was just his Teaching Assistant in an introductory economics course for a couple of semesters, and that too, one of several. All the logistics of the large course were handled by a head TA, a more senior graduate student, so we junior TAs had little direct contact with Art. I didn't take any graduate courses in macroeconomics and monetary theory with him, so I have no idea what other brilliance bounced in and off that shiny head. I only saw him perform a couple of days a week for a couple of semesters, and what he did in those outings was pure art.

Great teachers are not always great researchers, brilliant at coming up with new ideas, discovering things, and inventing new stuff. Great teachers are those who can convey ideas simply and excite students in ways that make them curious about things. They can inspire students to be critical of what has been said before and be creative in coming up with new explanations and solutions. It works differently at different levels of schooling and disciplines, but in my view, the three Cs—curiosity, criticality, creativity—make up the art of teaching.

I have no idea how good Art was at the more advanced undergraduate and graduate levels of economics, but at the introductory level, the one in which I saw him wield a chalk, he sure was the best.

I tried to be Art when I got to teach three sections of introductory economics at North Carolina State University for three semesters, and then again for a year at Davidson College. In those places, I mixed up Art's art with that of two other great teachers I encountered in graduate school.

One was Michael Salemi, who taught me macroeconomics for one semester in the first year of graduate school. He was a bit quirky but a brilliant teacher who could unpack a complex equation and explain every term, so it had economic meaning and meant more than a combination of Greek symbols.

And then there was Larry Kupper, from whom I learnt statistical theory for two semesters in the biostatistics department. He was unique because, besides delivering complicated material in straightforward ways, his homework assignments and exams consisted of real problems from his research work on modelling all kinds of toxicology phenomena. Walking in and out of his probability models of toxicology was hard work, but if you could do that, then you had built yourself a strong foundation of the core ideas of statistics. They were both brilliant and inspirational—because they packed the three Cs in their lectures.

I liked the art of teaching and would have liked to continue along that path, but when I went looking for a regular teaching job, I wasn't able to get one. I should have persevered but didn't, and instead ended up wandering about in the world of international development for 17 odd years. The only seriously satisfying bits in that period were the times I got to teach short, focused stuff in Vietnam, Mongolia, Mozambique, The Bahamas and Tanzania. What I taught wasn't highfalutin, but about the basic things governments should do to collect and analyse data on people's lives and the policies they design to impact those lives.

Somehow, and in a very roundabout way, the meandering professional life came back to its starting point when I landed up in New Zealand at Victoria University of Wellington and inched my way back into teaching. Whenever I think about how the teaching circle has been completed, it reminds me of a story my mother used to tell—which suggests that maybe teaching was pre-ordained. I used to find that story embarrassing when I was a teenager, but it is amusing now.

Amma said there was a time in Pantnagar when we had guests over for dinner and I, not much more than five, stood up on the coffee table and "lectured" to them—"*Main aloo hoon, mera bhai pyaaz hai,*" meaning "I am a potato, my brother is an onion." I have to guess that had come from watching my parents lecture in the College of Humanities and College of Agriculture in Pantnagar, and wanting to be like them. My parents were teachers through and through and masters of their art, though they practised it in different ways.

Amma's teaching was a gentler and broader variety that had at its core teaching English literature at women's colleges in Benaras, Mathura, Pantnagar and Delhi. Beyond that core, which paid her a regular salary, there was the *sitar* that she taught beginners, invariably young women in the neighbourhood. When she retired after 40 odd years in multiple universities and moved to Indore, I thought she was done with teaching. She wasn't. She continued teaching *sitar* and started something new—English conversation classes for children and adults.

Appa's teaching was more pragmatic— about animal husbandry and livestock-related livelihoods—and had at its core a quasi-scientific approach anchored in careful observation of the way the world functioned. He'd point that out repeatedly, the most memorable instance being something he said when he and I were standing in the front room of the house we were renting on Todarmal Road in Bengali Market and watching the street sweepers.

The street had an assigned sweeper—Angoori—and she had a large brood of children who camped on the street during the day and were allocated different stretches of the street and the neighbourhood to keep clean. It was a micro-enterprise of sorts, and she was the manager. Watching the sweeping, he said: "You can learn a lot from carefully observing the world around you, even from the way a *jamaadar* (street sweeper) sweeps the streets." Quite aside from its social dimension, significant in a society with rigid social and class distinctions, it was noteworthy for its emphasis on careful observation.

That bit of teaching of his was quite possibly the most significant bit of learning for me. Without knowing it, I employed it all the time, sometimes to great value and at other times to hilarious effect in numerous screwups. I later turned his "observing carefully" pointer into my own acronym ODA—observe, describe, analyse—and now employ variants of the basic idea in the introductory courses I teach. It works for those who have an open mind and are curious and willing to think differently, not for those who want to be told what to think and how to think. When it works, and I get an email like the following one, it is gratifying:

"I am not sure if you remember me or not, but I wanted to say thank you for two amazing courses this year ... I feel that my worldview has in some ways shifted this year, and I think your courses are a large cause of that."

This doesn't happen as often as I'd like, but when it does, it reminds me of a dream I had a couple of years ago in which I saw my father sitting in the second row of a class I was teaching. He looked young and muscular, as he was in his 40s and 50s. He was observing me and had a satisfied smile on his face. I think ... he liked my art of teaching.

51

Let the good times roll

It was only half an hour, but it was enough ... to feel the magic. For 30 minutes, BB King rocked and rollicked the blues and "let the good times roll" on one of several makeshift stages at the Louisiana state fairgrounds in New Orleans in April of 1988. There was music of all kinds at the Louisiana Jazz and Heritage Festival, and I did catch a lot of it, but his was ... well, just his. There is no other way to describe it. It was a moment to remember, and I have not forgotten.

The journey to New Orleans and BB King started with a somewhat random suggestion by the graduate program director in the economics department to take a demography methods course in the sociology department. That led to taking the second demography methods course (in the sequence) in the biostatistics department, which in turn led to a complete change in my academic trajectory, of which one part was a pre-doctoral fellowship at the Carolina Population Center (CPC). That place would end up becoming my academic home within the university for the next several years. It didn't lead to my becoming an economic demographer in the way the fellowship had intended, but the multi-disciplinary air of that centre would go on to shape my worldview in far more important ways. For that, I am forever in debt to CPC.

There was much to be admired at the "pop center." The computing facilities were great, the staff were helpful and fantastic, the weekly seminars were eye-openers, and the demographers from different academic departments were world leaders in population research. Other than the requirement to attend weekly brown-bag seminars, the fellowship was a free ride that allowed us "predocs" to focus on our own work.

The cherry on the topping of that fellowship was the all-paid trip to the annual meeting of the Population Association of America (PAA) held in a different city each year. We weren't required to attend those meetings, but ... it was a free trip, so why wouldn't you? Plus, in 1988, it was being held in "The Big Easy"—"Nu Orleans"—a place I heard had a culture unlike anywhere else in America. Of course, I was going. It was a given.

The timing of that visit couldn't have been more opportune. It was my sixth year in America, and just as my friend Jehan had predicted four years earlier, the country's culture had crept under my skin. I was living life on my terms in an independent efficiency apartment and rode a motorcycle, more to get around town and go beyond its confines than to drift in "Easy Rider" spirit. More than all of that, my music tastes had changed and gone from the pop and soft rock I used to tune in to in the early years to classical and jazz and blues and rock and more.

I want to say the transformation began in the third year of graduate school in the red brick house on Mallette Street with Patsy Cline and Paul Simon's Graceland and Bruce Hornsby's twangy southern rock album "The way it is," but it began earlier. The credit would have to go to my friend Adrian. Not only did he take me to see James Taylor in concert in 1984, but he also introduced me to

Bruce Springsteen and Keith Jarret and John McLaughlin and more. By the time I moved out of the Mallette Street house into the efficiency apartment on the side of a house on Elliot Road, my music tastes had expanded, and I did them justice by investing a chunk of money in a proper music system with an amplifier, dual tape player, CD player, and speakers.

Around the time I headed out to The Big Easy for the PAA meeting in 1988, I had discovered the Irish rock band U2, had listened to their albums, and formed a strong opinion that 'The Joshua Tree' was their best work. Wikipedia has a long entry on the album with details I had no idea of then and still know little about. I was vaguely aware that the album was based on U2's experience touring America and that the lyrics of songs like "Where the streets have no name" and "I still haven't found what I am looking for" had some special meaning to them.

Some of those lyrics also resonated with my struggles at that time, but my appreciation of 'The Joshua Tree' was simpler—the melodies and rhythm were beautiful, and the hard-hitting sound was unlike anything I had heard until then. Nothing captures that more than the first 15 seconds of "One tree hill," especially the transition at the eight-second mark when the change in sound and tempo creates the sensation of a cloud burst, dropping buckets of musical rain. On weekends, when my landlords were out of town, I would turn up the volume and listen to that section again and again. I still do that sometimes—in the car with windows closed!

It was in that musical frame of mind that I headed out to New Orleans for the PAA meeting. Arriving in the afternoon before the meeting started, the first thing I did on checking into the hotel was to get a map and head out to the French Quarter looking for places that were known to play great music. Over the next three evenings, I went to several, often staying late into the night to catch as much as I could.

At the PAA meetings, we doctoral students were expected to imbibe demographic research, but in the three days of the New Orleans meeting, I imbibed something entirely different. The city was all temptation with food and music, and I caved in to all of it. I don't think I went to more than a few sessions at the meeting.

Mornings were spent recovering from the night before— over beignets and coffee along the great Mississippi—and afternoons were spent ... I think attending sessions, but I am not entirely sure. Evenings were preparation for nights, and that's how it went. I soaked in the sounds of Nu Orleans, so much so, that in a postcard to my mother, I wrote: "This city seeps music from every pore."

Three evenings and three nights in that place would have been enough, but there was more to come. The Louisiana Jazz and Heritage Festival happened to be on the weekend of the PAA meeting, so I skipped the half-day of Saturday demography sessions and headed over to the state fairgrounds—to attend music sessions.

In terms of music, nothing has ever come close to that day. There were 50 odd stages set up all over the fairgrounds, and there was a continuous rotation of bands that played 30-min sets. There was all kinds of music on those stages—jazz, blues, rock, gospel, bluegrass, zydeco, what have you—and there was a printed schedule of who was going to play what on which stage at what time.

I could see several people walking about purposefully with a schedule on which they had marked what they wanted to hear when. I didn't know much about who-was-who in the world of music, so I just wandered from stage to stage listening to whatever was playing, all the while eating crawfish Po'Boys and drinking beer.

I did have a schedule in hand, and it had only one mark on it, and for that, I joined the long queue at the stage—where the great BB King was to perform. I had heard him on the radio and might even have bought an album of his, but just like it had been with the first time I heard James Taylor in concert, it was one thing to listen to him on the airwaves and another to hear him in person. There was, however, a huge difference—between JT and BBK. With James Taylor, the difference between recordings and live was in the purity of live singing. With BB King, the difference was his stage presence. No recording, on audio or even video, could capture that. It had to be experienced. I did, and it was a phenomenal experience.

No other place in America has ever felt like that, not even Nu Orleans on a revisit. I returned to the city in 2013—for the same meeting, this time to present a paper and impart and imbibe demographic research. In the evenings, I went to some places to listen to music, but it was not the same.

On the final morning of the meeting, I sat by the mighty Mississippi (river)—with a coffee and beignet. The river flowed just like it had done 25 years earlier, the water gently lapping the shores, a cool breeze blowing off it, and the sound of distant music wafting in from somewhere in the French Quarter. As I reminisced, a barge loaded with concrete debris floated by and had me smilin' and wonderin' … if the memory of the first visit was really about those 30 minutes with BB King.

It was about the great BBK, but maybe it was about more—about the blues of that stage in the typical journey of a doctoral student, when you are drifting, you have little, you wake up in a cold sweat in the middle of many nights … but once in a while still manage to "let the good times roll."

52

He's Not Here

When you spend seven years in a small place, go running in and out of almost every street in town and wander about here and there, you are bound to have some favourites, some places you are more likely to have been found in than others. In the southern part of heaven, other than the places I lived in, and the places I picked up some learning from, there was really only one regular port of call—'He's Not Here', a classic college town bar.

I am not sure how the place got its name. Maybe it was just something cutesy to draw in college students, or maybe there is a real story about someone's girlfriend or wife calling up the bar to check on the whereabouts of their partner and being told—"He's not here." I don't know. Whatever the origin of the name, He's Not Here was anything but cutesy. It was as basic as bars go, with an entrance tucked away at the back of an open-air alleyway off the main drag through town—Franklin Street. I don't remember there being a sign to signal its position, but some places don't need signs and directions; everyone knows.

The gap-in-the-brick-wall entrance on the left of that alleyway led into an open-air stretch with a tree on either side of the concrete walkway that led to the two-storey structure. The ground floor, which I almost never frequented, had gaming stations. The first floor could be accessed from the enclosed ground floor, but the preferred access was from the outside via a black metal stairway. That first floor was where *the* bar was, and where you could find the essential large screen TV to watch Tar Heel basketball ... and hate Duke!

The bartenders were ordinary folk—college students and a somewhat older and bearded manager. All wore T-shirts and jeans, and the only protocol they had was what was needed to keep the place running in friendly ways. There was no fancy wood panelling, no fancy tables, no fancy food but chips and pretzels, and no fancy drinks other than beer, fizzy drinks and wine coolers.

I have several images of the place in my mind. If I rewind the memory roll a bit and think about weekend nights through the year and the steamy ones in summer—the big cup specials on Tuesdays, in particular—multiple storylines will surely emerge. You can't not have stories if you stay in the same town for seven long years, go to the same place again and again and drink a little too much beer. Here's one that came along some time back and got written up.

One summer, in what we graduate students in economics used to call the n-th year of the PhD, that being anything and everything past the four-year guaranteed university funding period, a cousin of mine came to town from California. He was in Chapel Hill for some conference and was staying at the lovely Carolina Inn. I hadn't seen him in several years, so when he called, I gladly agreed to meet him for a drink. Naturally, I took him to He's Not Here. If I had paid any attention to where he was living those days, and understood the world beyond Chapel Hill, I wouldn't have taken him there, but ... I didn't know much then. Of course, according to the women of my family, I don't know much now either.

It was a weekday, and there weren't many people at He's Not Here. Walking up to the bar, I asked for the standard beer, and cuz asked for "a Perrier with a twist of lemon." I heard that unheard it, and quickly lifted my head to take a big sip of the beer—just to look away, but it was not quick enough to escape the bartender's irritated eyes. The big fella, who knew of my existence because some of my Mallette Street housemates had worked at He's Not Here in the past, pulled me over and quietly said, "Jaiki, tell him we don't serve that shit here." I didn't relate the message in quite those words but told my cousin that they only served beer, soda pop and wine coolers. He politely agreed to have a wine cooler, but I had the sense he had never had one and had no idea what they were. Neither did I.

It being summer and all, I was already more than halfway through my beer, so I suggested I finish the rest, and we go somewhere else. He insisted we stay, but I insisted we leave, and to fortify my case, took another large swig of the daintily held bottle to show that I was already done.

I should explain the dainty holding. It was not a style statement (at HNH there was no such thing), and it was not out of any respect for the beer either. It was just my former housemate Mike's technique of holding a beer bottle by its neck, so body heat from the hand didn't compromise the beer's frostiness.

We extracted ourselves from He's Not Here, and I took him to Spanky's, the bar with wood-panelled ambience, the one where business school and law school students hung out, and the one that always made me feel somewhat uncomfortable. It was not just that I was a poor graduate student subsisting on a stipend. It was this sense that Spanky's was beyond my *aukaat*—that simultaneously comforting and limiting Hindi word that loosely translates to—a sense of worth and position in society. Occasional visits to Spanky's were fine, but my *aukaat* was more in line with He's Not Here. The years have moved on, and I have moved up the economic ladder and can spend longer at Spanky's-like places now, but I am always more at home at HNHs. It's not a statement or anything. That's just how it is.

Anyway, there we were at Spanky's. I ordered a beer and my cousin finally got himself a Perrier with a twist of lemon. We chatted and caught up on each other's lives. He told me he had given up drinking after being in a serious drunk-driving incident when he had crashed a car. I didn't know how to drive a car and couldn't relate to that but was reminded of an incident earlier that summer when I'd had my own run-in with drinks and cops.

My friend Tom lived in Durham, but like all UNC alumni, preferred the watering holes in Chapel Hill. One weekend, he wanted to go out on the town without feeling constrained, so he drove over to my place, parked his car there, and we went to He's Not Here on my motorcycle. He planned to crash on my couch that night and drive back home in the morning.

We had headed out quite late and had a few beers, and time had passed, as it always does on weekends. Soon enough, it was the last call and time to head home. I had parked the bike in the University Square parking lot near my office on the other side of Franklin Street, across from He's Not Here. We walked over there to get the bike.

Tom was much bigger than me, and I was concerned about balancing the bike with him on the back, so I had told him at the outset, on the way to He's Not Here, that he should be ready to put a foot down on the ground as soon as we stopped. Even though I did that instinctively whenever the bike came to a halt, I knew that with him on the back, my foot stabilization would not be enough to keep the bike upright—if he didn't do the same.

I started the bike and turned right on Franklin Street, and got in the turning lane to go left on to Airport Road. I had hoped that it would be a green light so there would be no need to stop, but unfortunately, the light was red. To stop the bike, I pulled in the clutch with the left hand and the break with the right and put my left foot down on the ground. The bike came to a halt, but Tom was a split second late in putting his foot down, and the bike tipped over to the side.

Tip overs had happened to me in the early stages of learning to ride a motorcycle, but that was on a 400cc Honda and never in the heart of town. This was on Franklin Street, at its most visible spot and at a time when the bars were closing and spilling people who were gathering themselves to go home. It was embarrassing, to say the least, but the bigger concern was getting the bike upright before the light turned green again.

A 650cc motorcycle is heavy, so it took a bit of effort to get it back up straight, but I was able to do that without either of us getting off the bike. All seemed fine, except … when I looked in the sideview mirror, I saw a police car right behind us. Even though I had been able to get the bike up reasonably quickly, there was no way the cop in the car would have missed the tip over. I let Tom know who was behind us and told him to stay aligned with me, and reassured him that we'd be fine. When the light turned green, I turned on to Airport Road and drove just under the speed limit with the cop car behind me.

All went well, but I knew that sooner or later, the cop would have to pull us over, and so he did, soon after we passed the police station on the upward stretch of Airport Road. He walked over and asked how much I had had to drink and then asked Tom to stand on the sidewalk so he could administer the manual tests that were required by law—before he could legally ask me to breathe into a mechanical breathalyser.

I hadn't had that much to drink, so I passed the tests without a hitch. He had to let me go, but he wasn't fully convinced, so he said he would follow us home to be sure we got there safe. He did—and we did. Thankfully, the next two lights were green, so no foot-stopping coordination was required till we got home.

I didn't relate this story to my cousin. I didn't think he would have understood it. When we were done—me with my beer and him with his Perrier and twist of lemon—he walked back to Carolina Inn, and I went back to He's Not Here for an ordinary beer, to be held daintily but drunk quickly before the heat of a North Carolina summer night sapped its fizz.

53

Syrupy sleep

"If a man does not keep pace with his companions, perhaps it is because he hears a different drummer. Let him step to the music which he hears, however measured or far away."

I am not much for quotes. I have a hard time remembering who said what, but this one from Henry David Thoreau, the great 19th century American philosopher, naturalist, poet and much more, is one I have not forgotten. It comes from 'Walden', a longish essay Thoreau wrote in the year or two he spent in the woods around Walden Pond in Massachusetts. The individualistic spirit of the quote resonated with me the very first time I read it, but the essay was tough going ... because it always came along on Tuesdays and Thursdays when maple syrup would drag down eyelids and put me to sleep.

I was at the stage of the PhD program when the four-year funding from the university had dried up, and I was doing whatever on-campus work I could do to get by. The research assistant job I had with a family doctor studying Alzheimer's patients in specialized clinics was winding down, and I was looking for something else. A more senior research associate position was on offer, but then in a casual conversation with the director of the international student office, I found out that under a student visa, I could work off-campus if he certified that it was going to contribute to professional development. Till then, I had understood practical training as being possible only for the post-degree phase, but apparently, it was also available pre-completion. That meant I could do what a lot of stragglers at UNC did—teach introductory economics at North Carolina State University in Raleigh.

NC State had a clever strategy—a classic economist approach. To teach three sections of an introductory economics course, they offered us twice what we could typically earn as research assistants. To make it even more tempting, they scheduled classes on Tuesdays and Thursdays, so it would only take two days away from our own thesis work. They further sweetened the deal by having exams set up with multiple-choice questions and a machine-readable answer sheet. All you had to do was prepare once, deliver three times, write up exam questions, and you'd get double the money.

It was great for State's economics department because they got introductory economics taught in small class settings for a third of what they would have had to pay regular assistant professors. In the language of economics, it was 'an efficient outcome,' and so it continued year after year. Markets are like that—they are about narrowly defined value and the efficiency of the outcome. They are not about equity, fairness, ethics and all those other things that really, really make us who we are. My economist brethren and sistren are often so thoroughly tangled up in efficiency, they forget that the ultimate social goal is the humanity of human beings, not the efficiency of their existence.

In the fall of 1988, I started teaching at State. There were five of us who would pack into a car and drive over to Raleigh. Interstate

40 hadn't opened up yet, so it was North Carolina Highway 54. The first class was the early morning one, so we would leave in the dark, around 6:30 or so. The second tended to be around lunchtime and the third was mid-afternoon. By the time we headed back, it was late in the evening, and all you wanted was a cold beer. At first, I tried to see if the beer wanted thesis research for company, but it didn't much care, so I gave up on getting them to tango on those two days.

A regular part of the Tuesday-Thursday routine was breakfast after the early morning class. We would head over to this nondescript restaurant on Hillsborough Street, the main stretch running along State's rather nondescript campus. I'll admit that is a UNC bias that applies with even greater vehemence to Duke's out-of-period Gothic buildings. When you spend six and a half years in Chapel Hill, you lose all objectivity and learn to never apologize for any disparaging remarks about State and Duke. It is somewhat juvenile but in a harmless way.

At breakfast, I always got the stack of three pancakes. It was the best deal on the menu, a notch better than 'Pigs in a blanket' which was the same stack but with sausages. Much as I liked the salty interlude, I was quite happy to skip the pigs and go with a small glass of cold milk to wash down the sweetness of the syrup. The blankets soaked in butter and maple syrup hit many spots—in the gut and the heart—and were eminently satisfying, especially as the temperature dropped further in the fall.

Breakfast done, we'd walk back to our shared temporary office and do time till the next class. I would begin with Thoreau's Walden, which I had picked up at Bull's Head, the UNC campus bookshop, but the reading never lasted long. I would invariably succumb to the soporific pull of the syrup-soaked blankets and either put up my feet on the desk or put my head down on it and shut shop for a few minutes. Nap done, I would get back into Thoreau and take an imaginary wander with him in the Walden woods and try and make sense of his prose.

The "different drummer" quote is a line in "Walden" that appears at the very end, in the "Conclusion" chapter. It is not set up with a flourish and dramatic distinction and positioning—to be a quotable quote (someday). It is simply the second line of a paragraph that appears at the end of a long and, at times hard to follow, essay of 18 chapters. Given the syrupy-sleep interrupted reading over many weeks, I am not sure when I got to the "drummer" line, but I am very sure that when I did—it resonated. It had to have reassured me that in stepping to a different drummer, time and time again, I wasn't the fool that periodic doubt made me feel sometimes. Thirty-plus years later, more can be said about all of that, but I'll leave that for another time; best to get back to this story and complete it.

A couple of years back, on Father's Day, the women in the house wanted to go out for brunch. I don't much care for Hallmark 'days,' but sometimes I am happy to go along with the way things roll. We went to Mama Brown, a basic restaurant in foody Wellington that serves delicious brunch food in an easy-going setting. It usually takes me ages to figure out what to order, but that day it took but a second—one look at the menu, and I ordered the waffles. If pancakes had been on the menu, they might have posed a bit of a dilemma, but I am quite sure I would have still gone with waffles because of a preference for their crispiness – of texture and memory of daily encounters with them, six years before the one with Tuesday-Thursday pancakes.

In my first year in America, at Davidson College, I was on a 19-meal plan in the large self-serve cafeteria called Commons. The variety and unlimited quantity of food available at the cafeteria were mindboggling. It took me a while to adjust to that, but once I settled in, I discovered that at breakfast, they had two waffle makers set up on a side table with batter and spray cans, and you could make as many waffles as you wanted. On cross-country road trips, I had gotten to know the crispy, golden Belgian waffle very well, and we had become good friends. Discovery of the waffle makers at the Commons meant waffles didn't have to be road-trip food but could be part of regular breakfast fare, and so they did—with cold milk as accompaniment. You see, the syrupy pancake-and-cold milk combination habit indulged in while teaching at NC State had its origins in that syrupy waffle-and-cold milk combination at Davidson College!

Back to Mama Brown, being a man of combinations, I naturally looked at the menu for cold milk. To my great disappointment, they didn't have any. Mama Brown only does milkshakes, and while I have a story for those too, a milkshake doesn't go with syrupy pancakes—too much sugar. When the waitress came along, I hesitantly asked if I could get a small glass of cold milk with the waffles. She must have been southern, American, that is, for she smilingly said: "I am sure that can be arranged."

So, I had waffles and cold milk and then, with a "what the heck" mindset, ordered a side of southern fried chicken. I don't know why, but maybe because of the name of the restaurant ... and its association with Mama Dip's, a heavenly "southern cooking" restaurant on Rosemary Street in Chapel Hill that I had eaten at more than once in graduate school years. The fried chicken that came along at Mama Brown was otherworldly and, with apologies to my Carolina cousins and fans of Mama Dip's, better than any I ever had in the southern part of heaven. The net outcome of all that consumption was a snooze on the couch with feet propped up on the coffee table—kinda like it used to be when syrupy blankets used to put me to sleep in Raleigh, North Carolina.

54

Satanic Verses

Amma had a habit of signing, dating and place-marking the books she owned. I have only a few of her books, and most of them have her beautiful rounded open-spaced signature, the year of the book's acquisition, and the city it was acquired in. When I started buying books in graduate school, I did the same. The nice thing about that habit is that the dates and places noted on the books help reconstruct memories, though that isn't always needed for books like Salman Rushdie's 'Satanic Verses'—they imprint without ink.

There is a long, long list of controversial, challenged, banned books in the English language. Put in the term "controversial books 20th century" in a search engine, and you might be surprised by the titles that show up and the ones amongst them that are now considered classics of literature. 'Satanic Verses' is on that list. To say it was controversial when it was published is an understatement. It was the equivalent of the prophet cartoons of recent times, though, unlike the cartoons, it did not take a direct pot-shot at Islam. It is allegorical, not literal, but … to illiterates and intemperates, it is all the same.

The book was published in Britain in September 1988 and immediately generated controversy. Its import was banned in India, but somewhat strangely, its possession was not a criminal offence. In those days, I used to subscribe to the monthly Indian news magazine, 'India Today.' In it, I read about the protests and the ban and was not entirely surprised by the typically spineless response of the Indian government, then led by the Congress party and its so-called modern leader, Rajiv Gandhi.

For those who vent their anger and frustration at the current state of affairs in India, it is worth spending a few minutes thinking about what preceded it and who weakened the secular foundations of the country and enabled the emergence of "the new republic." What politicians did then, and still do, is not particularly surprising, but what was appalling was that even a venerated writer like Khushwant Singh advocated the ban.

After the initial disappointment, I forgot about the whole issue because at that stage, I was more concerned with my own floundering in graduate school. In a classic case of hubris, I had decided to do a masters in biostatistics while working on the proposal for the doctoral thesis in economics. The additional academic work was entirely manageable, but the course work in biostatistics became the excuse for not focussing on some of the challenges that arose with the proposal. The result was that student life had dragged on past the planned four years in graduate school, and in 1988 I was into a sixth year with the masters mostly done, but with no end in sight to the PhD I had started with.

Things turned around by the end of that year—after a couple of hearty Johnnie Walker Black Label sessions with my friend Madhav in Manhattan over the New Year break. When I got back to Chapel Hill, I got more focused, and by the time spring came along had matters under control. I would do serious research work during the day and then read fiction at night. That was, in many ways, a perfect year, one in which the yin and yang in my head were at peace with each other.

Those were solitary years. After two years of living in a group house, I had decided that the only way I would finish graduate school would be if I got away from all distractions and lived on my own. I had been prepared to pay more for going solo but got lucky when I found a professor's advertisement for an efficiency apartment on the side of a house—built around a swimming pool. For a rent not too much more than what I was paying in the group house, I had an air-conditioned efficiency apartment with one side made of glass that looked out onto trees on the property. The apartment had its own bathroom and a separate entrance but no kitchen which, in some ways, was no different to my earlier group house arrangement where I did not use the common kitchen.

The only catch was that I had to agree to stay in town every weekend and walk the dog, feed the cats, and bring in the mail. The owners had a beach house in the Outer Banks in North Carolina, and they drove out to it every weekend and needed someone to watch the house while they were gone. On the weekends, I could access the house, the pool and the large kitchen. I wasn't going anywhere on the weekends anyway, so it was a great deal.

I had been living in that apartment for two years when, in the summer of '89, 'Satanic Verses' came back into consciousness. Earlier that year, Iran's supreme religious leader, Ayatollah Ruhollah Khomeini, had issued a *fatwa* (a death warrant) against Salman Rushdie. That was big news, especially in liberal Chapel Hill. I wanted to know what the fuss was all about and was tempted to get a copy of the book and find out right then, but resisted the temptation, for once staying focussed on my academic work.

When summer came along, and things were even more firmly under control, I went over to an alternative bookstore on Rosemary

Street and bought a hardbound copy of Satanic Verses. It was a typically hot and steamy summer weekend. Instead of going to the Carolina Population Center to work on statistical analysis of survey data, I stayed closeted in the efficiency apartment and uncloseted my mind by following Farishta and Chamcha, the two protagonists of the novel.

'Satanic Verses' is the only book I have ever read non-stop. I was completely mesmerized by Rushdie's imagination and wordsmithery. Earlier in the year, I had read "One Hundred Years of Solitude" by Gabriel Garcia Marquez, and this rode the same wavelengths of magical realism. The next couple of days, I walked around in a daze, and the next couple of years led to reading more of the same, including Rushdie's even more masterful 'Midnight's Children'.

I wanted to share the book with my mother, but it was banned in India. I didn't want to wait till my next trip home, so I decided to send it to her by post. She was leading a quiet retired life in Indore, and it wouldn't have been such a big deal for her to receive a banned book by post, especially since its possession was not a criminal offence in India. But I didn't want to get her into any trouble, so I photocopied the entire book and sent it to her in three separate manila envelopes spaced a few days apart. Deviance had always been pleasurable, and to employ it to share the genius of imagination—well, how could I not?

She read it but didn't like it. She said the modern style of writing, particularly its use of sexual imagery, didn't appeal to her. She preferred the more classical stuff she had taught for 40 years. According to her, the writing in that literature was understated and left imagination unfettered. My preferences were different; back then, my imagination needed a helping hand. These days it doesn't, but I still like to fly about with the masters of the written word.

It has been more than 30 years since I read Satanic Verses. Over time our collection of books has grown and moved with us—from one dwelling to another, from one city to another, from one continent to another. Each time the books have been boxed and unboxed, I have looked for the hardback copy of 'Satanic Verses' bought on Rosemary Street in Chapel Hill and have not found it. Each time I have told myself I should get a replacement copy but never gotten around to it. Finishing this story has led to ordering it from an on-line store. I'll be eager to see if it holds me spellbound now as it did 30 plus years ago. I am sure it will.

55

Baseball

The LA Dodgers lost the World Series to the Boston Red Sox in 2018. That was big news to some people, little news to others, and no news to most. I am in that last category. I don't follow baseball, finding it almost as painful to watch as cricket. To aficionados of those sports that might sound like blasphemy, and in the offended-by-everything world we live in, that might be hurtful and insensitive to some. So be it. I "ain't apologizin' to nobody."

Most years, I have no idea who is on bat and who is not, but in October 2018, I tuned in. It came about because one day, I happened to be lolling around on the internet, saw the score of the second Dodgers-Red Sox game on ESPN and read a short article on the series. I might not be able to bear watching some sports, but I thoroughly enjoy sports writing of all sorts, and as a result, I often tune into sports I have little interest in. The article said the Dodgers were down by two games in a best-of-seven series against the Red Sox, and there was a chance of them getting swept in four.

That article hooked me in, and I paid attention to the epic third game, which went all the way to infinity. Doing that while watching a regional rugby championship and the beginnings of a New Zealand All Blacks rugby game says something about the hook and that third game. Eventually, the Dodgers caved, and the Red Sox won, and in itself that wouldn't have meant a thing, but the games and the contestants had triggered invitations to wander back in time, and so I went along—first to 1982, then to 1990—to my two stints at little Davidson College in North Carolina.

The first wander through Davidson was as a student, and of the two, it was the more meaningful one because that is when I learnt to think—carefully in the box and also out of it. The years before, at St Stephen's College and Modern School, were about doing well in exams, not really about thinking - independently, critically or creatively (ICC). It really did begin at Davidson, partly in economics courses, but mostly in philosophy, political science and American literature. That ICC way of thinking has progressed, regressed, and digressed to the point where I am now—so thoroughly without box that I doubt Davidson would want to acknowledge my expression of gratitude.

It was during that first run through Davidson that I encountered the Dodgers. Not long after getting there, I was invited to Charlie Ratliff's house one evening. He was a highly respected professor of economics but was on sabbatical that year, so I couldn't take any courses with him, but he was in town, so I got to meet him a couple of times. Tall, with a thick mop of hair and glasses, he reminded me of Gregory Peck in 'To Kill a Mockingbird', though, unlike the more stern-looking Atticus, he was disarmingly friendly. He and his wife, Mary Virginia, were home-bred southern folk but had also wandered the world. They had spent a year or more in Pakistan and had a particular fondness for south Asia. That's how I, along with a couple of Pakistani students, ended up at their house that evening.

At that time, I was reading the Swedish economist Gunnar Myrdal's tome, 'Asian Drama'. It is an exploration of development issues in Asia, so I had a lot of questions for Professor Ratliff. We sat around and chatted, and I wondered aloud if my plan to go on to do a PhD was pointless and if I shouldn't just head back after Davidson and join the administrative service to tackle the "soft state" problem Myrdal had highlighted. He dissuaded me, arguing that ideas were just as important as actions.

It went on like that, one topic to another, education in an evening. At one point, Mary Virginia excused herself to go to the back porch, saying, "I have to catch up on the day's action." I must have looked puzzled, so Dr Ratliff clarified: "She has to catch up on the baseball scores of the day." I thought that was amusing. I knew what baseball was, but I had no idea how deeply ingrained it was and is in American storylines.

When she came back to the living room, I tried to make polite talk by asking her about the sport and teams, and that's when she told me that while baseball was of interest, her real focus was the Dodgers. It wasn't because she had anything to do with Los Angeles, where they were based, but because at one point they had been the Brooklyn Dodgers and had been the first team to integrate by signing the great African American baseball player Jackie Robinson. I didn't know anything about any of that, but that little tidbit stuck.

Over time, I would learn more about America's original sin—the colour line—and about the 60s, integration, civil rights, and Jackie Robinson. And I would also meet and befriend several more Mary Virginias and Charlies in North Carolina and Washington DC, and elsewhere. Their commitment to inclusion, respect, dignity, and human values—for all humans—impressed me and had a huge impact.

If you are who you think you are—more than what others think you are—then one foundation of my identity was laid in that fall of 1982 and then nurtured in Chapel Hill. Of course, the real foundations were laid much earlier. I was born to parents who had married outside their communities and grew up in an India in the infancy of independence when nation-building was of paramount importance and the founding myth— 'unity in diversity' —was more about unity than diversity. Sadly, the current atmosphere of divisiveness with the wearing of religion and language and origin and whatnot on one's sleeve, celebratory as it may be of cultural pride, is the antithesis of that age of innocence I grew up in. I miss that.

That first encounter with the Dodgers didn't lead into baseball. Davidson led to Chapel Hill, and in the southern part of heaven, only one ball—basketball—was king. There were other sports, and I did watch American football, soccer, field hockey, lacrosse, and track and field ... but never baseball. It didn't have a chance, though it did get another entry point.

Summers in small university towns in the southern part of America are slow. Most students are away, temperature soars, and the humidity is stifling. About the only game in town is cold beer and minor league baseball games if there is a team nearby. There was one —the Durham bulls—in nearby Durham, and while I did go along to a couple of their games, it was more for the outing than for the baseball. Even 'Bull Durham,' the hugely successful romcom movie based on that team, and released in 1988, didn't get me going.

The best chance for baseball came the following year with the movie 'Field of Dreams.' I wouldn't have known about it, but my friend Tom wanted to see it, so I went along, not expecting anything more than a typical Hollywood movie with Kevin Costner, who had also starred in Bull Durham.

Five minutes into the movie and I was hooked into the dreamy storyline with the cornfield scene and—"If you build it, he will come." That line is not much more than a whisper that Ray Kinsella, the Berkeley-attending 60s liberal, hears as he is walking through the cornrows with a baseball bat in hand. At first, Ray doesn't understand it, but when it comes, again and again, he figures it means he should mow down a part of his cornfield and build a baseball diamond. His fantastical reasoning is that if he does that, "he"—Shoeless Joe Jackson— will come. Shoeless Joe was the White Sox player banned from baseball for his alleged association with fixing the World Series, the finals of American professional baseball, in 1919.

Field of Dreams is set in the late 80s, and Shoeless Joe had been dead and gone a long time, so if you are looking for logic and reason, the storyline makes no sense. But in a fantasy story with crazy, zany dreams, reason and time don't matter. What matters is … well, whatever you want the dream to mean.

Ray Kinsella follows the voice and clears part of his cornfield, and builds a baseball diamond in the middle of nowhere—that timeless place where pointless dreams are born and live lives full of point. And Shoeless Joe does come, as do several other baseball players from the past—all men whose dreams came to nought.

The movie grabbed me like no other. It made little difference to me that it was about baseball, and even after seven years in America, I still didn't know much about the game. It was because the story was about more than baseball. It was about dreams and reconciliation, and I knew a thing or two about that. I don't know whether I watched 'Field of Dreams' again that year; it would not be the least bit out of the ordinary. What I do know is that soon after the movie was released on VHS, I bought it—even though I didn't have a VCR! I must have figured that someday I would buy a VCR and want to watch the movie again, and likely choke up at the end, as I always have.

That purchase remained a bit of an embarrassment, but of a quirky innocent sort that I ended up mentioning to one of my colleagues when I joined Davidson College's economics department in August of 1990 for a one-year teaching stint. Allison had joined at the same time, and we both had to teach one section of introductory economics each semester. In the second semester, hers turned out to be the early morning class and mine the afternoon one. Not being a morning person, she offered to buy me a VCR in exchange for trading course times. I was tempted and might even have gone along—except I didn't have a TV!

A TV and a VCR did come along later, and the tape I had bought was watched, and like a lot of other possessions, travelled back and forth to different cities and continents and countries. It is still there in the TV cabinet, and there is a TV on top of that cabinet, but now there is no VCR. Time has moved along, and technology has obsolesced the VHS tape ... but not the memory. Working on this story has compelled me to stream the movie and watch it again. It still grabs me as it did in 1989, but I don't see it leading me to baseball any time soon!

56

Cinema Paradiso

If I hadn't had a dinner plan with a friend ... nothing would have changed. My life trajectory would not have altered, and no counterfactual 'if-then' would have been set up for reminiscing, reflecting, regretting. Really, it wouldn't have made any difference at all if I had done what I was tempted to do—walk right back into the Dupont Circle movie theatre I had just come out of and seen Cinema Paradiso a second time. Such was the magic of that delightful movie that I seriously considered calling Marvin and cooking up an excuse.

It was the summer of '90, and I had ridden up my black 650cc Suzuki motorcycle from Chapel Hill to Washington DC to scope out a job for the following year. I had a one-year teaching gig lined up at Davidson College for the year ahead, but I was looking beyond that year and had come up to the big city, chasing up a couple of leads at the World Bank that one of my advisors had given me.

I had called up one of the leads, and out of courtesy to my advisor, more than interest in me, she had agreed to meet. It wasn't much of a meeting other than the formalities of—hullo, how is so and so, what are you doing, and I don't have anything on right now, but I'll take your CV if something comes up. I had the sense nothing would come of it. It didn't matter. The mojo that had gone missing for a couple of years was back, and I had the feeling that it would all work out. That great Indian saying that provides false assurance aplenty—"*ho jayega*" (it will get done)—was the spirit of that time, so it didn't bother me much that my CV likely ended up in the trash not long after I left that meeting.

It was a hot summer day, a bit less humid than usual for July. I didn't have anything else to do after that meeting for the next few hours, so I walked back up the way I had come—towards Dupont Circle. Downtown DC is a fairly logical grid of lettered and numbered streets that criss-cross each other at right angles, with a few diagonal avenues to throw you off a bit, but not by much. Navigating the grid is not that difficult because getting from A to B means going along straight lines and turning a few straight-angled turns. That's for normal people. Then there are those like me, who intend to go that way, but end up wandering off to C and D and 'hereandthere' in between because, well, because our minds wander off with dreams and themes that aren't always logically angled. It is anxiety-ridden in the moment but amusing in retrospect.

The wandering off course that day didn't matter much. I had time, and time had let me loose to walk my walk, and when it is that way, you don't care much about detours. They are, in some way, part of the intended route. It took a little bit longer than normal, but eventually, I got to Dupont Circle with a couple of hours to spare.

There was a movie theatre right there at the meeting point of Connecticut Avenue and 19th street, and I did what I had often done since turning 13—I walked into the movie theatre all by myself to see Cinema Paradiso. For some, movies are a social experience. For me, they are that, but more about stepping into a story and being in it, not as one of the characters but as an onlooker, a wide-eyed villager blown away by city lights. You could say it is the reverse of that thoroughly delightful Woody Allen movie, 'The Purple Rose of Cairo', wherein one of the characters, Tom Baxter, walks out of the movie he is in to meet Cecilia, the waitress who goes to watch movies to get away from her bleak life.

The fact that I had no idea what the movie was about made no difference. There was a poster that said something about all the Best Foreign Language Film awards the movie had picked up, and that probably was how I chose it over the Hollywood alternatives on offer. The motorcycle ride up to DC, the pointless CV-dropping, and the stage of life I was at—all had me in a dreamy state of mind. You could say Cinema Paradiso was pre-ordained.

The tape rolled, and within minutes, had me hooked. Two hours later, when I walked out of the theatre, I was in a daze and considered going rogue, like little six-year-old Salvatore in the movie and calling off the dinner date. But I didn't; a rebel with a cause is not quite the same as a rebel without one. I had come up to DC on the motorcycle wearing a James Deanesque brown leather jacket I had bought off a Spiegel catalogue for 150 dollars, but unlike James Deane in the movie Rebel Without a Cause, I wasn't a teenager, and I had a cause that wouldn't let me go rogue.

Dinner was lovely, the night that followed was even more fun, and the next day I headed back to Chapel Hill to pack up and move further south to Davidson, the small town with two signal lights. The haze of the daze cleared as a new act of my own movie opened up. It was a hard life of an end-stage doctoral student teaching full time and squeezing in work on the thesis. I didn't have a TV and did little else but prepare to teach, teach, and work on my thesis. The simple pleasures were a crazy, rebellious puppy named Maria and occasional outings with friends.

With no TV and no movies with stories to walk into, there wasn't much happening on the entertainment scene ... till I ran into Cinema Paradiso again. It came about because American colleges and universities used to have this wonderful set-up where they contracted with a movie consolidator and got a chunk of movies that they showed once or twice a week, either free or for a token dollar or two. I had seen some great movies as a student at Davidson and then in Chapel Hill, but I wasn't in student mode anymore, so I don't know how it came about that I ran across the year's movie list.

Imagine my delight—three screenings of Cinema Paradiso over two weeks! I told myself I would attend at least one and also told students in the senior courses I was teaching that if they wanted to watch a great movie, they should check it out. I showed up twice, and several of them did too.

What was most interesting about this iteration of Cinema Paradiso was that after the screening, a couple of the students insisted on discussing the movie with me. They wondered if, at the very end, there is a hint that Salvatore gets back together with a girlfriend he had as an adolescent. I hadn't paid any attention to that angle the first time, or even these two more times. There is a bar scene at the very end of the movie that could be interpreted that way, but I was quite happy with the ambiguity of it all. To me, stories don't have to have happy endings or any ending at all; they can just stay unfettered strands that can go any which way the 'mindwinds' blow.

That's how it stayed till life turned another chapter, and I got a proper job and had some money and ended up at a record store and impulsively bought a videocassette of the movie. Unlike the earlier purchase of a tape of 'Field of Dreams'—the movie that had grabbed me the year before Cinema Paradiso—this time around, I did have a VCR, so I watched it yet again. Later, when I got married to Sumi, we watched it together, but only one time. I must have forgotten about the conversations in Davidson because I didn't look for the signs students had pointed out in either of the post-Davidson viewings.

The repeat-watching paused, and that story gathered dust ... till I ran into the movie again in a record store in Bangalore. By then, technology had obsolesced out videocassettes and replaced them with DVDs, and there in front of me was a DVD of Cinema Paradiso with the added lure of being the director's cut—the longer uncut version of the movie. I was older by this time, had a bit more money, so I bought it. I should never have.

The uncut version shows the older Salvatore at Alfredo's funeral spotting a girl who looks exactly like the younger Elena, who was his love in adolescence. He follows her and meets the now older Elena, who is her mother, and there is reminiscing and regretting and other details that ... if you haven't seen the uncut version, can cut straight to Wikipedia and find out.

I didn't like the director's cut—at all. At first, I thought the ending tarnishes the 'paradiso' (paradise) because it takes away ambiguity, but now I think what it actually does is somehow tarnish the 'paradiso' of the first viewing in Dupont Circle. The firsts of anything are special in ways no seconds or thirds or more can be.

I still have the DVD but have never watched it again, and probably won't. I also have the VHS tape, and while I don't have a VCR to play it, I have no intention of tossing it. I like keeping old memories.

57

Beautiful Maria of my soul

When she came to me, I was reading Oscar Hijuelos' 'The Mambo Kings Play Songs of Love.' It is a richly textured story of two Cuban musicians who emigrate to New York in the 1950s. The older one, Cesar, is flamboyant, while the younger one, Nestor, is soulful and yearns for a girlfriend back in Cuba. He writes a song—'Beautiful Maria of my soul'— to her memory, and it is one of many that the Mambo Kings play in bars and clubs in New York and elsewhere.

Hijuelos wove magic in that novel and justly won the Pulitzer Prize for it. You can watch a Hollywoodized movie version of the novel, but it has none of Hijuelos' word mastery in it, just snazzy Armand Assante and Antonio Banderas putting it on, but not putting it out.

I had just started teaching at Davidson College and, for some inexplicable reason, told some colleagues at a 'new faculty' orientation that I wanted to get a dog and learn to play the saxophone. They were both great ideas but bad for the times because besides teaching a full load of courses, I was also working on my doctoral thesis. In that set-up, saxophone and dog wouldn't have fit, but things had been said, and all I can say is that while I deeply regret my lips not touching a saxophone, I am glad they didn't. "Dawg"—well, that story followed its own trajectory.

Just about when I had settled into the semester and got a routine going, she came along on a fateful Tuesday, or possibly Thursday. That day, after finishing an early lecture, I walked over to the café in the student union to get a coffee and doughnut. The coffee was American-style paper-filter drip coffee and always crap, but the honey glazed doughnut was always divine.

On that walk over to the café, I had seen a black-and-tan puppy running around outside the entrance to Chambers, the main Davidson College building, but not paid much attention. Back in the office, I was just settling into the bad coffee and the good doughnut and looking at notes for the next lecture when Catherine, one of the academics in the French department, walked into my office and in her very French accent said, "Jaiki, you wanted a dog, here is a dog." She had that same black-and-tan puppy in her arms. She was the local finder of cats and dogs and was doing what she did. I had opened my stupid mouth, and now there was a little puppy running around in my narrow office.

At that point, I could have said no, but I didn't. Instead, I carried the puppy over to Catherine's house to get a leash and then walked her over to my place. The dog-cat finder put up lost-and-found posters around town but didn't expect anyone to claim the abandoned puppy. No one did. That's how I came to have a live-in companion while teaching and working on my thesis.

She came when I was just getting into the Oscar Hijuelos story, so naturally, I named her Maria. Being a teething puppy, she ripped up Mambo Kings and chewed on my running shoes and many other things. The book, I was able to tape up and finish reading, the shoes, I had to keep on top of the closet all year. The rest, well, we got by somehow. The damage she did to the box springs under the mattress when she went under it and ripped out the lining, the window blinds she chewed while sitting by the window watching Davidson's slow world pass by the gas station directly in front, and the carpet she so thoroughly peed through, even three steam cleanings didn't fix? That was all permanent. It was the cost Davidson College absorbed for renting me that indistinct single-bedroom brick house on zero deposit back in 1990-91.

She was black and tan, and short and long, or as a friend who tried to help me in my futile attempts to learn French a year later, often said—"petite et grosse." People would ask me what breed she was, and I could never answer that well. Her big paws and low centre of gravity said she was Basset Hound, but she wasn't as dopey eyed and restful as them. Her colours said she was more likely a mix of Beagle and Rottweiler, and that might be right because she sure did carry the traits of both breeds. The Beagle bit would light up at the sight of a squirrel, and the Rottweiler bit would chew into anything.

Of all her genetic strains, the Beagle part was the most fun and frustrating. In Davidson, I would take her for walks on the trails and let her off the leash. She'd stay close for a while and then sight a squirrel or a cat or a wild rabbit or a deer or anything and take off. It was fun to watch her get excited and chase them, but frustrating when no calling, cajoling would bring her back. It was the same in dog parks in DC in subsequent years, on the beaches in Mozambique, and back in the woods behind our house in Carrboro in later years. Anything chaseable was chased. She never caught any of them but never gave up.

I can rewind the tape on many of those chases and smile now, as I always did at their start, but they always ended up tearing my hair out. On more than one occasion, I gave up trying to find her, but she always did come back—when she felt like it. In the first two years, I tried to train her, but I was stressed and didn't have patience. A couple of days of training would go well, and I'd see progress and start feeling confident enough to let her off the leash... only to have a squirrel come along somewhere distant and have her take off after it. Eventually, I just gave up trying to train her. The dog had too much character to fall into prescribed patterns. That's just how she was.

Those chases may have been because of the Beagle gene she carried, but ultimately what dominated was the phenotypic strain emerging from her developmental environment—she was a stray and never lost the instinct for garbage. Goodness, the crap she would get into, anywhere and everywhere, from the garbage can at home, to the dog droppings in parks she would roll on, to what the tide brought in at the Costa de Sol beach in Maputo, Mozambique. It was remarkable. The number of times I shampooed the stink out of her fur, only I know.

She was a family member, or as I liked to mimic Cheech Marin, as Tito the street dog in the animation movie, 'Oliver': "(s)he's family, (s)he's 'bluud'." She moved with me to Washington, DC the year following Davidson, and then to Maputo, Mozambique after Sumi and I got married, then back to the US—to Baltimore, then DC, then Chapel Hill.

She was, in some ways, my firstborn and was there when the girls came along in DC. People say dogs are great companions for little kids and are gentle and watchful. Maria wasn't really like that at all. For her, the girls were sources of food, nothing more. She would sit under their highchairs and wait for them to drop food and wouldn't hesitate to grab it from their hands. She had no other interest in them, and they too learnt to leave her alone.

When we decided to move from Chapel Hill to Bangalore in 2003, there was no question she was coming with us. A dog crate was purchased, and as with her previous cross-continental travels to Europe and Africa, she was given two sleeping pills for the 23-hour journey from Raleigh-Durham airport to Frankfurt and then on to Bangalore. That was the longest she had travelled, but it seemed to make no difference. She picked up right where she had left off, searching for food scraps in the apartment building we lived in and sniffing around at garbage on walks in the neighbourhood. The only thing that changed was the leash let-offs—there was no scope for those in India.

At that point, she was 13 years old, had started having epileptic seizures and was on strong medication with a poor prognosis for the future. The remarkable thing about the move to India was that instead of declining in health, she actually got better. The incredible vet who came by every few months put her on a combination of liquid vitamins and altered her diet to have more vegetables, and that brought her phenobarbital dosage down for a couple of years.

Life, unfortunately, has only so many legs to run on, and by mid-2005, hers were giving in. She had difficulty walking and would stay on the balcony most of the day. Most importantly, for a dog that had always been interested in food, she no longer seemed interested in picking up scraps. That summer, we went to the US to wrap up our lives there and left her in a kennel on the outskirts of town. She was happy to see us when we returned from that trip but looked weaker than before.

Within a month of returning, I had to turn around and head out to Geneva for a week on some consulting work. The first night back, I brought her in from the balcony, having to carry her because she couldn't get up. I sat with her on the floor that night with her head in my lap and stroked her for a bit. She seemed to like that.

By the time the next day dawned, she was gone—chasing squirrels somewhere else. It was almost as if she had waited for me to come back from Geneva to make her final dash off the leash. That morning I sat with her, coffee in hand, tears and smiles and all, and thought—not many a dog gets to traverse three continents, leave her mark in three countries, vacation in the Algarve in Portugal and on the beautiful beaches of Mozambique, and make more stories than can fit in one book chapter.

She sure was beautiful Maria of my soul!

58

Fishing in familiar waters

I met him in the summer of '83, in the mountains of western North Carolina at Camp High Rocks, a land tucked away from the road that runs somewhere from Brevard to ... nowhere, really. Roads and pathways in the mountains are like that. If you are there, you better be in their frame of mind—happy to go from somewhere to nowhere—else the mountains won't like you, and you won't like them, and you'll want to leave, and they'll be all too happy to have you gone. Most of those who spent time at Camp High Rocks were in that happy-to-be-there frame of mind, and the mountains liked having them there.

Lee was an upper senior camper, which in the age classification of High Rocks meant he had just about come to the end of the journey as a camper and needed to move on. Most upper senior campers had been at camp for several years and knew the ropes. They understood the simple culture of High Rocks but were also at a point in life where it grated against the consumerist and competitive world

316

they inhabited most of the year. It was tough for all the campers who were from well-off families, but it might have been particularly tough for those adolescents.

I didn't really have much interaction with him that first time around, but the following summer, when I had been promoted to head junior counsellor, and he had transitioned from paying camper to junior counsellor, we interacted a bit more. He was engaged in outdoor activities like hiking and riding while I stayed on camp doing the artsy stuff. In those small interactions, I found out that his real passion in life was not camping, riding, or hiking, but fishing. He didn't get to do that at High Rocks, but that's what moved him. His friends joked that his photo album was filled with captions like "the fish I caught when I was 6" and "the fish I caught at 14." Everything else was incidental to Lee. I thought that was amusing but didn't think much more than that.

Life moved on, and I forgot all about him and High Rocks for the next several years till I landed up at Davidson College in the late summer of 1990—this time to teach. It was then that I ran into him again. I was teaching economics, and one of my students was friends with him, and one day brought him along to my office. Lee remembered who I was, which is not that unusual because I would have been the only Indian he would have encountered during his many summers at High Rocks. Somewhat embarrassedly, he asked if I remembered him. Of course, I did. How could I not—remember the boy and the fishes he had caught at different ages?

Once I was done teaching the first semester, I invited the two of them to dinner in the quirky little one-bedroom house I was renting from the College. It was a rectangular house positioned right on South Main Street, just after the road had passed the college campus and the few shops that sold ... I don't remember what. It was oddly positioned, with one short side facing the road and the long one (with the front door) steps away from a small gas station with a repair shop. I have to guess that before the college bought the property, the gas station owner must have lived in that house.

The house was as barebones as you could get with a small bedroom, a functional bathroom, a tiny study, and a living room with a kitchenette. You'd be tempted to think it was a step down from the place I had last lived in—an apartment in a house built around a pool in an upscale neighbourhood of Chapel Hill—but I didn't think of it that way. To me, it was a step up. It was one block from the college campus, had space enough for me and my dog and the friends who came over occasionally, and was a standalone "single-family home." What more did I need?

I had a very focused life at that time with only a handful of friends, mostly colleagues at Davidson. I would meet up with two of them, Barbara and Arnold, a historian and a psychologist, once a week at the one restaurant in town. We'd talk about this and that and … thisandthat, which somehow always came around to the oddity of a progressive liberal arts college in a small conservative town only 20 miles from the largest city in North Carolina. If you've lived in one of those places, you'll know what I mean; if you haven't, you won't, and I am not sure whether that is good or bad.

The historian and psychologist introduced me to the multi-disciplinarian—Jack Daniels—and we became friends, not in a needy way but in a somewhat spiritual way. You may be tempted to think Jack Daniels is whisky or whiskey with the extra e—if you are of Irish inclination—but that is on a technicality. In fact, Jack Daniels is bourbon. I didn't know that back then, and it wouldn't have mattered even if I had. The taste of JD on ice was a balm of sorts in that challenging year, and I appreciated his occasional company.

I must have mentioned Jack Daniels to Lee and his friend because they showed up for dinner with a bottle. Lee had come in a tie. I poked fun at that, and he said he was coming to a professor's house, and so he figured he should dress appropriately. I wasn't professorial then and am still not, but that's how he thought, so who was I to say.

I had cooked Indian food, and we sat around a small round dining table and talked and ate in Jack's company. The talk went here and there, and I don't remember much of it, except for two bits. At one point, I asked them if what I had heard was true—that at Davidson college parties, there was lots of underage drinking, and the college knew about it and didn't just condone it but actually facilitated it. They said it was true.

The story was that a couple of years earlier, an underage student had gone partying in nearby Charlotte, got drunk and flipped the car on the way back, and either died or was seriously injured. That is when the college authorities got together with lawyers and campus security and devised a plan—not to prevent underage drinking but to prevent its serious consequences.

They had figured out that in the pressured academic environment of Davidson, students were bound to let off steam on the weekends, and that would involve alcohol. You couldn't stop them from going to Charlotte to drink, but what if you made it available on campus in a legal way? That was safer because there would be no driving after drinking. So what started happening was that at each congregational party—mostly in fraternities and eating houses—the kegs of beer were kept in the basement, and only those with valid licenses were allowed to go down there. What the "legals" would do is go down, grab a couple of plastic cups of beer, bring them up, put them down on a table already set up, and turn away. The "illegals" could then pick up the cups and walk away, and there would be no direct link between dispenser and consumer and thus no legal liability. I didn't know anything about law and individual and collective liability; I just thought that was a clever solution to a knotty problem.

I could well imagine Lee in that set-up. I must have kidded him about that, which is when he said to me, "Jaiki, you know, the reason I am going to graduate this spring is that I came to a place like Davidson College. It is like an extended boarding school, and I needed that. Quite a few of my high school friends went to big state schools like the University of Florida, Florida State University and the University of North Carolina, and had such a loose rein that they partied all the time, got completely lost, and ended up dropping out. The only reason I am going to graduate is that the parties here are smaller, and Charlotte is too darn far away, and if I miss a class, someone calls and checks up on where I am. Without that, I would not have made it."

His friend, my economics student, wasn't like that, but no two people are ever the same, a simple fact that we all know but easily forget when we go about preaching what people should and should not do. Different people need different environments to flourish, and the small liberal arts college had clearly served both well.

By dinner's end, the bottle was empty, we'd had a couple of bowls of Breyer's Heavenly Hash ice cream, and as the saying goes, "tongues were tired." It wasn't that late, but after a full day of working on the thesis and preparing dinner and chatting with them, I was ready to go to sleep. They were just getting started and left to go to frat parties and continue with what young people do on weekends. Later, I heard that Lee had been spotted walking around with his tie in a beer cup … possibly a fishline looking for a catch. I could only smile at that.

59

Ships at a distance

"Ships at a distance have every man's wish on board. For some they come in with the tide. For others they sail forever on the horizon, never out of sight, never landing until the Watcher turns his eyes away in resignation, his dreams mocked to death by Time. That is the life of men.

Now, women forget all those things they don't want to remember, and remember everything they don't want to forget. The dream is the truth. Then they act and do things accordingly"

That's how Zora Neale Hurston begins the novel 'Their Eyes Were Watching God.' It's the not-yet-completed life story of Janie Crawford in central and southern Florida in the early decades of the 20th century when Jim Crow laws were still in force, and the Harlem Renaissance was in full flow. The story is a gritty one and peppered with dialogue you have to initially work at understanding but can settle into if you just speak and imagine it all through the characters' eyes. Do that, and you just might be the god their eyes are watching.

I crossed paths with the novel in the year I taught at Davidson College. It was the last decade of the 20th century when Jim Crow laws were long gone, and the older George Bush had just about started the Gulf War, but conservatives hadn't yet completely lost head and heart. That's not to say they had much back then, not in North Carolina, where the long-time conservative senator Jesse Helms was running a nasty and racist re-election campaign against the African-American Democrat Harvey Gantt. I have never forgotten being in the grocery store in Cornelius, the town next door, and seeing a white man in a white T-shirt with Harvey Gantt's face on the front and a bullseye overlayed on it.

Encounter with the novel was somewhat serendipitous. At the start of the academic year, I ran into a friend from Camp High Rocks on South Main Street as I was walking back home from my office. Like me, he had been a camp counsellor, and we had become good friends but then not had any contact after I stopped working at the camp. While we were catching up on each other's lives a friend of his came along, and as these things go, I became friends with her.

At some point in the fall semester, she told me about a college essay she was writing on the novel. I had not heard of Zora Neale Hurston and had no idea what the novel was about, so she gave me a synopsis and told me that her essay had a menstrual cycle take on it. I didn't quite understand the connection but wasn't surprised at her interpretation. Even though I had been trained in mainstream economics, which tends to look at the world with a monofocal lens, I had been exposed to the multifocal lenses of demographers and appreciated that different eyes can watch things in different ways.

The first semester at Davidson was a crazily busy one, with preparing for teaching, teaching, and squeezing out time to work on my thesis. It was a double-time full-time life in dual teacher-student mode. Those who have done a PhD and had to hold down a full-time job while working on the thesis know how dark those days and nights can be.

Caught up in a busy life and busily applying for academic jobs for the following year, I forgot all about the novel but then ran into it during the winter break in a bookstore in Washington, DC. I had gone to DC to attend the annual meetings of the American Economic Association, the formal marketplace for jobs in economics, but didn't have a single interview lined up and didn't see any prospects for picking one up.

Not wanting to hang around the meetings in low spirits, I walked out of the venue in Dupont Circle and continued along Connecticut Avenue to Woodley Park—to a movie theatre showing "Dances with Wolves." It was a brilliant movie and had me spellbound. When I emerged from it two hours later, the streets were covered with snow. The movie and the snow lifted my spirits, but only for a little bit. Walking back to Dupont Circle, I wandered into a bookstore, saw a copy of 'Their Eyes Were Watching God' and bought it without a second thought.

The second semester was more challenging than the first one. Life was still "double-time full-time", but now hope had to contend with disappointment. Those days were tough. I'd often listen to Sting's brilliant third album, "Soul Cages," in the evenings; the sombre music fit the mood. The best advice I got during that time was from a colleague—"Hang in there." I have never forgotten those three words; they've served as good guideposts in other tough times.

I had made progress on the thesis, but there was still lots to do. When my teaching contract with Davidson College ended in May, and a colleague offered to sublet me a room in a house he was renting in Durham that summer, I took him up on it and moved. For two months, I worked night and day on the thesis while staying closeted in a bedroom in a big house next to ... the east campus of Duke University! Having "learnt" to hate Duke in six and half years at Carolina, I would be lying if that location didn't make me cringe at times. Every time I would catch myself thinking that way, I would have a good laugh at myself. If you have spent time in those parts of the country, you'll know what I mean. If not, you won't. There is no rational way to explain that way of thinking and feeling, so I am not going to try.

I was no longer actively looking for a job but had my eyes and ears open. One came along at the Cornell University Food and Nutrition Policy Project in Washington, DC, and it involved working on food security issues in the context of structural adjustment reforms in Africa. That meant a move away from the economic demography that was the focus of my research, and it also wasn't the type of academic job I wanted, but I had no options at that point. I took the job thinking of it as a stopgap measure for a year, maybe two. That it would take 25 odd years to stop the gap is not something I could have envisioned then, but... that's how the dice rolled.

By the time I moved up to DC at the beginning of July to take up the new job, it had been six months since I had bought 'Their Eyes Were Watching God', and I still had not gotten around to reading it. Looking back on things now, I wonder what I would have made of the novel—if I had read it while I was at Davidson. Would it have resonated with me? In a way, yes, and in a way, no. I would have likely read it at night after a days' worth of teaching and work on the thesis. Like other great literature that I had gotten into the habit of reading at night, Janie Crawford's remarkable story and Zora Neale Hurston's wordcraft would most certainly have grabbed me. But I doubt I would have looked for deep meaning in the story, not in the way my friend had in her essay. I wasn't in that type of mind space then.

Would the "ships at a distance" quote have provided perspective? Maybe, though I am not sure what I would have made of it. I hadn't yet gotten to that stage in life when you start thinking about the ships that have come in with the tide and the ones that sail forever on the horizon. I was still looking more ahead than behind. My eyes were on the horizon, but instead of waiting for the tide to come in, I was actively swimming out to the ships. I suppose, in Zora Neale Hurston's eyes, I was living the life ... not of men, but of women!

I only got to read the novel a year or so later, still very much in that previous century, but in a big city, while flitting between big and small countries. At that point, Bill Clinton was boss, and even though he had done some shady stuff and looked away from the killing fields of Rwanda, he had done plenty good within the country for invisible people, so some referred to him as the first black president. Things could have stayed that way in the new century if Al Gore hadn't changed his tie as often during the campaign and tagged his presidential aspirations to those partially punched ballots called 'hanging chads'.

You can string a storyline through all of that and hang your clothes out to dry on it, but I am pretty sure it will cross someone else's, and random winds will still blow them all here and there, and time will march on. Time always does.

60

Peaches

You can cut a peach this way and that and eat slices and squares elegantly and sophisticatedly as they do on TV food shows and in fancy restaurants. Or you can eat it the way nature intended, which can't mean anything other than eating it whole because, well, because who the heck knows what complex and dynamic nature intends—in the way we humans think of intent? So, if you were to eat a peach whole, how would you do it? I hadn't thought much about that till Paul insisted there was a peachy way, and when someone insists that way, then you just have to desist doing it the way you thought "nature intended" and get more deliberate.

It was the summer of '91. After a challenging year of teaching at Davidson College and two months of highly focussed work on the thesis in Durham, I moved to DC on a hot July 4th weekend. A friend was driving up to DC and agreed to give Maria, the dog, and my few belongings a ride in her air-conditioned car. I rode my motorcycle up interstate highways I-85 and I-95 in 100F-degree heat with an army duffle bag on my back resting against the pillion backrest.

It was already hot when we left Durham late that morning, and it just got hotter on the wide-open interstate. A storm seemed to be gathering steam as we drove into downtown DC. Not wanting to keep my friend from getting to her destination, I unloaded my stuff from her car as quickly as possible and then hurried to get it up to the first-floor apartment I was renting on 18th and Q Streets in Dupont Circle.

By the time I got everything, including Maria, up to the apartment, I was wiped out. But there was a measure of relief in having completed the locational transition from North Carolina to Washington, DC. I wasn't done with the thesis and still had work to do on it, but that anxiety was not in play at that point. There was a day to recover from the move and figure out the neighbourhood, an important part of which came about that evening itself.

A friend, Barb, lived a couple of blocks away from my apartment, and once I had showered and caught my breath, I called her up to see if she wanted to catch a bite and a beer. She was going to have dinner with her sister nearby and invited me to join them, so once I had settled in Maria with food and drink, I headed over to Café Luna, which was a block and two turns away.

It was late by the time the relaxing Italian dinner was over, and I had started walking back the three short stretches of sidewalk I had come on. The first right turn on to 17th street went fine, and I happily walked by the bars and restaurants, oblivious of others walking along the sidewalk. It was when I missed the next left turn on to Q street and had to backtrack that I had the feeling someone might be following me.

I was too tired to be suspicious, so I walked on without thinking much about being stalked. It was when I went through the lobby of the apartment building, and the man followed me in that I got concerned and then genuinely worried when he got into the elevator with me. At that point, a sensible person would have gone to a different floor, walked out and taken the stairs to their apartment, but a mixture of fatigue and cluelessness led me to take the elevator to the first floor and walk straight to my apartment, which was right in front of the elevator. As I turned the key and walked in, I remember thinking: "Yeah, smart, really, really smart move."

Maria was happy to see me, and I was relieved to see that the year-old puppy had behaved like a mature dog and not chewed anything. Her greeting soon turned to sniffing at the door and then barking as she pawed on a metro transit card that had been slipped under it. I waited a bit and then picked it up. On one end of the card was scribbled—"I'd like to meet you"—with a phone number below it. I was relieved that it wasn't anything sinister and threatening and also somewhat amused at the new experience.

My grad school friends who had helped me find the apartment might have told me about the neighbourhood—that it was an easy-going one with gay bars and restaurants—but I had completely forgotten and not realized that I had just passed those on 17th street and piqued someone's interest. The message on the card was of no interest to me and didn't bother me either, so I tossed it into the trash can. Over the next few months, I got used to occasional remarks from men, though they did make me somewhat uncomfortable and more aware of how it must be for women—more generally. It was a real-life education that helped break me out of the university cocoon I had existed in for nine years.

My apartment was just two blocks from the office, so I was in and out as it suited me. It was the end of summer, and several of the young analysts at the organization were moving on. I was sharing an office with two others, and one of them was Paul, a smart fella and what I now think of as—a classic Washington liberal—very sure of left and right, and right and wrong, and who is on and who is off.

I wasn't one of 'them' but became one within a few months. With the brilliance of conveniently rearranged memory, I like to think … I was 'not as bad as them.' That tendency to overestimate oneself is called the "Lake Wobegon effect" and comes from Garrison Keillor's brilliant radio program, "News from Lake Wobegon," in which he describes the fictional town, Lake Wobegon, as a place—"where all the women are strong, all the men are good-looking, and all the children are above average."

Like many good liberals, Paul lived in Mount Pleasant, which is where the ethnic folk—meaning low-income Central and South Americans—lived in DC. Liberals like to mingle, the real ones up close, the others from a distance. That's not just in DC but everywhere in the world. In DC, you could go further out of town towards Virginia and up in Takoma Park in Maryland, and you would find "ethnicity," but Mount Pleasant was closer and walking distance to downtown DC. Why black people and white people and others are not ethnic is a mystery I wonder about now, but back then, I was too stupid to think about those things. I was a development economist, and my halo was holier than thou and … that's just how it was.

So there we were in that three-person office, and then the third analyst left, so it was just Paul and me. When you are squeezing multi-faceted reality, as captured in household survey data, into parsimonious statistical models, there isn't much space for crunching conversations, so we didn't really talk much except at lunchtime. I'd usually walk home for lunch, eat a bite, and then come right back. Those were the days I was desperately trying to finish my thesis, and lunch was no more than a necessity.

One day, when I got back from a quick bite, Paul was still eating lunch. He had finished his sandwich, and we got talking, and then he took out a peach. It was big. Summer is peach season on the east coast of the US, and they come in by truckload, some from Georgia and some from wherever tries to have 'Georgia on [my] its mind'. I must have said something about the size of the peach because he proceeded to tell me how he had *not* bought it at Safeway, the chain grocery store, but at the farmer's market.

That first year in DC, I learnt how important farmers markets are to being a good liberal. In reality, those markets, like all markets, have no political ideology, and sales and purchases are largely driven by people's assessment of relative prices and quality of produce. But farmers markets do have a feel-good factor that liberals feel more than conservatively inclined folk. I don't know enough conservatives, so I am not sure. Just sayin.'

Had I brought back a peach from the apartment, and was I eating it somewhat messily? Or did I say something about his peach eating? I don't remember. Whatever it was, something led him to tell me that there was a proper way to eat a peach—you had to bite and suck at the same time. The little pods in juicy peaches burst open when bitten into, and if you didn't suck on them simultaneously, they'd dripple on down … not quite all the way to Georgia, but everywhere else not very convenient to analyst functioning.

Then, without much of a prompt, he demonstrated the technique. Always interested in the details of things and the peculiarities of human beings, I watched in amazement and with some amusement. Later, or maybe even right then, if I had a Safeway peach with me, I tried it myself and found the lesson—in the peachy way of eating peaches—quite useful.

I have since tried to pass that valuable technique on to my family but without much effect. Their intent always seems to be to slice and dice a peach and not eat it the way nature intended. I, on the other hand, always go with nature's intent—modified by Paul's intentful technique. It always brings a smile, even when the pods are dry.

Epilogue

"There are years that ask questions and years that answer."

I like this first sentence in Chapter 3 of Zora Neale Hurston's novel, "Their Eyes Were Watching God" because it prompts reflection. At the end of journeys, like the writing of this book, it is worth looking back at the road travelled—to assess how things went and to look ahead at the road in front.

"So, what do you think, Jackman?" That's the latest entry in a journal where I periodically jot down musings, some of which are self-deprecatingly directed at me and use this namesake, which is not mentioned in the first chapter of this collection.

I gotta say … writing this book has been one heck of a ride. It's been fun, challenging, and rewarding, all things you'd want in a memorable journey, but it has also been more than what I bargained for. That doesn't come as a surprise, because I am good at building castles-in-the-air, *"hawai kile"* in Hindi, but not very realistic about the journey to get to them.

I have thoroughly enjoyed putting this book together by going through Facebook posts written over several years, smiling at their quirkiness, selecting a set to fit the parameters of the book and expanding the posts to book-length chapters. The beautiful thing about this process is that tickling memories' toes brings forth forgotten details and opens windows and doors to other memories. Interaction with friends, during this journey and the longer Facebook-posts one that led up it, suggests my writings do the same for others. That adds to the satisfaction derived from the journey.

There is also no denying that writing this book has been challenging. The Facebooks posts that are the starting point for several stories in this collection were just musings, some short, some long, some standalone pieces, some with overlapping content—all written casually over several years. Reworking them into coherent chapters and arranging them in a book is a bit like taking a bunch of music riffs, developing them into compositions, and putting together an album of those compositions. Except, 60 chapters are more pieces than what you get in a music album, and working out their details and arranging them is, quite possibly, harder.

At times I've wondered if it would have been easier to write a typical memoir—with a continuous narrative that strings together a set of deliberately selected memories. In a way, yes, though reworking the posts to fit a particular narrative would have presented its own challenges and working with a clean slate would have been a non-starter. I am sure that if I had gone in that direction, this book would have never gotten to this last page.

So much for reflection. On to projection—where to from here? Well, that welcome mat laid out in April of 2011 is very much there. New memories continue to float in, and the suitcase of eager beavers (Prologue) keeps getting bigger. Those fellas will want to find space to stretch their legs, especially the more numerous ones from the 30 years not covered by this book. How can I deny them the words they need to tell their stories? It would not be fair.

How and when will that come about? Will I walk the (typical) memoir path in the future? I don't think so. All my life I have followed the sounds of a different drummer. Why change now, especially when self-publishing offers an aid to deviance? With several stories already written but left out of this collection because of its limiting parameters, and more likely to get written—to be fair to the eager beavers—it is fair to say there will be another collection of "Imagined Memories." As to when, well there is a paying job to do, and two analytically oriented books to write in the coming year, so there's no saying when. Best to go along with the cautiously optimistic tone of the very last words of the delightful movie, 'The Lunchbox'— "Dekhte hain" (let's see).